AF538922

The Right to Education

The Right to Education

Bharti Satsangi

RANDOM PUBLICATIONS
NEW DELHI (INDIA)

The Right to Education

ISBN 978-93-5111-509-0

Published in 2015 in India by

RANDOM PUBLICATIONS

4376-A/4B, Gali Murari Lal, Ansari Road
New Delhi-110 002
Phone : +9111-43580356, 011-23289044, 011-43142548
e-mail: sales@randompublications.com,
info@randompublications.com, randomexports@gmail.com

Reprinted 2021

Type Setting by : Friends Media, Delhi-110089
Printed at : Replika Press Pvt. Ltd.

Preface

Education is a fundamental human right and essential for the exercise of all other human rights. It promotes individual freedom and empowerment and yields important development benefits. Yet millions of children and adults remain deprived of educational opportunities, many as a result of poverty. Education is a powerful tool by which economically and socially marginalized adults and children can lift themselves out of poverty and participate fully as citizens.

Normative instruments of the United Nations and UNESCO lay down international legal obligations for the right to education. These instruments promote and develop the right of every person to enjoy access to education of good quality, without discrimination or exclusion. These instruments bear witness to the great importance that Member States and the international community attach to normative action for realizing the right to education. It is for governments to fulfil their obligations both legal and political in regard to providing education for all of good quality and to implement and monitor more effectively education strategies.

This book provides an analysis of the content and development of the right to education at the international and regional levels. It refers to the provisions on the right to education found in instruments of international law and discusses challenges faced by the international community to effectively implement the existing stock of standards and how to bridge the gap between the international obligations undertaken by nations and the performance of their governments in fulfilling them. It also brings together the current thinking and practice on human rights-based approaches in the education sector.

The content of book will be of interest to students, teachers, researchers, legal practitioners and officials dealing with human rights law.

Author

Contents

Preface

1. The Right to Education **1**

Right to Education as a Universal Right 3

Inclusive Dimensions of the Right to Education 4

International Obligations 7

Right to Education for All its Beneficiaries 8

Future Action and Key Tasks 16

2. Instruments and Mechanisms for the Right to Education **22**

Rights at Stake 24

Key Assistance Agencies 25

Standard-setting Instruments 26

Beneficiaries of the Right to Education 37

Implementation of the Right to Education 47

Means Required for the Exercise of the Right to Education 53

Sanctioning the Right to Education 56

Normativity of the Right to Education 58

Monitoring and Follow-up Procedures 63

Monitoring Measures 65

3. Primary Education as a Fundamental Right **79**

Achieving Universal Primary Education 79

Factors Contributing to Lack of Access and Poor Attendance 81

Normative Action for Universalising Primary Education 83

Right to Free Primary Education 85

Principle of Nondiscrimination and Equal Access to Education 88
Principle of Equity and Positive Measures 89
Educational Rights of Children Belonging to Minorities 90
Right to Standard and Quality of Education 91
Financing Free Primary Education 92
Preserving Public Interest in Education 93
School Feeding Programs 93
Current Efforts 94

4. Right to Lifelong Learning 98

Lifelong Learning: Moving beyond Education for All 99
Lifelong Learning and the Right to Education 103
What Lifelong Learning is Not 104
Building Learning Societies 106
Fundamental Education and Adults 107
Eradication of Illiteracy 110
Expanding Vision of Educational Opportunity 118
The Hamburg Declaration on Adult Learning 123

5. Human Rights-based Approach to Education For All 130

Education As a Human Right 132
Human Rights-Based Approaches to Development 134
Adopting a Rights-Based Approach to Education 136
Applying a Rights-Based Approach to Policy and Programming 138
Addressing Tensions in Fulfilling the Right to Education 143
A Rights-Based Conceptual Framework for Education 149
Rights-based Education Through Sector-Wide Approaches 160
Importance of Rights-based Approach 164
Building A Rights-based SWAp 173

6. Literacy and Human Rights 181

Importance of Literacy 182
Literacy Programmes 186
Literacy and gender 188

Literacy for Poverty Education 189

Literacy in Conflict-affected Areas 191

Making Policy for Literacy 192

Putting policy into Practice 196

Promoting Quality Literacy 197

Developing Capacity for Literacy 201

Literate Environments 203

United Nations Literacy Decade 206

7. Convention against Discrimination in Education 209

Fulltext of the Convention 210

Aim and Scope of the Convention 217

International Recognition of the Convention 222

8. The World Declaration on Education for All and the Framework for Action to Meet Basic Learning Needs 224

Preamble 226

Education For All: The Purpose 228

Education For All: An Expanded Vision And A Renewed Commitment 229

Education For All: The Requirements 232

Framework For Action: Meeting Basic Learning Needs—Guidelines for implementing the World Declaration on Education for All 234

9. The Dakar Framework for Action— Education for All: Meeting our Collective Commitments 255

The Full text 256

Expanded Commentary on the Dakar Framework for Action 263

Bibliography 287

Index 289

1

The Right to Education

The right to education is at the heart of the Education For All (EFA) programme as UNESCO's priority. It responds to the constitutional mandate of the Organization - ensuring "*Full and equal opportunities for education for all*" (emphasis added). The Dakar Framework for Action, adopted at the World Education Forum (2000), at which the right to education was reaffirmed, and the EFA goals were set, expresses the political commitment of the whole international community to:

- expanding and improving comprehensive early childhood care and education, especially for the most vulnerable and disadvantaged children;
- ensuring that by 2015 all children, particularly girls, children in difficult circumstances and those belonging to ethnic minorities, have access to, and complete free and compulsory, primary education of good quality;
- achieving a 50 per cent improvement in levels of adult literacy by 2015, especially for women, and equitable access to basic and continuing education for all adults;
- eliminating gender disparities in primary and secondary education by 2005, and achieving gender equality in education by 2015, with a focus on ensuring girls' full and equal access to and achievement in basic education of good quality.

However, the EFA agenda is falling behind, as the current pace of progress is not sufficient to meet the EFA goals. The target of eliminating gender disparities in primary and secondary education by 2005 has already been missed in a large number of countries and the target of achieving free and compulsory primary education of good quality for all, which is a Millennium Development Goal agreed upon at the Millennium Assembly (2000), also seems unlikely to be attained by 2015.

Making good quality basic education accessible to all is an important objective of the EFA. As regards the Dakar goal for universalizing free and compulsory primary education by 2015, the Joint Expert Group UNESCO (CR)/ECOSOC (CESCR) on the Monitoring of the Right to Education has expressed its concern over the process of weakening the right to education – a process which needs be reversed. As the EFA Global Monitoring Report 2008 (henceforth referred to as the GMR 2008) shows, countries facing conditions of fragility – especially those that suffer the consequences of conflict or disaster - call for particular attention, as over one-third of out-of-school children live in such countries. These conditions continue to take a heavy toll, denying millions the right to education. Education systems remain affected by conflicts, natural calamities and instability.

The United Nations Committee on Economic, Social and Cultural Rights (CESCR), in its Concluding Observations has, for example, identified various *reasons why some groups have limited access to education*, ranging from traditional attitudes preventing girls from attending school to the limited availability of schooling, including teachers, in rural areas. A further ground of exclusion represents the limited financial means of persons living in poverty, who frequently may also be members of minority or indigenous communities. Within some vulnerable groups, parents can be a decisive factor preventing their children from attending school. Language can be another major factor in limiting access to education, and, therefore, of the exercise of the right to education. At the same time, those without permanent residency status may not have access to education in general.

As the *Global Monitoring Report (GMR)* (2008) states, for various social, cultural or political reasons, certain population groups - such as migrants, indigenous people, ethnic minorities and those with disabilities – find themselves excluded from mainstream society, which often results in reduced access to formal education and literacy programmes.

The magnitude of the challenge was expressed in the communiqué issued at the Ministerial Round Table on Education and Economic Development (organized in October 2007 during the 34th session of the UNESCO General Conference), in which the Ministers of Education urged that: "(...) access to education is addressed, and this *right* urgently realized, especially for the poorest and most marginalized, including more than 72 million children not in school and 774 million adults without literacy skills" (Emphasis added).

It is, therefore, imperative to give further momentum to the EFA process. Advocacy of the right to education as a fundamental human right, with a focus on its inclusive dimensions, and with greater emphasis on the obligations of Governments for its more effective implementation, is indispensable for advancing the EFA agenda.

Right to Education as a Universal Right

The *Universal Declaration of Human Rights* (1948) which lays the moral foundation for human rights, proclaims that "every one has right to education" (Article 26 (1)). The legal framework of the right to education is laid down by UNESCO's *Convention against Discrimination in Education (1960)* which is the first instrument in the field of education. The Convention establishes the entitlements to the right to education for various beneficiaries at all levels of education, including the right to universal primary education free of charge. It has been recognized by UNESCO's Executive Board as a key pillar of EFA.

Several other instruments in the field of education, elaborated by UNESCO, develop the right to education in its different dimensions: the right to technical and vocational education established by the *Convention on Technical and Vocational Education* (1989), and the *Revised Recommendation concerning Technical and Vocational Education* (2001); the right to adult education, literacy and lifelong learning by the *Recommendation on the Development of Adult Education* (1976), and the *Hamburg Declaration on Adult Learning* (1997); the fundamental right of every child to quality education by the *Recommendation concerning the Status of Teachers* (1966); and the right to the pursuit of higher education by the *World Declaration on Higher Education for the Twenty-first Century* (1998).

The right to education is provided for in several human rights conventions adopted by the United Nations. It is comprehensively covered by the provisions in article 13 of the *International Covenant on Economic, Social and Cultural Rights* (1966), which was drafted at the suggestion of UNESCO's Director-General and which draws extensively upon the *Convention against Discrimination in Education*. The General Comment 13 on article 13 of the International Covenant, which was elaborated by the CESCR in collaboration with UNESCO, elucidates the nature and scope of the right to education. Moreover, article 14 of the International Covenant provides for "compulsory education free of charge for all." There are several other United Nations human rights treaties and declarations which provide for the right to education.

The right to education thus laid down is an internationally recognized right. It is an overarching right: *a human right in itself and indispensable for the exercise of other human rights*. Its main attributes are:

- Universal access to primary education free and compulsory for all;
- Accessibility to secondary education in its different forms as well as technical and vocational education which should be made generally available;
- Capacity-based access to higher education;
- Opportunities for continuing education and literacy programmes and lifelong learning;
- Minimum international standards of quality education and of the teaching profession.

Inclusive Dimensions of the Right to Education

In order to fully understand the nature and the scope of the right to education as being universal, it is necessary to shed some light on its *all-inclusive dimensions*.

Rights of 'national minorities' to carry on their own educational activities, while remaining respectful of *understanding the culture and language of the community* as a whole are provided in UNESCO's *Convention against Discrimination in Education* (article 5.1.c). While the Convention was being elaborated, the expression 'national minorities' was employed to denote the rights of cultural, ethnic and linguistic minorities. The United Nations *Declaration on the Rights of Persons Belonging to*

National or Ethnic, Religious and Linguistic Minorities, elaborated later, covers the rights of such minorities.

The "right of *equal access* to technical and vocational education" is laid down in the *Convention on Technical and Vocational Education* (emphasis added), which provides that the Contracting States "shall guarantee that no individual who has attained the educational level for admission into technical and vocational education shall be discriminated against" (Article 2, paragraph 3). Under the provisions of the Convention, States are required to "take appropriate measures" to enable the handicapped and other disadvantaged groups to benefit from technical and vocational education (Article 2, paragraph 4).

The inclusive dimensions of the right to education are reflected more elaborately in the *Revised Recommendation concerning Technical and Vocational Education* which provides that technical and vocational education is available to persons with disabilities and to socially and economically disadvantaged groups and groups such as immigrants, refugees or minorities (including indigenous peoples), and underprivileged and marginalized youth in order to integrate them more easily into society.

Similarly, these dimensions are reflected in the *World Declaration on Higher Education for the Twenty-first Century*, which stipulates that education shall become "accessible to all throughout life." The Declaration provides that "Access to higher education for members of some special target groups, such as indigenous peoples, cultural and linguistic minorities, disadvantaged groups, peoples living under occupation and those who suffer from disabilities, must be actively facilitated (...)" (Article 4).

Principles for adult education and literacy are laid down by the *Recommendation on the Development of Adult Education* which stipulates that measures should be taken with a view to "making access to all levels of education and training more widely available." Similarly, the *Hamburg Declaration on Adult Learning* contains the main principles and concepts adopted so far in the context of the right to education and makes them generally applicable to the population as a whole. These instruments give primacy to norms and standards for wider access to education. The *Hamburg Declaration* postulates that "The State remains the essential vehicle for ensuring the right to education for all, particularly for the most vulnerable groups of society, such as minorities and indigenous peoples, and for providing an overall policy framework", and enumerates various categories of the most underprivileged groups.

In this respect, it is important to note that the principle that education is a human right and its provisions should respond to the necessity of wider access to educational resources worldwide, is reflected in the *Recommendation on the Recognition of Studies and Qualification in Higher Education* (1993). Besides, the right to education of children requiring special educational treatment, and the need to pay due attention to it, is recognized by the *Recommendation concerning the Status of Teachers*. It provides that education is *the fundamental right of every child* "to be provided with the fullest possible educational opportunities."

Various conventions and recommendations in the field of education, elaborated by UNESCO, thus reflect all-inclusive dimensions of the right to education. They lay down the normative bases of universalizing access to education for all without discrimination or exclusion and express the international obligations and political commitments for the right to education for all: for national, ethnic, religious and linguistic minorities, for indigenous people, for the socially and economically marginalized, for vulnerable groups, for immigrants, for the disabled and handicapped, for refugees, for the rural-urban poor and for millions of those deprived of education by poverty. They embody the key concepts of universal approaches, which should be all-inclusive, and also provide the normative bases for education in its diverse forms such as adult education, community education, special education, etc.

Inclusive dimensions of the right to education are also covered in the United Nations instruments. The General Comment 13 on article 13 of the International Covenant, mentioned above, states that "education must be accessible to all, especially the most vulnerable groups, *in law and fact*, without discrimination on any of the prohibited grounds" (para. 6(b)). Similarly, the General Comment 11 on article 14 of the International Covenant, elaborated by CESCR, lays down the principle of compulsory education free of charge for all and stresses the need for action with a view to securing the implementation of this right.

The right to education for the benefit of its specific population groups has been emphasized by other United Nations instruments – for children in the *Convention on the Rights of the Child* (articles 28-30) - for women in the *Convention on the Elimination of All Forms of Discrimination against Women* (article 10); for migrants in the *International Convention on the Protection of the Rights of All Migrant Workers and Members of their Families* (articles 12, 30 and 45) and for disabled and handicapped in the *Convention on the Rights of Persons with Disabilities* (article 24). In addition to these United Nations human right conventions, some United Nations declarations, mentioned above, such as the *Declaration on the Rights of Persons Belonging to National or Ethnic, Religious and Linguistic Minorities*, and the *Declaration on the Rights of Indigenous Peoples* (article 14) cover the right to education of minorities and of indigenous peoples.

The right to education is thus universal and does not admit of any exclusion or discrimination. It needs to be upheld more emphatically, and its all-inclusive dimensions need to be brought into prominence in order that all those who remain deprived of it become its beneficiaries. In fact, promoting the right to education universally in that perspective is an obligation of Governments.

International Obligations

The legal framework for the right to education, highlighted above, carries international obligations. Like all human rights, the right to education imposes three levels of obligations on States parties: the obligations to respect, protect and fulfil. In turn, the obligation to fulfil incorporates obligations to facilitate and promote, and obligation to provide. The State obligations remain, even in the case of the privatization of education, so that there is a regulatory framework as regards standards, quality and contents of education, and, above all, for full respect of the fundamental principle of non-discrimination in education.

The legal or political nature of obligations depends upon whether they emanate from conventions or recommendations. The *conventions* and treaties have *binding force for States* which are parties to them. States are obliged to *incorporate their obligations* into their domestic legal order. On the other hand, the *recommendations* do not have binding force, they *reflect standards of political commitments* by Member States and have moral force. States are expected to take measures to bring them into effect through national legislation. Moreover, recommendations can be taken into account in administrative practices and judicial pronouncements. Education as a human right, reaffirmed at the World Education Forum, carries an obligation for

Governments to ensure that basic education is made accessible to all. The *Dakar Framework for Action*, adopted at the World Education Forum, insofar as it was based on rights recognized in existing international instrument, can be taken as imposing legal obligations on signatories.

In the context of EFA, it is necessary to place special emphasis on States' *core obligations* for universalizing access to primary education, free of charge for all, without discrimination or exclusion. Accordingly, the Joint Expert Group, mentioned above, has underlined the need for full compliance with such *core obligations*. Having regards to the recommendations by the Joint Expert Group, UNESCO's Executive Board adopted in October 2007 a decision, by which it invites all Member States "to fulfil their respective commitments and international obligations relating to universalizing access to free primary education for all" (177 EX/decision 37).

The obligation to take immediate steps aimed at providing primary education *for all* is also expressed in the General Comment 13 (on the right to education). This General Comment states that "the States parties to the International Covenant are obliged to prioritize the introduction of compulsory, free primary education" (para. 51). This obligation is reinforced through the immediate nature of the non-discrimination clause (article 2 (2) of the Covenant), which applies "fully and immediately to all aspects of education and encompasses all internationally prohibited grounds of discrimination" (para. 31). The CESCR has also confirmed that "the principle of non-discrimination extends to all persons of school age residing in the territory of a State party, including non-nationals, and irrespective of their legal status" (in conformity with article 2 of the *Convention on the Rights of the Child* and article 3 (e) of the *Convention against Discrimination in Education*) .

In conformity with these obligations, it is necessary to give a renewed momentum to EFA as a global drive and urge Governments to fulfil their obligations to implement the right to education, giving priority to all those who remain deprived of basic education of good quality.

Right to Education for All its Beneficiaries

For the right to education to become all-inclusive, cultural, ethnic and linguistic minorities, socially and culturally marginalized and disadvantaged individuals and groups, other vulnerable groups, and especially children from poor households should become its full beneficiaries.

Cultural, ethnic and linguistic minorities as beneficiaries of the right to education are conventionally recognized categories in the international law of human rights. Their right to education is not always respected. Moreover, 'new minorities' (resulting from present-day migrations) raise new problem dimensions for cultural, ethnic and linguistic minorities. What is important is to ensure that the rights of minorities to education are given effect in a way that it promotes, at the same time, integration and social cohesion in the context of EFA. Questions related to segregation and integration are complex and deserve further consideration. Inclusion implies *respect for diversity* – of different cultures and languages and of those from different racial, socio-economic and cultural backgrounds – in a spirit of mutual understanding and appreciation. While protecting the rights of national minorities, respect for the diversity of national education systems, and for cultural pluralism must be maintained.

The normative bases of protecting the right to education of cultural, ethnic and linguistic minorities, laid down in the *Convention against Discrimination in Education*, provide a legal framework for action at national level. In its article 5.1.c), the Convention provides for the educational rights of *national minorities* to carry on their own educational activities, including the maintenance of schools and, depending on the educational policy of each State, the use or the teaching of their own language. It requires that the exercise of this right by the members of minorities should be respectful of the *culture and language of the community as a whole* and should not be prejudicial to national sovereignty. The Convention further requires that (i) the standard of education in minority schools should not be lower than the general standard laid down or approved by the competent authorities; and (ii) that attendance at such schools is optional. In this respect, reference should also be made to the Declaration and the *Integrated Framework of Action on Education for Peace, Human Rights and Democracy*, adopted and endorsed by the International Conference on Education (October 1994): "In order to create understanding between different groups in society, there must be respect for the educational rights of persons belonging to national or ethnic, religious and linguistic minorities, as well as indigenous people, and this must also have implications in curricula and methods as well as in the way education is organized."

Persons belonging to ethnic minorities are often prevented from fully enjoying their right to education. This has been addressed by the CESCR in various Concluding Observations. In some countries, they suffer from irregular access to education. The CESCR has referred States parties to its General Comment 11 (1999) on plans of action for primary education and General Comment 13 (1999) on the right to education when calling upon States "to take effective measures to ensure that all children, including (...) ethnic minority children, have access to free compulsory primary education." *Persons of African descent* have been identified by the CESCR as one specific ethnic group likely to be prevented from access to education for example in Costa Rica, and in being prevented from equal access to university education in Canada. In order for the State party to remedy this, the CESCR has recommended an overall assessment of the situation of the community, in particular regarding education, "in order to adopt and effectively implement a targeted programme of action to realize their rights under the Covenant."

As regards linguistic minorities, special emphasis is given in many countries - Australia (Indigenous people), Brazil (Afro-Brazilian), Croatia, Czech Republic, Hungary, Latvia, Norway, Slovakia (Roma), Slovenia (special educational rights for Italian and Hungarian) and Spain (immigrants) - to the legal and policy framework relating to educational standards in institutions run by minorities. Offering language facilities is an important issue. Language often constitutes a barrier to access to education. Therefore, CESCR has recommended that where this constitutes a problem, States parties should allocate sufficient funds for *bilingual education*. Higher education should also be accessible, i.e. it should not only be provided in one language if other official languages exist. Children belonging to minorities or indigenous communities are entitled to have *equal opportunities* to receive instruction in their mother tongue; any distinction between different minority and indigenous groups must be justified by reasonable and objective criteria (such as numerical criteria, etc.). Despite the trend towards requiring instruction in or of the main minority languages within a State party, CESCR clearly *rejects* the establishment of *separate schools* for children belonging to different ethnic groups and asks States parties to teach *one over-arching curriculum* to all classes, irrespective of ethnicity. It goes without saying that such curricula should provide for instruction in the official language of States parties.

The language of instruction as well as knowledge of languages plays a key role in learning. As the GMR (2008) mentions, bilingual education has been found to improve the schooling outcomes of children from indigenous communities in many countries (p 120). It suggests the need to "recognize the importance of *mother tongue* instruction in early childhood and the first years of primary school" (p 4). The contemporary issues in language and the right to education call for practical solutions with a view to operationalizing the existing normative framework, established in several United Nations human rights conventions, mentioned above.

Roma children constitute another group suffering from limited access to education. In the reports submitted to UNESCO for the seventh consultation on the measures taken for the implementation of the Convention and the Recommendation against Discrimination in Education, several Member States have indicated the progressive measures as well as obstacles encountered as regards the realisation of the right to education for Roma children. Their integration into the education system, while respecting their cultural identity as also the principle of non-discrimination, can be promoted by drawing upon practical examples.

CESCR has recommended in its Concluding Observations regarding the Ukraine, for instance, the adoption of "special measures, including subsidies for textbooks and other educational tools" to increase their school attendance at all levels. The obligation of the State party also comprises the provision of language classes, the combating of discrimination against Roma students and the need to "raise awareness among Roma families on the importance of education, including for girls." The provision of mother tongue education for minorities, including Roma, has also been interpreted as obligatory under the Covenant, as postulated in the Concluding Observations adopted by CESCR concerning Slovenia. The conditions of Roma children in Europe are a key concern, as there are over 10 million Roma population affected.

Indigenous communities are also frequently denied access to education. The GMR (2008) indicates that "Experiences in diverse contexts show that children of indigenous population are less likely to enrol in primary education and more likely to repeat than non-indigenous children". Among the main needs to be met in order for indigenous children to have access to good quality education are appropriate and accessible schooling opportunities, adequate resources in schools and the cultural relevance of the education offered.

In its Concluding Observations, the CESCR regularly reminds State parties of their obligation to ensure the access of indigenous children to education. States parties must ensure that there are adequate numbers of teachers in primary and secondary schools attended by indigenous children, that school attendance by indigenous children as well as their comparatively poor performance is raised, and that their illiteracy rate is reduced. The CESCR has also specified that States parties are obliged to "strengthen and upgrade schooling programmes" for indigenous children, and "to report on the progress made in achieving universal access to compulsory primary and secondary education" to the CESCR.

In this respect, it is pertinent to note that the United Nations *Declaration on the Rights of Indigenous Peoples* (2007), which states that "Indigenous individuals, particularly children, have the right to all levels and forms of education of the State without discrimination", provides the normative bases for addressing the educational needs of the indigenous people and promoting their right to education. The Declaration sets promising international standards for the protection and promotion of the rights of indigenous peoples within the larger human rights framework and, more specifically, highlights their rights related to culture, identity, language and education.

Women and girls are frequently excluded from education. In such cases, CESCR reminds States parties of the obligation to achieve gender equality in the access to education in different regions. In some countries, this disparity between women and men can even be greater in rural areas, as addressed in the Concluding Observation on Morocco. The obligation of States parties in this regard has also been interpreted to comprise the elimination of traditional attitudes which frequently prevent girls and women from the enjoyment of their right to education.

As the *GMR* (2008) states, women constitute 64 per cent of illiterate adults (1995-2004) and their literacy is crucial in addressing wider issues of gender inequality. Stating that the gender equality remains elusive, it addresses various issues as regards equity and gender disparities and inequalities and underlines the need to promote gender equality through teacher training, the curriculum and textbook content.

It is, therefore, of critical importance to intensify advocacy for non-discrimination based upon gender, in line with the *Convention against*

Discrimination in Education, and give full effect to the provisions in Article 10 of the *Convention on the Elimination of All Forms of Discrimination against Women* (1979), which establishes the obligation of the States Parties to the Convention to "take all appropriate measures to eliminate discrimination against women in order to ensure them equal rights with men in the field of education." An important area of action relates to the need to give follow up to the Concluding Observations adopted by the CEDAW-Committee.

Disabled and handicapped children – of which there are more than 600 million today – are an important segment of the population which remains victim of discrimination and/or deprived of education. Actions aimed at giving effect to the *Convention on the Rights of Persons with Disabilities* would ensure their access to education. The Convention provides that, with a view to realizing this right without discrimination and on the basis of equal opportunity, States Parties shall ensure an inclusive education system at all levels and lifelong learning. In its article 24 (2), the Convention provides that "In realizing this right, States Parties shall ensure that: (a) Persons with disabilities are not excluded from the general education system on the basis of disability, and that children with disabilities are not excluded from free and compulsory primary education, or from secondary education, on the basis of disability; (b) Persons with disabilities can access an inclusive, quality and free primary education and secondary education on an equal basis with others in the communities in which they live." The measures aimed at fulfilling obligations under the *Convention on Technical and Vocational Education* cover basic skills and would contribute to such education for the handicapped.

Rural and illiterate populations constitute a majority of those left behind and excluded from education. There are over 700 million illiterate adults in the world today, of which more than 60 per cent are women. These figures indicate the scope of the challenges lying ahead in combating illiteracy. In order to universalize access to basic education, accelerated momentum needs to be given to promoting adult education and continuing learning for youths and adults deprived of education. This calls for measures aimed at promoting the right to literacy and improve adult learning situations and both formal and non-formal adult education. There is greater need to ensure the right to education of rural populations, especially those who live in remote areas. Promoting the quality of teaching and learning, with special attention to the strategies for placing, supporting and retaining qualified and trained teachers in rural areas and improving their working conditions is of crucial importance. In its Concluding Observations concerning Morocco and China, CESCR recalled the obligation of States parties to ensure the availability of sufficient numbers of teachers in rural or remote areas.

Literacy as a right, linked to adult or continuing education, has further evolved towards the concept of lifelong learning. The EFA Global Monitoring Report 2006 has highlighted the main issues in literacy "as a right" and its interpretation as a foundational universal life skill. In that perspective, it is necessary to intensify action at national level in line with the right to adult education and literacy, as provided by UNESCO's *Recommendation on the Development of Adult Education and the Hamburg Declaration on Adult Learning*, for providing continuing education and learning opportunities for youth and adults. The *Recommendation on the Development of Adult Education* stipulates that "The place of adult education in each education system should be defined with a view to achieving a rectification of the main inequalities in access to initial education and training, in particular inequalities based on age, sex, social position or social or geographical origin." Besides, the legal obligations of States must be underlined in keeping with the *Convention against Discrimination in Education* which enjoins States to "encourage and intensify by appropriate methods the education of persons who have *not* received any primary education or *who have not completed the entire primary education* course and the *continuation of their education* on the basis of individual capacity" (Article 4 c). The International Covenant contains similar provisions, and employs, in its article 13 (2) (d), the term "fundamental education" which extends to all those who have not yet satisfied their "basic learning needs".

Nomad populations including pastoral nomads, and Roma populations, are spread over a large number of countries, in all regions of the world. Enabling these populations to exercise their right to education, recognized by the *Recommendation on the Development of Adult Education*, is an area which deserves much more attention. The role of public authorities as regards the obligation of parents to ensure that their children attend schools, which they frequently change raises particular problems and imposes responsibility on public authorities in regard to the obligation of those parents as Nomad populations frequently move.

The need for special attention to be paid by Government to certain specific categories of population has been recognized in the course of recent development on modernizing national legislation, with UNESCO's technical assistance – for instance, positive measures in favour of the children from the Arid and Semi-arid Lands (ASALs) in Kenya; the *alma-jiri* in Nigeria (the Act on Compulsory Free Universal Basic Education of the Republic of Nigeria (2004) provides for basic education including the education of special groups such as nomadic and migrants, girl-children and women, *almajiri*, street children and disabled groups (article 15 (1)); and the Kuchi population in Afghanistan who form around 8 per cent of population of which nearly 40 per cent have never attended a primary school.

Migrant workers, refugees, internally displaced persons (IDPs), and asylum-seekers represent groups whose right to education raises critical questions. The recent concern of many European countries to counter discrimination in education based on race and national origin has been prompted in part by the growth of immigrant populations and influx into the schools of large numbers of children of immigrant families. States have adopted a variety of approaches to meet this challenge. The exclusion of migrant workers, refugees, internally displaced persons (IDPs), and asylum-seekers from education has regularly been addressed by CESCR in its Concluding Observations. Children of migrant workers, in the case of China, particularly in relation to internal migrant workers, are entitled to education on an equal basis as nationals. With regard to immigrant children, States parties have been encouraged to reduce linguistic barriers through intensive language training and "to offer appropriate catch-up classes, and to increase family awareness about the importance of education for future professional careers." The Covenant has also been interpreted as requiring equal access to all levels of education by asylum-seeking children. Uncertain residence status and limited access to personal identification documents frequently precludes refugees and IDPs from access to education as such documentation is usually required to register for schooling.

It is, therefore, important to promote measures as a follow up to the *International Convention on the Protection of the Rights of All Migrant Workers and Members of their Families*, which provides that "Migrant workers shall enjoy equality of treatment with nationals of the State of employment; and access to educational institutions and services (...)", and that "each child of a migrant worker shall have the basic right of access to education on the basis of equality of treatment with nationals of the State concerned."

Children from poor households are most affected in exercising their right to education. Millions of those living in poverty suffer multiple disadvantages. An *unequivocal political commitment* is needed so that the children living in poverty are not relegated to the most disadvantaged schools. Providing education to the poor, to the excluded and to the disadvantaged – the rural poor but also children and youths in teeming urban slums – is a priority concern, as poverty is the greatest obstacle to realizing the right to education.

The right to education has close links with the right to development and is a powerful tool in poverty reduction strategies. To achieve the EFA goals, the governments, organizations, agencies, groups and associations represented at the World Education Forum pledged themselves "to promote EFA policies within a sustainable and well-integrated sector framework clearly linked to *poverty elimination and development strategies*" (emphasis added). Without accelerated progress towards education for all, national and internationally agreed targets for poverty reduction will be missed and inequalities between countries and within societies will widen.

The international norms of non-discrimination and equality, which demand that particular attention be given to vulnerable groups and individuals from such groups, have profound implications for anti-poverty strategies. As such, a human-rights approach to poverty can enforce anti-poverty strategies and make them more effective. The need for accelerated momentum for the achievement of literacy and the eradication of poverty - "based on the recognition of the fundamental importance for enjoying the right to education" and its promotion through 'legal discourse' on literacy and normative action as part of EFA process is urgent.

The above categories are not limitative as regards those who could be deprived of basic education – marginalized and vulnerable would also include demobilized soldiers, children in conflict areas, street children, child workers, exploited children and those victims of child labour as well as stateless persons/those without official papers, etc.

Future Action and Key Tasks

The challenges of ensuring that the EFA goals are met and every one is enabled to receive basic education are indeed daunting. The right to education, which is inviolable, is of paramount importance and its sanctity must be maintained everywhere. Advocacy for fulfilling the right to education in all its inclusive dimensions is fundamental to the theme of the International Conference of Education: *Inclusive Education: The way for the future.*

Ensuring equality of educational opportunities is a continuing challenge faced by Member States, as has been shown by the results of the seventh consultation of Member States on the measures taken for implementation of the Convention and the Recommendation against Discrimination in Education. Even in countries where educational opportunities are in general widely available, inequalities remain in the ability of all social groups to fully avail themselves of such opportunities, giving rise to early drop-out from education and failure to obtain a useful qualification. Ensuring that children from differing socio-economic backgrounds, born with different advantages and disadvantages, have equality in educational opportunities, is a key element in facing this challenge. Inclusive dimensions of the right to education are important both as regards access to education and the way it is dispensed.

In countries facing severe resource constraints and caught in widespread poverty, inequalities in educational opportunity are often more pronounced and have led States to adopt different kinds of compensatory measures. Fundamental changes are required in the distribution of educational resources, along with positive measures in favour of the children from poor households deprived of basic education. Normative action at national level for the benefit of the poorest and most marginalized children, youths and adults should be promoted through "better school infrastructure, elimination of tuition fees, provision of additional financial support to the poorest households and flexible schooling for working children and youth". *Equity, quality and financing* as key areas in pushing forward the

EFA agenda have been highlighted in the EFA Global Monitoring Report (GMR, 2008), which states that "Education expansion does not necessarily translate into reduced inequality" and "Most countries, even those with relatively high primary enrolment ratios, need to address equity issues".

The work of all United Nations human right treaty bodies contributes to promoting the fundamental principle of equality of educational opportunities - laid down by the *Convention against Discrimination in Education*, and also expressed in the United Nations human rights treaties.

Where stark contrasts in quality and opportunities between education in public and private institutions exist, such as identified in Morocco by the CESCR, States parties are under an obligation to ensure that low-income sectors of society are not denied equal opportunities.

Emphasis on all-inclusive dimensions of the right to education is critical in eliminating existing *inequalities* and *disparities* in educational facilities, both as regards various beneficiaries of education as well as *inequalities* and *disparities* in different regions in a country. For education to be all-inclusive, everyone must be given the opportunity to achieve and maintain an acceptable level of learning. This requires the removal of all 'educational disparities' and attention as an 'urgent priority' to categories suffering from exclusion or discrimination, even if the achievement of equity involves positive discrimination or granting priorities to certain groups. As the GMR (2008) states,"Despite overall enrolment increases, sub-national disparities in school participation persist between regions, provinces or states and between urban and rural areas. Children from poor, indigenous and disabled populations are also at a systematic disadvantage, as are those living in slums". Therefore, as is stated in the Concluding Observations adopted by CESCR, any disparities in school enrolment rates between girls and boys and between rural and urban areas must be eliminated.

For children from social, cultural and ethnic groups or families that do not offer favourable conditions for the development and education of their children, the equity of education implies a set of "positive" measures. Such temporary special measures may be a suitable action in cases of longstanding or historical and persisting forms of discrimination. They may be justifiable until full equality of treatment is reached. As the Communiqué issued at the Seventh Meeting of the High Level Group on EFA in Dakar states, "Governments should strive to ensure that no child is excluded from school because of the financial burden (...)." At this meeting, the Ministers underlined that poverty and social exclusion remain the major barriers to achieving the EFA goals, and they committed themselves to further measures in support of the poorest populations, such as abolition of school fee and cash transfers, as well as policies to promote inclusion. *Affirmative action and promotional measures* are highly necessary in order to eliminate existing inequities and disparities in education. Some practical measures reported to UNESCO on the Seventh Consultation of Member States, mentioned above, are significant in terms of available experience.

There is need to clearly address the educational needs of poorer sectors of society as well as economically and socially-marginalized and vulnerable groups. Special consideration must be given to such educational needs. Articles 3 and 4 of the UNESCO's *Convention against Discrimination in Education* contain provisions for this purpose for granting scholarships and other forms of assistance, etc. The *Convention* covers "matter of school fees and the grant of scholarships or other forms of assistance to pupils." Similarly, Article 13 of the *International Covenant on Economic, Social and Cultural Rights* includes "an adequate fellowship system" among its provisions on the right to education. The nature and scope of the right to education as provided for in Article 13 have been elucidated by the General Comment 13 on the right to education: this General Comment states that "the requirement that 'an adequate fellowship system shall be established' should be read with the Covenant's non-discrimination and equality provisions; the fellowship system should enhance equality of educational access for individuals from disadvantaged groups."

In its Concluding Observations, the CESCR has, for example, recommended that States parties upgrade schooling programmes for indigenous and migrant children, child workers and children belonging to other disadvantaged and marginalized groups, in particular girls, take effective measures to promote school attendance by Roma children and children belonging to other minority groups, as well as refugee and internally displaced children, by increasing subsidies, scholarships and the number of teachers instructing in minority languages, and promote equal access by Roma children to primary education, e.g. through the grant of scholarships and the reimbursement of expenses for schoolbooks and of travel expenses to attend school, and to closely monitor school attendance by Roma children. Similarly, minority and indigenous children and their families may be entitled to temporary special measures, including scholarships and financial subsidies such as reimbursement of expenses for schoolbooks and of travel expenses.

The right to education needs to be monitored with greater concern for quality imperatives. Quality stands at the heart of EFA. "*Minimum educational standards*" must be ensured as a follow up to the *Convention against Discrimination in Education* which recognizes the importance of norms, standards and quality of education. Poor standards of education – both in public and private schools – can, *inter alia*, be attributed to lack of qualified teachers and lack of respect for their professional status and working conditions. The *Recommendation concerning the Status of Teachers*, which "*applies to all teachers in both private and public schools*" (Article 2, emphasis added), provides a legal framework for measures to that end. Greater emphasis needs to be placed on action at the national level on universalizing access to quality education for all, and on equitable deployment of teachers in rural, urban and remote areas.

The state obligations for fully respecting the right to education as a universal right must be reflected in national legal systems, in education policies and strategies and in education programmes. Some recent developments in national legislation, reported to UNESCO on the Seventh Consultation of Member States are exemplary. While promoting UNESCO's normative action, aimed at more effective implementation of conventions and recommendations in the field of education, greater emphasis on all-inclusive dimensions of the right to education is required. It is important

that Governments fully abide by their legal and political obligations and adopt necessary measures and intensify action with a view to meeting the challenging tasks in the full implementation of the right to education as a universal right. Greater attention should be given to the measures taken at the national level while emphasizing the need for wider access to education in order to foster the full realization of the right to education. The decision taken by the Executive Board at its 177th session (177 EX/Decision 36) and the resolution accordingly adopted by the General Conference at its 34th session in October 2007 (34 C/Resolution 13) request the Director-General of UNESCO to "intensify his efforts to encourage Member States to adopt effective domestic measures intended to secure education for all without discrimination or exclusion as part of the EFA process."

As mentioned above, the right to education is universal and does not admit of exclusion or discrimination. It must, as such, be incorporated into national legal systems. While examining the foundations of the right to education in national legal systems, the Joint Expert Group, mentioned above, had underlined the need for analysing the international legal framework of this right as well as the constitutional provisions and laws, so that policies are accordingly evaluated and developed. As such, the inclusive dimensions of the right to education would be an important aspect, while undertaking analytical studies and dissemination of the knowledge on its constitutional and legislative bases. The Ministers of Education at the

Seventh Meeting of the High-Level Group on Education for All (December 2007, Dakar, Senegal), mentioned the need "to determine more precisely the characteristics of excluded groups, their circumstances and needs and thus inform more inclusive educational policies", and to "identify steps to strengthen and harmonize, where necessary, the *legislative framework within which the right to education is guaranteed*".

Strengthening normative action with a focus on the all-inclusive dimensions of the right to education requires new policy and programmatic approaches so that the right to education can be enjoyed universally, it is effectively enforced and becomes justiciable. Central to the reform process is the need to ensure stronger integration of education-sector planning with that for broader development objectives, at both national and international levels. There is need to encourage all actors in the field of education to pay due regard in their undertakings to the need for equity, inclusion and social cohesion in today's societies. All-inclusive dimensions of the right to education must be brought into focus while raising the profile of EFA in development, as a human right and as a fundamental tool in economic growth and poverty reduction.

References

Bernstein Tarrow, Norma, ed. *Human Rights and Education.* Oxford: Pergamon Press, vol. 3, Pergamon Comparative and International Education Series, 1987.

Beiter, Klaus Dieter. *The Protection of the Right to Education by International Law.* The Hague: Martinus Nijhoff. 2005.

Right to Education project. "Right to education – What is it? Acceptability". Retrieved 2010-09-11

UNESCO and UNICEF. *A Human Rights-Based Approach to Education for All.* 2007.

2

Instruments and Mechanisms for the Right to Education

Education is a fundamental human right and essential for the exercise of all other human rights. It promotes individual freedom and empowerment and yields important development benefits. Yet millions of children and adults remain deprived of educational opportunities, many as a result of poverty.

Normative instruments of the United Nations and UNESCO lay down international legal obligations for the right to education. These instruments promote and develop the right of every person to enjoy access to education of good quality, without discrimination or exclusion. These instruments bear witness to the great importance that Member States and the international community attach to normative action for realizing the right to education. It is for governments to fulfil their obligations both legal and political in regard to providing education for all of good quality and to implement and monitor more effectively education strategies.

Education is a powerful tool by which economically and socially marginalized adults and children can lift themselves out of poverty and participate fully as citizens.

The right to education is a fundamental human right. Every individual, irrespective of race, gender, nationality, ethnic or social origin, religion or political preference, age or disability, is entitled to a free elementary education. This right is explicitly stated in the United Nations' Universal Declaration of Human Rights (UDHR), adopted in 1948:

> "Everyone has the right to education. Education shall be free, at least in the elementary and fundamental stages. Elementary education shall be compulsory. Technical and professional education shall be made generally available and higher education shall be equally accessible to all on the basis of merit. ..." (Article 26)

Ensuring *access to education* is a precondition for full realization of the right to education. Without access, it is not possible to guarantee the right to education.

Quality of education is the other side of coin. Providing access to schools secures only one part of the right to education. Once in school, children can be subjected to indoctrination (e.g., in communist countries). As stated, in the UDHR:

> "... Education shall be directed to the full development of the human personality and to the strengthening of respect for human rights and fundamental freedoms. It shall promote understanding, tolerance and friendship among ... racial or religious groups. ..." (Article 26)

The right to education does not limit education to the primary or the first stage of basic education, or among children of a particular age range. The right to education is also not an end to itself, but an important tool in improving the quality of life. Education is key to economic development and the enjoyment of many other human rights. Education provides a means through which all people can become aware of their rights and responsibilities, which is an essential tool for achieving the goals of equality and peace.

Katerina Tomasevski, former United Nations Special Rapporteur on the right to education, points out: "There is a large number of human rights problems, which cannot be solved unless the right to education is addressed as the key to unlock other human rights. Education operates as multiplier, enhancing the enjoyment of all individual rights, freedoms where the right to education is effectively guaranteed, while depriving people of the enjoyment of many rights and freedoms where the right to education is denied or violated."

As part of the United Nations Literacy Decade (2003-2012), the Commission on Human Rights urged member states:

> "(a)To give full effect to the right to education and to guarantee that this right is recognized and exercised without discrimination of any kind;

> (b) To take all appropriate measures to eliminate obstacles limiting effective access to education, notably by girls, including pregnant girls, children living in rural areas, children belonging to minority groups, indigenous children, migrant children, refugee children, internally displaced children, children affected by armed conflicts, children with disabilities, children with human immunodeficiency virus/acquired immunodeficiency syndrome (HIV/AIDS) and children deprived of their liberty." (Resolution 2002/23)

Thus, *education about human* rights is closely related to the right to education. International and regional human rights noted in various documents (declarations, resolutions, and conventions) emphasize that the knowledge of human rights should be a priority in education policies.

Rights at Stake

The human right to education entitles every individual to:

1. Free and compulsory elementary education, and to readily available forms of secondary and higher education
2. Freedom from discrimination in all areas and levels of education, and to equal access to continuing education and vocational training
3. Information about health, nutrition, reproduction, and family planning

The human right to education is inextricably linked to other fundamental human rights ? rights that are universal, indivisible, interconnected, and interdependent including the right to:

- Equality between men and women and to equal partnership in the family and society
- Work and receive wages that contribute to an adequate standard of living
- Equality between the boy-child and girl-child in all areas, including education, health, nutrition, and employment
- Freedom of thought, conscience, religion, and belief
- Freedom from discrimination in all areas and levels of education
- Learn in one's own language
- Education for children of migrant workers
- Education for persons with disabilities and the freedom from discrimination in access to education
- Share in the benefits of scientific progress

Key Assistance Agencies

Several agencies around the world are working to make education available to all:

United Nations Educational, Scientific and Cultural Organization (UNESCO)

The main objective of UNESCO is to contribute to peace and security in the world by promoting collaboration among nations through education, science, culture, and communication. This will further universal respect for justice, for the rule of law, and for the human rights and fundamental freedoms that are affirmed for the peoples of the world, without distinction of race, sex, language, or religion, by the Charter of the United Nations. The United Nations Literacy Decade (2003-2012) aims to extend the use of literacy to those who do not currently have access to it. More than 861 million adults are in that position, and over 113 million children are not in school and therefore not in a position to learn to read or write either.

United Nations Children's Fund (UNICEF)

Created by the United Nations General Assembly in 1946 to help children after World War II in Europe, UNICEF was first known as the United Nations International Children's Emergency Fund. In 1953, UNICEF became a permanent part of the United Nations system, its task being to help children living in poverty in developing countries. Its name was shortened to the United Nations Children's Fund, but it retained the acronym "UNICEF," by which it is known to this day.

Believing in quality education for all, UNICEF helps children get the care and stimulation they need in the early years of life and encourages families to educate girls as well as boys. UNICEF supports young people, wherever they are, in making informed decisions about their own lives, and strives to build a world in which all children live in dignity and security. UNICEF's work is geared toward ensuring that all children realize their right to education, and that every child has the opportunity to develop to his or her full potential. Working with national governments, non-governmental organizations (NGOs), other United Nations agencies and private-sector partners, UNICEF protects children and their rights by providing services and supplies and by helping shape policy agendas and budgets in the best interests of children.

World Bank

Since it began funding education funding in 1963, the World Bank has provided over U.S. $30 billion in loans and credits. It currently finances 153 projects in 79 countries. Working closely with national governments, United Nations agencies, donors, NGOs, and other partners, the Bank helps developing countries in their efforts to reach the Education For All (EFA) goals of achieving universal primary education for all children by 2015 and reducing the education gap between boys and girls by 2005.

International Labour Organization (ILO)

The ILO is the UN specialized agency that seeks the promotion of social justice and internationally recognized human and labor rights. Founded in 1919, it is the only surviving major creation of the Treaty of Versailles, which created the League of Nations. It became the first specialized agency of the UN. The ILO is known for its long-standing work on vocational training policy and structures, but it also has an active program in education. The ILO's specialty lies in its detailed technical knowledge of what constitutes good employment practices — recruitment, career development, salaries, working conditions, and labor relations — as the basis for education reform and quality. Since the 1950s, ILO's work has focused on researching, promoting, and sharing information on standards and best practices. It is important (though often overlooked in education sector work) because the salaries of educational personnel take up 60 to 95 percent of governments' annual expenditures on education; it is highest in developing countries.

Standard-setting Instruments

Today the international community is faced with increasingly serious problems: proliferating acts of violence and conflicts; poverty and illiteracy; the gap between rich and poor; and marginalisation and social exclusion in a world where one quarter of all human beings live in poverty. The right to education is an invaluable tool in the bid to eradicate poverty and to tackle these problems. How great the challenge is can be seen from the fact that some 113 million children, 60% of them girls, have no access to primary education; at least 880 million adults, including a majority of women, are illiterate. There is a need, therefore, for "a global renewal of and recommitment to Education for All as a bedrock of peace and all forms of development.

UNESCO is convinced that resolute action in favour of education for all, such as is now indispensable, should be carried through with greater energy and better cooperation at the national and international levels. The Organisation, which was called immediately upon its inception to play a pioneering role in promoting the right to education, needs to redouble its efforts to respond to the fundamental educational needs in the world today. UNESCO's programme, as adopted in 1952, is concerned with the measures that need to be taken so that the right to free and compulsory education, as set forth in Article 26 of the Universal Declaration of Human Rights, is actually honoured. In this way, UNESCO establishes the fundamental principle of equality of opportunity for the children of the world. "It is just and it is necessary that all the children of the world should have the right to equal opportunity. This ideal is the motivating force which has led UNESCO to undertake a campaign for compulsory education."

Today, as UNESCO's vocation for education for all is renewed, the ideals set forth in its Constitution are as relevant as ever. Under its mandate, the Organisation must "contribute to peace and security by promoting collaboration among the nations through education, science and culture in order to further universal respect for justice, for the rule of law and for the human rights and fundamental freedoms which are affirmed for the peoples of the world." To do so, UNESCO must "give fresh impulse to popular education and to the spread of culture by collaborating with Members, at their request, in the development of educational activities; by instituting collaboration among the nations to advance the ideal of equality of educational opportunity without regard to race, sex or any distinctions, economic or social; [and] by suggesting educational methods best suited to prepare the children of the world for the responsibilities of freedom".

To fulfil its mission, UNESCO has drawn up numerous standard-setting instruments over the last decades in the field of the right to education, collaborating with Member States in educational activities as provided in the Constitution. Member States thus subscribed to the successive commitments intended to assert the right to education. There is no doubt that giving concrete expression to the right to education, in all its various aspects—"extending from initial or basic education to lifelong learning"– is best achieved by means of standard-setting activities coupled with follow-up mechanisms.

The right to education, characterised as a fundamental right, can be considered an "upstream" right in the sense that it determines whether other rights can actually be exercised. None of our civil, political, economic and social rights can be exercised by individuals unless they have received a certain minimum education, without which their access to such rights remains illusory and theoretical. What scope can freedom of opinion and expression have for those who, because they have not obtained, through education, the means of access to knowledge of the full range of opinion (under any but a totalitarian regime), are unable to form any opinions of their own? Again, of what use is freedom of expression to individuals who have not acquired, again through education, the tools they really need for self-expression? One could give many such examples.

Among economic and social rights, therefore, the right to education holds a central place. No one will deny that education is the basis for development, and no State desiring to foster its development can fail to be concerned with that long-term, but unavoidable, investment that is the education of the people, which will generally receive priority. Nor will anyone deny that education, which implies receptiveness and access to others, is the best instrument to combat all forms of discrimination, particularly as affecting women, children, minorities and others. Finally, so central to the human condition is knowledge that the search for democracy, the culture of peace, the protection of the environment, in short the quest for human well-being, all incontestably involve providing individuals—all individuals—with an effective, suitable education, in as much as knowledge and skills are proper to human beings. Education is therefore to be understood in the broad sense, as continuous, ongoing education taking place in a great variety of professional, social and community fields and places.

As part of its education mission and, therefore, with due regard for the principle of speciality, UNESCO has sought to cover all aspects, orders and elements of the right to education, whether the traditional three levels of education (primary, secondary, higher), the nature of the teaching (initial or continuing training, general, technical or vocational training), the recipients (children, adolescents, adults), the conditions under which the right is exercised (respect for the principle of nondiscrimination, attention to vulnerable groups: women and girls, minorities, refugees, displaced persons or to States or regions in difficulty—developing countries, least developed countries and those suffering conflicts), or the content of education (basic schooling, fundamental education, literacy). UNESCO also works on all aspects of the subject in an organised, planned and systematic manner.

The major instruments, of varying legal weight, which have been adopted and are annexed hereto, in full or in part, testify to this very complete perception of the issue. According to this outlook, the right to education can be said to acquire a dual dimension, both individual and collective, with progress in either sphere determining progress in the other. Because of its crucial importance, this right was first affirmed—and often at length, with a wealth of detail—in the great founding texts, then made part of the domestic and foreign policy of States so that it could be developed and adapted to the rapid changes in the world context, and affirmed and reaffirmed in ever more numerous conventions, declarations and action programmes. One might be tempted to see in this proliferation of texts an abdication of responsibility, an affordable way for the international community to salve its collective conscience. Though the incantatory function of this series of texts cannot be completely ignored, they also, and primarily, serve to keep up the pressure by reaffirming the commitment to achieving an essential objective through the implementation of a right whose content is constantly being reconsidered and updated; for that reason, questions can always be raised about their legal value, and hence about the scope and actual enforcement of the commitments made.

To affirm the right to education, States have adopted a number of international legal standards which fall into various categories and, as they follow one after another, give the impression of being links in a chain. They indisputably give rise today to a fairly comprehensive, if evolving, *corpus*, so that one may rightly speak in that regard of a truly "progressive development" of this right, in the sense that the expression is used to refer to innovative aspects in the formulation of the legal rule. Owing to a set of standards, right to education is established. It then becomes necessary to ensure that it is really enjoyed by individual right-holders and by the society, the State and the international community, which cannot make progress without education.

The right to education was included from the outset among the human rights listed in the major texts adopted by the United Nations: the *Universal Declaration of Human Rights* of 10 December 1948, the *International Covenant on Economic, Social and Cultural Rights and* even the *International Covenant on Civil and Political Rights* of 16 December 1966.

In this "Charter of Human Rights", the right to education holds a key position and is the subject of more precise and detailed provisions than the other rights. Moreover, the longest article of the *International Covenant on Economic, Social and Cultural Rights* is Article 13, which deals with education, setting out its aims and purposes, system and content, while Article 14 deals more specifically with the provision of free primary education. It will be recalled that, as indicated in analyses at the time, as the 1948 Universal Declaration was merely a United Nations General Assembly resolution, it was not recognised as legally binding, however great its political and moral scope. It was therefore necessary, in order to make it binding in character, that its major principles be taken up in an instrument of conventional nature, which was the purpose of the "Covenants". No doubt, as will be seen later, conceptions have changed today regarding the legal nature of General Assembly resolutions, and the analysis of the scope of the Universal Declaration has also changed, so that the "legal construction" may be somewhat different. But according to the canons of conventional international law, the method followed is the right and only really possible one. Moving from the general to the particular and from the affirmation of great principles to practical procedures designed to permit their implementation, conventions have therefore succeeded the Universal Declaration and, subsequently, the conventions themselves have been joined by other, more specific conventions, proclamations, programmes of action, etc. The basic texts may have aged in respect of one particular aspect or another. This observation does not in any way call into question the basic principles which they express and on which the right to education rests; it is merely intended to underline the need to devise new instruments on specific aspects derived from those principles so that the requisite adjustments can thus be made.

The major texts (conventions, declarations and programmes of action) adopted by UNESCO on the right to education are therefore of great importance in several respects. First, they reaffirm certain principles enshrined in the basic texts and give them concrete substance; otherwise, they would remain mere "principles" whose application would not be clear. Next, they make it possible for Member States' commitment to the right to education to be enlisted by updating the principles and procedures for exercising that right so as constantly to adapt to individual and collective needs. Among the regulatory texts established by UNESCO, a key place is given to the *Convention against Discrimination in Education* that was adopted in Paris by the General Conference of UNESCO at its 11th session on 14 December 1960, and which came into force on 22 May 1962. Referring to the *Universal Declaration of Human Rights*, which asserts in Article 7 the general principle of nondiscrimination and proclaims in Article 26 that every person has the right to education, and to the *Constitution of UNESCO*, the Convention, while respecting the diversity of national education systems, pursues the twin objectives of not only proscribing any form of discrimination in education but also of promoting equality of opportunity and treatment for all in that field. It is clear that if the two objectives are attained, enjoyment of the right to education is assured.

UNESCO's method of first adopting a convention on the subject was therefore a good one. It was also desirable to keep a firm line on these principles and ensure that they were not watered down. Reservations to the Convention are therefore excluded in Article 9, and Article 15 provides that it can be applied not only to the metropolitan territory of each State but also to territories whose international relations are the responsibility of that State, thus preventing the clause known in treaty law as the "colonial clause" from coming into play.

The question of technical and vocational education is also covered by a text that is a convention, namely, the *Convention on Technical and Vocational Education* adopted by the General Conference of UNESCO at its 25th session, in Paris on 10 November 1989. Referring to the *Universal Declaration of Human Rights*, in particular Articles 23 and 26 relating to the right to work and to education, and to the 1966 Covenants, the 1989 Convention also draws on the 1960 *Convention against Discrimination in Education* in considering that everyone should be able to enjoy this type of education on the grounds that it gives individuals access to employment and professional activity while contributing to the development of the State and to its collaboration with other States. The Convention lays emphasis on cooperation between UNESCO and the International Labour Organisation since the right to education and the right to work are very closely linked in this particular type of education known as vocational education. In this connection, the Convention is one of the international treaties adopted to complement and clarify the Universal Declaration of Human Rights and the Covenants of 1966. Like the 1960 Convention against Discrimination and by its legal nature as such, it therefore holds a central place in the standard-setting machinery of the right to education. These conventions are necessary as sources of rights and obligations. Such obligations may lead to strengthening international cooperation and exchanges, as in the present case, since the Convention contains several provisions on this point. As this concerns the specific field of human rights, there is greater scope for action, which will be considered later. It includes enabling the judge, before whom such matters can easily be brought by a private individual, to impose sanctions on a State Party for not fulfilling its obligations.

Besides these conventions, there is a set of standard-setting instruments of a less straightforwardly legal nature. These are the various recommendations, declarations, charters and frameworks for action adopted by conferences of representatives of States, sometimes together with members of civil society such as delegates from non-governmental organisations (NGOs), held within the framework of UNESCO or under its auspices.

As far as the principles are concerned, mention may be made of the *Declaration on Race and Racial Prejudice* adopted by the General Conference at its 20th session in November 1978. It proclaims that "the principle of the equality in dignity and rights of all human beings and all peoples, irrespective of race, colour and origin, is a generally accepted and recognised principle of international law" (Art. 9) and establishes "the right to be different" as well as the role of education.

The World *Declaration on Education for All* and the *Framework for Action to Meet Basic Learning Needs* adopted by the World Conference on Education for All, which met at Jomtien (Thailand) from 5 to 9 March 2000, and, more recently, the *Dakar Framework for Action Education for All: Meeting our Collective Commitments* adopted by the World Education Forum, which met at Dakar (Senegal) from 26 to 28 April 2000, are two comprehensive texts of a more uncertain standard-setting character than the conventions but of indisputable political importance. In Jomtien, the representatives of 155 States, officials from some 20 international organisations and the 150 or so NGOs represented adopted by acclamation these texts, whose overall goal was to define the role of education in human development policies and to express the concern to implement the principle of the *Universal Declaration of Human Rights* which states that "everyone has a right to education" in a world that is grappling with growing burdens such as debt, recession, population growth and environmental degradation, besides civil conflicts and crime. The *World Declaration on Education for All* recalls that "education is a fundamental right for all people, women and men, of all ages, throughout our world". It recognises "the necessity to give to present and coming generations an expanded vision of, and a renewed commitment to, basic education to address the scale and complexity of the challenge [of ensuring education for all]" (Preamble). The Declaration reaffirms the right to education: "We, the participants in the World Conference on Education for All, reaffirm the right of all people to education. This is the foundation of our determination, singly and together, to ensure education for all".

The views that emerge from the Jomtien Declaration, while being consistent with the basic texts, tend towards a modernisation and broadening of concepts such as basic education as well as reflection on the necessary conditions for basic education.

The Framework for Action resulting from the Declaration is intended as a reference and guide for governments, international organisations, bilateral aid agencies, NGOs and all those committed to the goal of education for all in formulating their own plans of action for implementing the World Declaration. The Framework for Action is decidedly pragmatic in that it envisages "three broad levels of concerted action: (i) direct action within individual countries, (ii) cooperation among groups of countries sharing certain characteristics and concerns, and (iii) multilateral and bilateral cooperation in the world community".

At the end of the decade of efforts to achieve education for all, the World Education Forum, which was held in Dakar from 26 to 28 April 2000 and marked their culminating point, can be considered as being the largest evaluation ever undertaken in the field of education. One hundred and sixty-four countries were represented, besides 150 "civil society groups", including many NGOs, amounting to some 1,500 participants altogether. As a "stocktaking meeting", the Dakar Forum was all the more important in that, as the preparations for it had been particularly thorough, a considerable mass of information was available, emphasising a highly contrasted situation from one country to another, with some countries having made remarkable progress in ten years while others were experiencing growing difficulties in various areas of the education sector. Owing to the precision of the objectives and strategies set out in the Framework for Action and the commitment made on those bases by the main partners to achieve education for all by 2015, the Dakar Framework for Action is of decisive importance as far as commitment on the part of the international community is concerned. Unlike the basic texts that perforce affirm principles, one finds here a level that is both more modest and more ambitious - more modest in terms of the status of the text adopted and the approach to the issue of the right to education; more ambitious in terms of the clear commitment, time-bound targets and the setting out of specific measures. The way in which these texts are interlinked and form a coherent whole geared to a clearly identified and defined objective is therefore evident. The right to education, hitherto affirmed in the form of a basic principle that remained somewhat abstract and therefore difficult to put into practice, takes on a clearer meaning as it is given concrete substance. As the efforts to be made are thus better identified, the course of action for attaining the objectives is mapped out more effectively and incentives for taking such action can be found.

Lastly, the *Receive Declaration of the E-9 Countries*, adopted by the E-9 Ministerial Review Meeting, Receive, Brazil, on 2 February 2000 with a view to the setting of an agenda for the next millennium, reaffirms "basic education as a human right". It stresses the importance of "effecting changes in legislation to extend basic education and include education for all in policy statements" and affirms for the future that "universal access to education will allow our peoples to participate more effectively in an interactive world".

The meaning and scope of the right to education have thus been clarified, but other texts play a similar clarifying role by dealing with more specific or sectorial aspects. Some may lay the foundations of an issue that will be taken up later in a convention, a method which is followed rather frequently in international law. This was true, as far as technical and vocational education was concerned prior to the 1989 Convention, of the *Revised Recommendation concerning Technical and Vocational Education*, adopted by the General Conference of UNESCO at its 18th session in Paris on 19 November 1974. Technical and vocational education is considered here in connection with the various skilled occupations, and therefore implies studying related techniques and sciences together with practical skills in addition to general education. It is, moreover, perceived as the gateway to continuing education and learning, and indeed to the various paths that tend to lead to skilled professions.

Certain other texts may update or modernise themes that have already been covered. This category includes, again in technical and vocational education, the recommendations of the Director-General of UNESCO contained in the document Technical and Vocational Education and Training: A Vision for the Twenty-First *Century*, adopted at the Second International Congress on Technical and Vocational Education, held in Seoul from 26 to 30 April 1999. This text takes up a question already considered at length by UNESCO, but which admittedly requires constant updating, particularly following the emergence of the new concept of "education throughout life" which is currently of great importance since it underpins all continuing training and lifelong education. In the twenty-first century, education is no longer a train that must be caught at a certain time of life and can no longer be caught if it has been missed.

Access to education has become permanent, and no opportunity should ever be considered lost, while at the same time technological development and the speed of scientific and technological change necessitate an updating of knowledge and regular retraining. The Seoul Recommendations, in which the Congress participants considered that technical and vocational education had a "crucial role to play" in the radically different society of the twenty-first century, deal with such learning throughout life.

The *Salamanca Statement* and the *Framework for Action on Special Needs Education*, adopted in Salamanca (Spain) on 10 June 1994 by the World Conference on Special Needs Education: Access and Quality, aims to facilitate access to education for persons with special needs still un-reached. It proclaims that "every child has a fundamental right to education, and must be given the opportunity to achieve and maintain an acceptable level of learning".

The Declaration reflects new lines of thinking on principles, policies and practices in special needs education. In recognising the need to work towards *schools for all*, it marks an important contribution to efforts to achieve education for all and to improve the effectiveness of regular schools. "Those with special educational needs must have access to regular schools which should accommodate them within a child-centred pedagogy capable of meeting these needs".

Other texts that are not legally binding also deal with specific matters. The Hamburg Declaration, adopted at the end of the Fifth International Conference on Adult Education, which states in a somewhat strangely worded phrase that "adult education is more than a right; it is a key to the twenty-first century", develops the new conception of education that extends "throughout life". The ultimate stated goal is "the creation of a learning society committed to social justice and general wellbeing".

Supplemented by an *Agenda for the Future*, which sets out in detail the new commitments to the development of adult learning called for by the Hamburg Declaration, the Declaration contains the main principles and concepts adopted so far in the context of the right to education and makes them generally applicable to the population as a whole, which demonstrates the relevance of adult education efforts made by UNESCO from the outset. Moreover, in 1976, UNESCO adopted a very important recommendation on the development of adult education, but the deep-seated changes that had occurred since then warranted the inclusion at the Hamburg meeting of the new concepts highlighted by the International Commission on Education for the Twenty-First Century, chaired by Jacques Dealers, stating that the concept of learning throughout life "goes beyond the traditional distinction between initial and continuing education. It links up with another concept that of the learning society, in which everything affords an opportunity of learning and fulfilling one's potential". Everyone can thus adapt to a changing world so that each person is involved in society and can contribute to its development.

Education also has a physical and sports component, which UNESCO catered for when it adopted on 21 November 1978, in Paris, at the 20th session of the General Conference of UNESCO, the *International Charter of Physical Education and Sport amended* in 1991. The term "Charter" is used here to give the instrument an official character but does not confer on it the legal status of a convention. It is only a recommendation, to which great political and moral importance is nonetheless ascribed since it aims at urging "governments, competent non-governmental organisations, educators, families and individuals themselves to be guided thereby, to disseminate it and to put it into practice". A large number of those beneficiaries, whose legal status is heterogeneous, and the nature of the requirements addressed, obviously make it no more than strictly a guide and a recommendation.

Prompted by a constant concern to adapt the right to education to all political, economic and social changes in the world, UNESCO, at the 28th session of the General Conference, held in Paris in November 1995, endorsed the Declaration adopted in Geneva in October 1994 at the end of the 44th session of the International Conference on Education, together with an Integrated Framework of Action. Observing the "manifestations of violence, racism, xenophobia, aggressive nationalism and violations of human rights, by religious intolerance, by the upsurge of terrorism in all its forms and manifestations and by the growing gap separating wealthy countries from poor countries", the authors of the Declaration were convinced that appropriate, properly conducted education policies would lead to mutual tolerance and understanding and therefore to the development of human rights and the building of a culture of peace and democracy.

Lastly, in recent years, higher education has in turn received particular attention with the Recommendation concerning the Status of Higher-Education Teaching Personnel of 11 November 1997, the World Declaration on Higher Education for the Twenty-First Century and the *Framework for Priority Action for Change and Development in Higher Education* adopted on 9 October 1998 by the World Conference on Higher Education for the Twenty-First Century: Vision and Action. These texts, which also have the character of recommendations, take into account the new and widespread emerging demand for higher education. That demand implies that frameworks for action should be developed which take into account the specific difficulties posed by the provision of higher education, the quest for quality and the need for rights to be matched by responsibilities arising from imperatives specific to that level of education, the vital role that it plays in development and the correlative need for access to it to be as broad as possible on the basis of the key principles of the right to education that must now be examined.

Beneficiaries of the Right to Education

The philosophy underlying Article 13 of the *International Covenant on Economic, Social and Cultural Rights is* to establish a right to education so that everyone accordingly receives a suitable education consistent with the needs of the society in which it is provided. What is significant is that the authors of the Covenant considered the right to education from two standpoints: the individual (conducive to the "full development of the human personality") and the collective (enabling "all persons to participate effectively in a free society").

Furthermore, it fulfils an international cooperation function by promoting "understanding, tolerance and friendship among all nations and all racial, ethnic or religious groups" and encouraging "the development of the activities of the United Nations for the maintenance of peace". The right to education is clearly perceived as the fundamental, central right that conditions many other rights and without the full exercise of which individuals, the society to which they belong and the world into which they are born cannot develop. Naturally, then, the right to education primarily benefits individuals in that they profit from the education that they have received. In that respect, the whole question is therefore how to make the exercise of that right both possible and effective, or how to enable every individual to enjoy maximum access to it. But with the extension of the right to education to the whole population it may also be seen in a more global perspective, in terms of the progress that this entails for the development of society, the State, and, beyond that, even the international community as a whole.

According to the modern view of the right to education, as expressed in the most recent texts, such as the *Dakar Framework for Action, the* object is to ensure universal access to that right for all children—regardless of their sex, their ethnic or cultural group, or any disability or particular situation—and for youth and adults, all of whom should have equitable access to appropriate programmes so designed as to enable them to acquire knowledge and the skills necessary for day-to-day life.

To begin by stating the obvious, the simplest way to achieve accessibility for all is by providing free education. But is it realistic to say that this can be done everywhere, if we consider the costs of universal provision, especially in certain States? This is a delicate issue and one that has not been addressed sufficiently consistently or in depth by the international community; instead there has been what has been called a "shift of emphasis", in other words emphasis has not always been laid upon the same aspects of the right to education since the Universal Declaration of Human Rights was adopted and, consequently, the commitment to one or other of the principles originally proclaimed– including free fundamental education, Article 26—may not have been total. In Article 4 of the 1960 Convention against Discrimination in Education the General Conference of UNESCO recognised that primary education should be compulsory and (by correlation) free, but did not apply the same principle to other levels of education. The *International* Covenant on Economic, Social and Cultural Rights provides for "the progressive introduction of free education" at the secondary and higher levels, while the 1989 *Convention on the Rights of the Child* calls for primary and secondary education to be made free, but not higher education. In paragraph 7(ii), the *Dakar Framework for Action requires* only compulsory primary education to be free.

But how meaningful is *equitable and unrestricted access* to education programmes unless there is a correlative recognition of free provision or assistance for the needy, which is the price to be paid for making these principles a reality. It must be said that less attention is paid to this point in the Dakar Framework for Action than in the World Declaration adopted at Jomtien in 1990. That said, the *Expanded* Commentary on the Dakar Framework for Action does broach the matter directly and in practical terms, asserting that no children should be denied the opportunity to complete a good quality primary education because their family cannot afford it. Child labour must not stand in the way of education. The inclusion of children with special needs, from disadvantaged ethnic minorities and migrant population, from remote and isolated communities and from urban slums, and others excluded from education, must be an integral part of strategies to achieve universal primary education (UPE) by 2015.

Making education free is not, however, the only way of making it accessible: nondiscrimination is no less essential since it enables those from disadvantaged or vulnerable categories to benefit equally from the right to education. There is an even greater obstacle to overcome here, as there are not only economic factors at play but also cultural and sociological constraints that cannot be overlooked and are difficult to circumvent.

It was in fact from this standpoint that UNESCO addressed the right to education when it asserted its desire, in the *Convention against Discrimination in Education* of 14 December 1960, to implement the principles of the Universal Declaration. For the purposes of the 1960 Convention (Art. 1) the term "discrimination" includes any distinction, exclusion, limitation or preference which, being founded on race, colour, sex, language, religion, opinion, economic condition or birth, might impair equality of treatment in education of any kind.

The Convention specifies, however, that organising separate education for the two sexes should not be deemed to constitute discrimination if the study courses are the same or equivalent and the teaching staff and premises are of comparable quality. Similarly, separate education systems may be established for religious or linguistic reasons if they apply the same principle of equivalence, and participation in them remains optional and is left to the free choice of the interested parties. Private education may coexist with education provided by the public authorities if the object is not to secure the exclusion of any group but to provide educational facilities in addition to those provided by the public authorities. These principles having been established, the States that have ratified the Convention (and, it should be recalled, no reservations are permitted) must, under their obligation to execute its provisions, take all necessary domestic legislative and regulatory measures to abrogate any texts that are contrary to the Convention and adopt those that bring their legislation into line with the Convention. Articles 3 and 4 offer the necessary guidelines for this purpose by indicating the measures to be taken in the matters of school fees, the granting of scholarships and other forms of assistance, standards of education, etc. Nondiscrimination also has to do with a very important principle of freedom, that of the right of parents to choose for their children the educational establishment of their choice when there exist institutions other than those maintained by the public authorities and the right to ensure, in a manner consistent with the procedures followed in the State for the application of its legislation, the religious and moral education of their children. And lastly, it has to do with the educational rights of minorities. The periodic reports that States are required to submit on the measures adopted are designed to ensure that the Convention is being effectively applied and that the obligations contained in it are being fulfilled.

Later texts support these principles and rules by complementing, specifying or illustrating them in such a way that, from both the economic and political standpoints, and even in terms of administrative practice, which is equally essential here, the principle of nondiscrimination is respected. The Jomtien World Declaration –significantly entitled “Education for All”—and the Framework for Action called for “universalising access and promoting equity” (Declaration, Art. 3). For that purpose “basic education” (not the same as primary education and possibly going beyond it, according to the options taken) must be provided to all children, young people and adults. For it to be equitable, everyone must be given the opportunity to achieve and maintain an acceptable level of learning. That also requires the removal of all “educational disparities” and attention as an “urgent priority” to categories suffering from exclusion or discrimination, such as girls and women and underserved groups (street children, working children, rural and remote population, nomads and migrant workers, indigenous peoples, ethnic, racial and linguistic minorities, refugees, displaced persons and people under occupation, and the disabled requiring special attention), even if the achievement of equity entails positive discrimination or granting priorities to certain groups.

The *Receive Declaration of the E-9 Countries*, adopted by the Ministers of Education of the nine-high population (E-9) countries, the world's nine most populated countries, in Receive, Brazil, on 2 February 2000, underscores the need "to draft a new visionary agenda for the new millennium that will reaffirm basic education as a human right". It recognises the challenge of addressing adequately existing inequities in education, particularly in regard to girls' and women's education. It therefore declares as one of its goals "effecting changes in legislation to extend basic education and include education for all in policy statements".

The Framework for Priority Action for Change and Development of Higher *Education* adopted along with the *World Declaration on Higher Education for the Twenty-First Century* provides that "States, including their governments, parliaments and other decision-makers, should (a) establish, where appropriate, the legislative, political and financial framework for the reform and further development of higher education in keeping with the terms of the Universal Declaration of Human Rights, which establishes that higher education shall be accessible to all on the basis of merit. No discrimination can be accepted, no one can be excluded from higher education or its study fields, degree levels and types of institutions on grounds of race, gender, language, religion or age or because of any economic or social distinctions or physical disabilities. [...]"

Mindful of the *Hamburg Declaration on Adult Learning* and the Agenda for the Future, adopted by the Fifth International Conference on Adult Education, the General Conference of UNESCO noted in 1999 that "effective lifelong learning can help address basic skills needs in literacy, widen participation in and promote access to learning, reduce inequality, improve employability, and contribute to community development and to social inclusion". It is significant that the same concerns were expressed by the United Nations General Assembly in the *Millennium Declaration*, in which the heads of State and Government resolved to ensure that by 2015 "children everywhere, boys and girls alike, will be able to complete a full course of primary schooling and that girls and boys will have equal access to all levels of education".

In the Integrated Framework of Action on Education for Peace, Human Rights and *Democracy*, too, particular attention is paid to "vulnerable population"; it states that specific actions and strategies are required for ensuring respect for their "educational rights" and that, if they are to enjoy their rights, that must also have implications in the curricula and methods and in the way education is organised. The *Hamburg Declaration on Adult Learning expresses* the same concern, in the sector that it covers, for "ensuring the right to education for all, particularly for the most vulnerable groups of society" [...], namely "the un-reached and the excluded", "indigenous peoples", and "disabled persons"; interestingly it asserts that education is not a matter of age since "basic education for all means that people, whatever their age, have an opportunity, individually and collectively, to realise their potential".

With regard to higher education, the *World Declaration on Higher Education for the Twenty-First Century* lays particular emphasis on nondiscrimination and addresses it at length. In this area the issue is a particularly important and delicate one since everyone agrees that higher education cannot be open to all without conditions of access. The difficulty lies in ensuring the strict implementation of the principles of Article 13 of the Universal Declaration of Human Rights, namely that higher education shall be equally accessible to all on the basis of merit. This is why Article 3 (Equity of access) of the World Declaration on Higher Education stipulates that admission should be based on "the merit, capacity, efforts, perseverance and devotion shown by those seeking access to it" and that it can "take place in a lifelong scheme, at any time, with due recognition of previously acquired skills". The conditions of access to higher education being thus defined and specified, no discrimination in granting access to higher education on the previously defined grounds (race, gender, language or religion, physical disability, etc.) is permissible. Indeed, the Declaration goes even further and seeks to ensure real equity, requiring as it does that mechanisms be created to improve the functional aspects of access to higher education, by means of reordering structures or improving linkages with secondary education. "Special target groups" (indigenous peoples, cultural and linguistic minorities, disadvantaged groups and people living under occupation) are the subject of Article 3(d). For their benefit access to higher education must be actively facilitated both in their own interest, to help them overcome the obstacles that they face, and in the interest of society as a whole, since their special experience can be a valuable asset.

Article 4 of the Declaration is specially devoted to the status of women, as despite significant progress women continue to be impeded by various socioeconomic, cultural and political obstacles from gaining access to higher education. According to the Declaration, sustained efforts in a number of areas are required in order to eliminate those obstacles.

In respect of technical and vocational education, according to the *Convention on Technical and Vocational Education,* adopted on 10 November 1989 by the General Conference of UNESCO, the Contracting States "shall guarantee" (Art. 2, para. 3) that there is no discrimination against individuals who have attained the educational level required for admission into technical and vocational education and "shall take appropriate measures" (Art 2, para. 4) to enable the handicapped and other disadvantaged groups to benefit from technical and vocational education. The *Revised Recommendation concerning* Technical and Vocational Education and the Recommendations of the Second International Congress on Technical and Vocational Education advocate compliance with the same principle of nondiscrimination and the same efforts to assist disadvantaged groups or other victims of obstacles to free access to education.

The principle of nondiscrimination even applies to physical education and sports. The 1993 *International Charter of Physical Education and Sport proclaims* free access by all to physical education and sport without discrimination in the sense of the Universal Declaration of Human Rights, and recommends guaranteeing such free access since it also declares the existence of a "right to physical education and sport" (Preamble) whose effective realisation requires considerable effort and recognition as a "fundamental right for all".

In Dakar, these essential themes were comprehensively addressed in the Framework for Action of 28 April 2000. As has been said, the Dakar Forum is a "stocktaking" meeting. The text adopted there describes as "unacceptable" that some 113 million children have no access to primary education, that discrimination continues to permeate education systems. Reasserting that education is a "fundamental right", it proclaims a collective commitment to ensuring that, by 2005, gender disparities will be eliminated in primary and secondary education, that gender equality in education will be achieved by 2015, and that, also by 2015, all children will have access to free and compulsory primary education of good quality, thereby apparently acknowledging that the latter two commitments will need more time. It is significant that the notion of "equitable access" features systematically in the wording of all the aims set for the different levels of education.

Benefits to Society

From the outset, there has been this inherent dualism in the right to education: as an individual right everyone is entitled to it but at the same time, according to Article 26 of the *Universal Declaration of Human Rights*, whereas education is intended to ensure "the full development of the human personality", it is also directed towards "the strengthening of respect for human rights and fundamental freedoms". The authors of the 1948 text did not wish to separate the individual right, which they intended to become universally accessible, from the collective benefit that the social corpus might gain from it: education for all would further the observance of human rights and fundamental freedoms within the State. And beyond the bounds of the State, in their view, education "shall promote understanding, tolerance and friendship among all nations, racial or religious groups, and shall further the activities of the United Nations for the maintenance of peace". This wording is reproduced word for word in Article 5. 1. A of the 1960 *Convention against Discrimination in Education, and* taken up again in Article 13 of the *International Covenant on Economic, Social and Cultural Rights.* Education lies at the heart of political, economic and social changes in our societies, which is why, over the years since 1948, the scope of its aims has broadened to encompass all "socialite values", the expression used in Article 1 (e) of the *World Declaration on Higher Education for the Twenty-First Century*. With variants and some shifts in emphasis—in particular by comparison with the *Universal Declaration of Human Rights*—the various texts have established linkages between education and human rights, democracy and peace, and between education and development.

Concerning the first aspect, the *Declaration* and the *Integrated Framework of Action on Education for Peace, Human Rights and Democracy brings* together the elements contained in the various texts of different kinds. It begins with a very broad overview of the world situation and, placing education at the heart of the provisions, assigns it the very general mission of improving troublesome situations. The aim is ambitious, not to say overambitious, but the text is nonetheless of considerable interest since it quite successfully sums up the contribution that education can make. "Citizens" are to be educated by means of education policies that "contribute to the development of understanding, solidarity and tolerance among individuals and among ethnic, social, cultural and religious groups and sovereign nations" and by an education that will ensure the promotion of "knowledge, values, attitudes and skills conducive to respect for human rights and to an active commitment to the defence of such rights and to the building of a culture of peace and democracy". The Integrated Framework of Action, following on from the Declaration, is replete with references to the promotion of the "values" that go into educating citizens; their personal identities are reinforced in the "convergence of ideas and solutions which strengthen peace, friendship and solidarity between individuals and peoples". In the same train of thought, emphasis is laid on the specific role to be played by higher education, which is probably better equipped for analysing and examining ethics, values and an appreciation of the "interdependence of States in an increasingly global society". At Jomtien in 1990 similar notions had already been included among the "basic learning needs" listed in Article 1 of the *World Declaration on Education for All.* This Declaration recommends tolerance towards different social, political and religious systems, the upholding of commonly accepted humanistic values and human rights and working for peace (Art. 1. 2), while considering that the transmission and enrichment of common cultural values help individuals and society find their identity and worth (Art. 1. 3). It is the satisfaction of basic learning needs that will enable the collective cultural, linguistic, spiritual and environmental heritage to be respected and built upon (Art. 1. 2). The fact must be faced, however, that not only will it prove difficult to implement these generous declarations of intent rapidly but they also are too general to be truly workable.

In that regard the *Dakar Framework for Action - Education For All: Meeting Our Collective Commitments* is probably more realistic. After boldly taking stock of the situation without any complacency, taking a typically very practical approach, the authors declare that, following a long succession of commitments solemnly proclaimed at various meetings, "the challenge now is to deliver on these commitments". In paragraph 3, they simply affirm that education includes learning "to live together" and enables people "to transform their societies" and "improve their lives". This is, all in all, a more down-to earth ambition but an essential one nonetheless, and one that ultimately conditions all other, loftier ambitions that cannot be fulfilled until people "improve their lives" –development by another name.

In fact the connection between education and development, the other aspect of the linkages referred to above, is an obvious one with a long history. Although investing in education inevitably produces effects only in the long term, nobody has ever disputed the fact that it is a necessity for States' development or that it is a priority. One of the recent pronouncements on development was the declaration concluding the World Summit for Social Development, held in Copenhagen in 1995, in which the heads of State and Government included among their ten "commitments" that of promoting universal and equitable access to (quality) education, confirming the well-established view of the role of education in the development process. But in fact a similar commitment was made earlier at Rio, in Agenda 21, and later in the *Agenda for Development* prepared by the Secretary-General of the United Nations in 1997.

Among the specific texts on the right to education, the *World Declaration on Education for All* and the *Framework for Action to Meet Basic Learning Needs*, both adopted at Jomtien, take a very clear stand in declaring that "time, energy and funding directed to basic education are perhaps the most profound investment in people and in the future of a country which can be made" and that "today, more than ever, education must be seen as a fundamental dimension of any social, cultural and economic design". These views are then taken up in the Framework for Action. The wording of these recommendations bears the strong imprint of the new concepts of development, which place more emphasis on social than on economic factors or, to be more precise, incorporate human and social parameters more fully into development, seen as the development of human beings rather than growth in GNP.

Perhaps more realistic, the *Dakar Framework for Action* does not stray from this general line when it designates education as the "key to sustainable development". In turn the *Expanded Commentary on the Dakar Framework for Action* states that "there is a powerful correlation between low enrolment, poor retention and unsatisfactory learning outcomes and the incidence of poverty". It underscores education's leading role in development by indicating, in paragraph 21, that "debt reduction programmes should offer governments an opportunity to give priority to education within overall poverty reduction frameworks". And the question acquires a new dimension when we look at current trends in world society and globalisation since, as is observed most judiciously in the text, "countries and households denied access to opportunities for basic education in an increasingly knowledge-based global economy face the prospect of deepening marginalisation within an increasingly prosperous international economy". Against that background, ensuring the exercise of the right to education becomes a real challenge for the poorest countries.

Implementation of the Right to Education

Thus recognised and accessible to all, the right to education must now be implemented. For this purpose, education systems must be organised around a specific content and be able to function through available resources.

Organisation and Content of Education

The general organisational principles, as established by a variety of texts, hold good whatever the type, level or context of the education in question.

Each State is of course responsible for organising teaching in accordance with its educational requirements. As stated in the *Dakar Framework for Action," the* heart of the education for all activity lies at the country level". National plans, taking into account each State's particular context, set out to define the strategies and resources required for their implementation. It can be beneficial for States to draw up such plans using the UNESCO frameworks for action as a reference. Thus the *Framework for Action to Meet Basic Learning Needs*, adopted in Jomtien in 1990, invites States to use these plans to "develop their own specific plans of action and programmes in line with their particular objectives, mandates and constituencies".

Similarly, it is recalled that the UNESCO Major Project in Latin America and the Caribbean operates along these lines. Without disregarding external support, the outcome of educational initiatives will therefore depend on the measures taken by individual countries, whose governments "are the key agents for improvement". Indeed, a document such as the *Framework for Action to Meet Basic Learning Needs* is by no means a substitute for States in their mission to organise public service education, but only an instrument containing guidelines, advice and proposed or suggested examples which States are free to follow or not. Hence the use of the conditional to express the fact that local plans "could" address various points. There follows a long list of no fewer than 14 items thus proposed.

In fact, such is generally the principal aim pursued by these various standard-setting instruments when they have no conventional legal value beyond advice and guidance for States in their choices and policies, on the basis of the—most probably correct –assumption that discussion, exchange and the knowledge of other models are essential in this area. The *Dakar Framework for Action does* not depart from this method and indeed calls for its general introduction in all States, suggesting that the development of national plans be as open and democratic as possible, by including a large number of actors, in particular representatives of the people, community spokes people, parents, learners, NGOs and civil society.

These plans, developed in a wider poverty reduction and development framework—such as the *Dakar Framework for Action* conceived them—reflect a conception of education for all which extends well beyond the simple process of acquiring knowledge and fits into the context of a genuine political and social programme for the joint benefit of individuals and society. Educational strategies are therefore intended to complement those applied in the fields of health, population, work, social welfare and even the production sector. Thus education is not confined to specialists but is a matter of concern for all. This is in line with thinking that a strong political commitment is necessary to achieve education for all in practice.

Therefore, although it is not the sole actor, the State remains the principal driving force since it is responsible for setting frameworks and guidelines. This mission is explicitly reaffirmed for instance in the 1989 *Convention on Technical and Vocational Education and* also referred to in the 1997 *Hamburg Declaration on Adult Learning* as the "essential vehicle for ensuring the right to education for all". Nevertheless, the latter text recognises that there is "a new role for the state", that it is not the sole vehicle and that education should now be organised into *partnerships*.

As stated in the *World Declaration on Education for All*, "Genuine partnerships contribute to the planning, implementing, managing and evaluating of basic education programmes. When we speak of 'an expanded vision and a renewed commitment', partnerships are at the heart of it" (Art. 7). The partnerships recommended and described at Jomtien are among the various subsection and forms of education, between education and other government departments, including planning, finance, health, labour, communication, social sectors and between the State and NGOs, the private sector, local communities, religious groups and families. In the Framework for Action that follows the Declaration, there is a lengthy passage on Undertaking Joint Activities, which would be recommended in contexts of regional cooperation. This would enable to take advantage of economies of scale and the comparative advantages of the various participating countries.

The concept of partnership is reiterated in the *Dakar Framework for Action*, which holds that the implementation of education for all can only be sustainable and effective through "broad-based partnerships within countries, supported by cooperation with regional and international agencies and institutions". The text highlights the need to build on and strengthen existing mechanisms with the support of all partners. By and large, this further strengthens the idea already expressed that education is a significant common venture requiring a united effort to ensure that the targets set are achievable.

Educational content of course varies from one country to another and differs in accordance with local circumstances, the objectives pursued, and even the resources available. *Respect for the diversity of education systems* is indeed a major principle supported and forcefully expressed by UNESCO in the various instruments adopted under its auspices. The Organisation recognises that not only each individual but also each people, each community and in fact each culture has an inherent dignity, worthy of respect. The *Mexico Declaration on Cultural Policies*, adopted by the General Conference of UNESCO in August 1982 proclaims that "the equality and dignity of all cultures must be recognised, as must the right of each people and cultural community to affirm and preserve its cultural identity and have it respected by others". Promoting the right to respect for differences and appreciating diversity must therefore be central to any educational project. Such an assertion is made particularly clear in the 1960 *Convention against Discrimination in Education whose* Preamble states that "consequently, the United Nations Educational, Scientific and Cultural Organisation, while respecting the diversity of national educational systems, has the duty to proscribe any form of discrimination.

The Preamble to the *World Declaration on Education for All*, requires to take into consideration "traditional knowledge and indigenous cultural heritage [that] have a value and a validity in their own right." Similarly, in the 1997 *Hamburg Declaration on Adult Learning*, it is stated that "Adult learning should reflect the richness of cultural diversity and respect traditional and indigenous peoples' knowledge and systems of learning". In other words, although there are common universal principles applicable to all States, namely the requirement for access to education to be universal and nondiscrimination, in contrast the means of implementing these principles may and must vary. As the *World Declaration on Education for All* (Jomtien) explains very well in Article 1. 1: "The scope of basic learning needs and how they should be met varies with individual countries and cultures, and inevitably, changes with the passage of time". Such demands for the respect for differences or specification are not only of an ethical or philosophical nature. They also aim to enhance the effectiveness of the education system, whose performance will be all the more significant since it will take on board values for which there already exists a firm commitment. Finally, such an initiative is also designed to attain the global objectives of a culture of peace only achievable through respect for values based on tolerance and the respect for differences, which are highly recommended teaching elements in the implementation of the right to education.

In paragraph 8 of the *Dakar Framework for Action*, the participants in the World Education Forum described all the measures for organising an education system that "governments, organisations, agencies, groups and associations" pledge to implement in order to reach the targets set in terms of education for all. A number of particulars on the potential content of these measures are to be found in the "Expanded Commentary on the Dakar Framework for Action". In addition to nondiscrimination and equality issues, and the drawing up of national action plans already mentioned above, these include:

— Linking poverty eradication and development strategies. It was considered in Dakar that evident asynergies existed between education promotion and poverty reduction strategies, which it was therefore necessary to exploit. Education strategies must be integrated into broader poverty reduction initiatives implemented at the national and international levels such as the United Nations Development Assistance Frameworks, Comprehensive Development Frameworks and Poverty Reduction Strategy Plans.

— The association of civil society and educational work. It is appropriate that at all levels of educational decision-making, governments develop mechanisms which are not only responsible for endorsing decisions already made by the State but, in contrast, through regular dialogue with citizens and civil society organisations, contribute to the planning, implementation and monitoring of educational activities.

— The characteristics of management and governance systems. The participants in the Dakar Forum consider educational management reform to be an essential requirement for progress from a highly centralised system to more decentralised and participatory decision-making, monitoring and implementation procedures at the lower levels of accountability. Better regulations and administrative mechanisms should therefore be set up, and responsibilities among different levels of government should be more sharply delineated. It is also important to ensure that decentralisation does not result in an inequitable distribution of resources, and to provide training for those in charge of school management and other education personnel.

— Dealing with the effects of conflict and instability situations. As such distressing situations take a heavy toll on education, governments should be made better able to carry out rapid assessments of educational needs in crisis and post-conflict situations and to restore destroyed or damaged education systems. Schools, for their part, should be in protected areas.

— The constitution of a healthy educational environment. The creation of such an environment fosters effective learning, namely for the benefit of the socially, culturally or economically excluded. In general, the *World Declaration on Education for All* had already emphasised the essential nature of the "supportive policies" in the social, cultural and economic sectors with a view to ensuring the full provision of basic education. Another important need is improvement of the "learning environment": "Societies, therefore, must ensure that all learners receive the nutrition, health care, and general physical and emotional support they need in order to participate actively in and benefit from their education".

— The use of new information and communication technologies. It is important for governments to design clearly defined policies in this field. The fact that these technologies are developing fast and falling in price has direct implications for learning. Nevertheless, they may also tend to increase disparities among individuals and these policies must therefore contribute to bridging the "digital divide", extending access and reducing inequality. Data gathering and management systems must therefore be devised at the various appropriate levels.

— National, regional and international monitoring systems. It is essential to have reliable data and statistics in the field of education if results are to be appreciated, progress measured, experience shared and lessons learned. These are decisive points when it comes to gauging the ability of partners in education for all to be accountable for their work. Monitoring and evaluation in this area are important and should be encouraged. Yet gaps and shortcomings have been observed in this field and the necessary steps should be taken to overcome them.

A further requirement is to organise quality education. Many texts insist upon this obvious necessity that is, nevertheless not always easy to meet. The *Dakar Framework for Action refers* to this in paragraph 7(vi) among the participants' "collective commitments" aimed at "improving all aspects of the quality of education and ensuring excellence of all so that recognised and measurable learning outcomes are achieved by all, especially in literacy, numeracy and essential life skills". In fact, the Jomtien Declaration and Framework for Action seek "quality", "effectiveness", "quality basic education", "effective basic education" and are committed to educational quality criteria. Such demands inevitably require resources and the selection of competent teaching staff. They must also be offered the opportunity to update their knowledge. States have been able to make commitments for this purpose. The search for quality education also entails the development of programmes which are adapted and specific to certain groups.

The Jomtien Framework for Action thus suggested taking this type of initiative for disadvantaged groups such as out-of-school youth or adults with little or no access to basic education services, for women and young girls in order to remove the obstacles they may encounter to attending regular training programmes, for refugees, displaced people, those suffering occupation or the illiterate. The same strategies are also reflected in other documents, such as the 1995 *Declaration on Education* for Peace, Human Rights and Democracy. Educational quality requires considerable attention for curricula and teaching methods. Articles 3 et seq. Of the 1989 *Convention on Technical and Vocational Education contain* detailed provisions and emphasise the need for revision and updates in this area. The concern to improve curricula and schoolbooks or other learning tools is very present in the texts, together with reflection on teaching methods, encouraged by discussion, exchange, dialogue within restricted groups, combating underachievement, etc. and the development of particular exchange-promoting activities such as learning foreign languages.

Means Required for the Exercise of the Right to Education

The *means* required for the exercise of the right to education are of various kinds. *Institutional support* is most certainly required, and UNESCO itself is playing a leading role in this regard. Education is its foremost field of action and its speciality, and it is therefore from UNESCO that such institutional support should first be sought. UNESCO has already done much, as is evidenced by its achievements, the extensive *corpus* of standard-setting instruments and the various documents and reports it has issued, as well as the numerous forums, meetings, working groups, etc. convened by the Organisation or under its auspices, the numerous activities of coordination and of collaboration with States, international intergovernmental organisations and NGOs. Further action remains to be undertaken, and in his important *Report on the outcome and implications for UNESCO* of the World Education Forum, the Director-General of UNESCO indicated that "UNESCO is prepared to join hands with governments and civil society, as well as with members of the international community in accelerating progress towards EFA, maintaining its expanded vision, finding new and more effective ways of achieving it, and dealing with the needs". "UNESCO through its mandate and its history of being a chief forum and interlocutor of education ministries, who trust its objectivity and non-partisanship, has a uniquely comprehensive and international perspective. Because UNESCO is concerned with the entire spectrum of the education sector, it is uniquely in a position to locate EFA efforts within it and articulate linkages with other education subsection".

UNESCO is thus the lead agency for international cooperation in education. The Director-General singles out four "most appropriate modulates" of exercising this competence, as follows: EFA support partnerships, as initiated at Jomtien, under the Organisation's *leadership*; policy dialogue and networks, which can be intensified and whose effectiveness can be improved by UNESCO; research and educational expertise, for which UNESCO enjoys a worldwide reputation as a credible source of information; capacity-building for the training of educational management personnel, empowering Member States to improve their human potential. The *Dakar Framework for Action* envisages that UNESCO will continue to co-ordinate EFA partners. To this end, it was decided to create a "small and flexible group" composed of "highest level leaders from governments and civil society of developing and developed countries, and development agencies". The group "will serve as a lever for political commitment and technical and financial resource mobilisation" and "will also be an opportunity to hold the global community to account for commitments made in Dakar".

UNESCO will serve as the secretariat. A great number of the initiatives fall under UNESCO's responsibility. An interesting illustration of this is provided by the 1998 World Declaration on Higher Education and Framework for Priority Action for Change *and Development in Higher Education, which* establish a list of proposed actions to be initiated by UNESCO with a view to the development and improvement of higher education.

The Dakar Forum was the outcome of the collaboration and mutual support provided by the "governments, organisations, agencies, groups and associations represented at the Forum", thus following the line adopted at Jomtien, where it was clearly established that foremost among the means required for the implementation of the right to education was collaboration—both internal and international. According to the Jomtien "trilogy", such collaboration should take place at three levels: at the national level, by means of partnerships with associations, unions, professional groups, the media, political parties, cooperatives, etc. ; at the regional level, by means of exchanges with neighbouring countries or countries belonging to the same geo cultural or linguistic region, and cooperation with regional organisations; lastly, at world level, with the cooperation of the specialised agencies of the United Nations which, in addition to UNESCO, whose lead role has already been mentioned, will provide support for the educational actions undertaken by the governments. These different means can be used for "strengthening international solidarity" *World Declaration on Education for All*, an action which is indispensable given that "meeting basic learning needs constitutes a common and universal human responsibility. It requires international solidarity and equitable and fair economic relations in order to redress existing economic disparities". The *Dakar Framework for Action* also expresses the conviction that education for all is a "responsibility that will be met most effectively through broad-based partnerships within countries, supported by cooperation with regional and international agencies and institutions".

Knowledge can be transmitted through the use of all the available *information and communication media.* Accordingly, the *World Declaration on Education for All* calls for the use, in addition to the traditional means, of all the potential offered by libraries, television, radio and other media, to which the Internet should now be added.

Attention must also be paid to the teachers who are at the sharp end of education. The Recommendation concerning the Status of Higher-Education Teaching Personnel concerns a particular category of personnel whose rights and freedoms entail specific characteristics, and states that "similar questions arise in all countries with regard to the status of higher-education teaching personnel and that these questions call for the adoption of common approaches and so far as practicable the application of common standards". It is these common standards that the Recommendation defines in terms of the "educational objectives and policies" in higher education which imply a very wide exchange of ideas and information, a research and publications component, and particular attention to the exodus of personnel, especially from the developing countries, a situation which requires the improvement of the status of teachers. In this context, the autonomy of the institutions and the recognition of academic freedoms are essential, with the corollary of the recognition of the individual freedoms of the teachers themselves in the exercise of their activities of knowledge transfer and research by enabling them to teach "without any interference, subject to accepted professional principles" [...].

The Recommendation finally deals, in great detail, with the terms and conditions of employment of higher-education teaching personnel. The *World Declaration on Education for All* insists on the need to improve the status of teachers, as "the conditions of service of teachers and their status constitute a determining factor in the implementation of education for all" (Art. 7), and calls for compliance with the 1966 ILO/UNESCO Recommendation Concerning the Status of Teachers. A similar concern is expressed in the *Declaration on Education for Peace, Human Rights and Democracy*, namely "to adopt measures to enhance the role and status of educators. (Art. 2. 5), while in Dakar, the World Education Forum included in the text of the *Dakar Framework for Action* the commitment of the participants (including governments) to "enhance the status, morale and professionalism of teachers". This therefore applies both to their training and to the qualifications which determine their ability to teach and hence their "professionalism" and their conditions of work, their status and their remuneration, which determine their "motivation" and define their "status". The *Expanded Commentary on the Dakar Framework for Action* states that, given that no education reform is likely to succeed "without the active participation of teachers", at all levels of the education system should be respected and adequately remunerated". In addition, "clearly defined and more imaginative strategies to identify, attract, train and retain good teachers must be put into place".

Lastly, in the material and financial context, in addition to having the right kind of buildings and the required teaching materials, the services of managerial personnel, planners, school architects, teacher educators, curriculum developers, researchers, analysts, etc., are also required, by the *Framework for Action to Meet Basic Learning Needs*, with a view to improving managerial capacities which also stresses the need to mobilise resources. In its turn, the *Dakar Framework for Action* stresses the need to mobilise financial resources and international cooperation, more particularly in favour of the developing countries, which should not be hampered in their efforts by financial constraints if they show a clear political will to work towards education for all. It goes as far as to proclaim: "We affirm that no countries seriously committed to education for all will be thwarted in their achievement of this goal by a lack of resources". Priority is given to the countries of sub-Saharan Africa and South Asia as well as to the countries in conflict or undergoing reconstruction, which should also be given special attention. All of this implies a substantial increase in international assistance, requiring firm financial commitments by national governments and "by bilateral and multilateral funding agencies, including the World Bank and regional development banks", civil society and the foundations.

Sanctioning the Right to Education

Discussing the matter of sanctioning the right to education raises questions as to the legal force of commitments made and the nature of the obligations imposed upon those in charge of its enforcement.

Before we go any further, it is important to differentiate between the beneficiaries of the obligations. As mentioned earlier in the field of the right to education, they fall into two categories: the individual and society as a whole. First, the individual is the direct beneficiary of the right to education since it provides bases for the underlying principle enabling him or her to follow a given programme of studies. When the right established for the individual's benefit forms part of a convention that is properly ratified and incorporated into a State's internal order, thereby rendering it legally binding on that State, he or she can use every available legal means to secure compliance: recourse to law courts, for instance, where the judge ultimately has the power to examine whether there is a breach of the States' legal obligations, and to come to a decision. Technically speaking, of course, individuals do not necessarily have to take such action themselves: groups enjoying legal status and with a stake in the matter (unions, public service users' or parents' associations, etc.) may take such action on behalf of their members. Furthermore, general international law—irrespective of whatever specific mechanisms any particular instrument may have additionally established to ensure compliance—provides similar means of sanctioning the right to education internationally within the realm of inter-State relations. If, for instance, individuals living abroad find themselves to be the victims of discriminatory measures in their State of residence that prevent them from exercising their right to education as laid down in a legally binding instrument, and failing domestic remedies, their State of origin will be free to exercise diplomatic protection on their behalf with a view to ensuring that the State of residence meets its commitments. Hence—and, in a sense, indirectly—one State can be compelled to meet its treaty obligations by another.

The situation is different with respect to the second category of beneficiary insofar as society, finds it to its advantage—for its development and for social progress, tolerance and harmony within the group—to ensure that its members enjoy generalised access to education. So the right to education has also, as said earlier, been devised to benefit society. Since society per se lacks legal status, however, it cannot claim the benefits of that right through the above-mentioned legal channels. As a matter of fact, the State tends to meet its obligations of its own accord because they help foster the well-being and progress for which it is responsible; and the only pressure that can be brought to bear is the political and moral influence exerted by society and its constituent parts. One witnesses that when the two beneficiaries of the right to education are identified, they cannot be placed on the same footing from either the legal point of view or that of the nature of the obligations.

After these preliminary points, the next step is to examine the scope of the obligations forming part of the right to education, on the one hand according to the types of standard-setting instruments that contain those obligations and reflecting a graduated normativity and, on the other, on the basis of the mechanisms designed to enforce compliance by States.

Normativity of the Right to Education

The right to education, as seen above, is established in texts of a varying legal nature such as conventions, declarations, frameworks for action and charters, which do not, legally speaking, involve the same obligations but which all serve the same end: the promotion and development of the right of every person, without discrimination, to enjoy access to education. So it is interesting to determine how and why, notwithstanding their differing legal nature, these texts still manage to organise efforts to achieve their intended goal in such a way as to preclude the possibility of only those of indisputable mandatory legal force being abided by, while others might easily be ignored.

Conventions are by far the most clear-cut example. Once a convention has been ratified, accepted or acceded to in sufficient numbers (as stipulated by the convention itself) to enable it to enter into force, it ultimately, after some possible delay, becomes binding on the State that has performed such a formality; and once incorporation procedures have been completed, it can be brought into force within that State's internal order. Details of this may be found in Article 14 of the *Convention against Discrimination in Education and* Article 10 of the *Convention on Technical and Vocational Education*. States are bound by the commitment they have made in ratifying or acceding to such conventions and are internationally responsible, according to the customary rules of international law, to account for any failure to comply with their obligations. Since Article 5, paragraph 2, of the *Convention against Discrimination in Education* requires States Parties to "undertake to take all necessary measures to ensure the application of the principles enunciated in paragraph 1 of this Article", any of them not adopting the appropriate regulatory framework to guarantee parents the freedom to send their children to the school of their choice would be in breach of their legal commitment and, hence, liable to face the consequences. This is backed by mechanisms designed to facilitate and lend weight to the enforcement and fulfilment of those obligations.

Determining the legal force of instruments other than treaties is somewhat harder. In the eyes of legal orthodoxy and according to the rules of traditional international law, they have no legal force and merely express a political or moral stance.

Traditional international law covers a period running roughly from 1648 to 1945. Those were times when international organisations did not yet exist or were not as developed as they are today; when the States were unquestionably the only subjects of international law. The only legal rule applicable to them was of a customary or contractual nature, to which they adhered voluntarily and which they had elaborated themselves. The past half-century, on the other hand, has seen the development of objective rules of international law, the emergence of new principles and the establishment of a certain hierarchy of norms. A typical illustration of these would be the rules of *jus cogens*, peremptory norms of international law from which there can be no derogation. The international organisations, meanwhile, have undergone significant expansion. Their often highly appropriate endeavours in their various areas of expertise, together with the thinking done with—or, under their auspices, by –Member States have led to the adoption of a number of instruments of undeniable importance. Given the horizontal structure of international society and the nature of relations maintained with States (save in the exceptional case of supernational structures), the international organisations' norm of general law remains an optional recommendation in the eyes of legal orthodoxy. And it is true to say that a State is strictly speaking not legally bound by such texts, even though its vote might have helped to have one adopted, since it will always be able to argue that its intention in so voting had been to endorse a mere recommendation rather than a legally binding document.

Yet the issue is not that simple, and one should no doubt be wary of overly cut-and dried or Manichaean points of view. When, on 19 January 1977, the arbiter delivered his award in the dispute between the Government of the Libyan Arab Republic and the California Asiatic Oil Company and Texaco Overseas Petroleum Company, for instance, he stated that the refusal to credit United Nations resolutions with any legal force whatsoever should be qualified in the light of individual texts. He went on to say that the court would bear in mind the usual criteria in its evaluation of the legal force of those resolutions, i. e. A review of voting conditions and an analysis of the prescribed provisions.

Such reasoning is still quite widely accepted today and, rather than a rift between what is obligatory and what is not, reflects a cursor or graduated rule ranging from the purely optional to the strictly mandatory, but with intermediate stages. It is important to examine, case by case, the voting conditions, the terms employed and the status of participants.

The commitments that States and governments make in adopting standard-setting instruments need to be considered in the light of the legal and moral force of declarations in modern international law. United Nations doctrine considers a declaration to be "a formal and solemn instrument, suitable for occasions when principles of great and lasting importance are being enunciated. In view of the greater solemnity and significance of a "declaration" (as opposed to a "recommendation"), it may be considered to impart, on behalf of the (United Nations) organ adopting it, a strong expectation that members of the international community will abide by it. Consequently, insofar as the expectation is gradually justified by State practice, a declaration may by custom become recognised as laying down rules binding upon States.

The full political and moral force of the declarations, recommendations and, also, decisions adopted by UNESCO with respect to the right to education warrants attention. Member States regard themselves as bound by the instruments adopted not only through General Conference decisions or within the framework of intergovernmental conferences, but also in the form of decisions reached by the Executive Board. A key example of this can be seen in the procedure for the examination of complaints received by the Organisation concerning alleged violations of human rights in its fields of competence, namely education, science, culture and information. This procedure is laid down in 104 EX/Decision 3. 3 of the Executive Board of UNESCO and implemented by one of its subsidiary organs, the Committee on Conventions and Recommendations (CR). When a State becomes a Member of UNESCO, it is automatically taken to have recognised the authority of the CR: "in practice, even non-Member States of UNESCO have of their own accord agreed to a communication concerning them being considered by the Committee". The CR considered 460 communications between 1978 and 1997 and in seven cases changes were obtained in specific education laws that discriminated against ethnic or religious minorities.

In common with United Nations General Assembly resolutions, the successive declarations and recommendations on the right to education adopted by States and governments illustrate the gradual development of the right's normative basis. Through persistent reiteration and reaffirmation of the right to education, the standard-setting instruments have also come to comprise an *opinion juris* component in international law. This makes for gradual consolidation of the normative basis of the right to education. Meanwhile, the considerable moral commitments formally assumed through such standard-setting instruments serve to further the enforcement of that right.

States and governments adopting these declarations and recommendations are also subscribing to moral commitments. These instruments clearly state their intention to implement them, even though, as in the case of United Nations resolutions, there are no legal penalties for noncompliance. They demonstrate an indisputable moral resolve to abide by the commitments assumed by those States and their partners when voicing their intention to adopt a given set of guidelines, as seen in the *World Declaration on Education for All* or the *Dakar Framework for Action*. The ethical basis and moral force of these declarations therefore needs to be recognised. Although not legally binding, agreed instruments have a normative character in their intent and effects and the States concerned regard them as political or moral commitments. The ethical value of such declarations is set to acquire increasing recognition.

It is worth noting in this respect the strong wording used in the *Dakar Framework for Action (which*, not being a convention, is strictly speaking nonbinding): "We affirm that no countries seriously committed to education for all will be thwarted in their achievement of this goal by a lack of resources"; "We will strengthen accountable international and regional mechanisms". Participants repeatedly underscored their commitment: "We hereby collectively commit ourselves to the attainment of the following goals"; "we pledge ourselves to and, moreover, the participants even go so far as to commit the international community itself by declaring that it "will deliver on this collective commitment. In the *World Declaration on Education for All*, the present tense is employed more often than the conditional and the text, which reaffirms the "right of all people to education", makes a number of strong statements. These "declarations", "recommendations" and "charters" generally tend to be adopted by acclamation and convey a clear sense of commitment. Yet do such commitments involve legal liability? Far from it. In actual fact, their unequivocal moral and political force contrasts with their legal frailty, which—apart from the reservations going with the above-mentioned stances—is largely due to the very mixed nature of the participants. One thing is the adoption of a resolution by State representatives acting individually and collectively within the framework of an international organisation; quite another is the adoption of a text by a "forum" that unites, in a joint declaration, government representatives (e. g. Education ministers) and international organisations within the ambit of the principle of speciality, but also representatives of NGOs, various other groups, civil society and so on. International law is therefore not omnipresent; and quite clearly, while the declarations, recommendations or frameworks for action adopted regarding the right to education may carry great political and moral weight, they are collectively and individually devoid of legal force.

But they cannot be regarded as totally insignificant. That would be tantamount to contempt for the often unequivocal stances taken by, among others, State representatives speaking on behalf of their governments. Moreover, it would mean undermining the role of UNESCO or diminishing the massive amount of work done up to now in its core area of expertise as mere politico-moral affirmation. So the legal force of instruments is not such a cut-and-dried matter. There is a natural tendency to liken international society to national societies with their legislation, judges and sanctioned law, and to transpose that model to world level. But should international society be necessarily conceived through comparison with national societies? And does international law, rather than being made up exclusively of a body of legally sanctioned obligations, not need to recognise the legal force of—and, hence, incorporate—guidelines and recommendations able to determine the behaviour of States? This applies particularly when such instruments have been elaborated by, or under the auspices of, a specialised international organisation, which represents a genuine "quality stamp" that can naturally and readily be conferred on this body of texts of graduated normativity arising within the purview of UNESCO and relating to what is, after all, its own sphere: the right to education.

On the other hand, while the convention process largely remains the route par excellence, owing to the certainty it generates as to the scope of the commitments involved, it is not entirely free of drawbacks or shortcomings since, in particular, conventions often take quite some time to come into force and may be weakened by the uncertainties of ratification and reservations. However, if the *Convention against Discrimination in Education* has been ratified by 90 States, the *Convention on Technical and Vocational Education*—adopted on 10 November 1989—garnered no more than 12 instruments of ratification or accession. It raises the question whether it is better to have texts that unite just a few States with a strong legal bond or texts approved unanimously yet of more uncertain legal force. It was in precisely these terms that a number of States brought the matter before the International Law Commission, where it was said that in some cases a declaration, which is more flexible than a convention and embraces a wider range of issues, could, if adopted by consensus, carry more weight than a convention ratified by just a few States. Current practice in international legal relations also shows at times relatively subtle interplay of balance and cross-referencing between recommendations and conventions, with the former paving the way for the latter and ensuring that people gradually grow accustomed to new rules that ultimately become binding once the process has reached maturity. So there is no standard, clear-cut answer to the question. As far as upholding the right to education is concerned, one can only observe that it is certainly likely to hinge more on governments believing in the need to develop education policy than on their being concerned to respect a legal obligation, especially whose sanction in any case is quite uncertain.

All in all, then, it is not so much an issue of instruments that are binding as against those that are not; what matters most is how they complement one another. Fortunately, UNESCO has understood this in employing the entire range at its disposal—albeit with a certain preference for recommendatory declarations and resolutions, in line with a brand of realism. This has also led to the development of procedures which, after long remaining unique, have since come into general use in the shape of monitoring and follow-up mechanisms.

Monitoring and Follow-up Procedures

The international organisations have long had monitoring and follow-up procedures in place, and UNESCO in particular has developed a set of mechanisms designed to permit more effective application of provisions adopted and ensure better fulfilment of obligations. It will therefore be useful to outline their main features. The periodic reports that States are asked to submit have the effect of informing UNESCO, and therefore all the States in the international community, of the measures they have taken domestically to fulfil their obligations under the conventions to which they are parties. Thus, to make it more effective, States Parties to the *Convention against Discrimination in Education*, must give information in their periodic reports to the UNESCO General Conference on the legislative and administrative provisions which they have adopted and other action which they have taken for the application of the Convention.

If there are no obligations under conventions because the principles and standards are laid down in simple recommendations, declarations or frameworks for action, the report is not meant to verify whether a statutory obligation is being properly fulfilled but to indicate measures that a State has decided to take, to implement voluntarily the principles adopted in recommendations. Such behaviour may set an example, and, conversely, a State failing to act may be placed in a politically difficult situation.

The reporting procedure therefore to some extent represents a means of applying pressure. It is, moreover, legally enshrined in the form of a State obligation under Article VIII of UNESCO's Constitution, which provides that each Member State shall submit to the Organisation a report on the action taken upon the recommendations and conventions adopted by the UNESCO General Conference. It is therefore apparent that the report produced derives from an obligation whose content will vary depending on the instrument to which it relates. Insofar that the report will give a precise account of the laws, regulations and practices adopted and it is known that all this information will be closely examined by UNESCO, it is clear that States will tend to give the maximum possible effect to the recommendations concerned. Furthermore, dissemination of information is always useful through the comparison it allows between systems that might possibly be taken as models or that provide answers to questions that arise. Lastly, this procedure reveals any problems that States may encounter in implementing measures. From this point of view, moreover, there is no reason to distinguish between a report on implementation of a convention and one relating to a recommendation, since the information value is the same in either case.

In order to ensure smooth operation of this procedure, UNESCO has set up subsidiary bodies responsible for examining the reports of Member States. Such is the role of the Committee on Conventions and Recommendations (CR) for the reports that are specifically entrusted to it by the Executive Board. Thus, for example, the CR examines the reports arising from the Convention against Discrimination in Education and those from the Joint ILO/UNESCO Committee of Experts on the Application of the 1997 Recommendation concerning the Status of Higher-Education Teaching Personnel. The General Conference then receives the Committee's report—accompanied by comments from the CR and the Executive Board—and Member States' reports. Unfortunately, in practice, not a large number of States reply to consultations, as noted by the Executive Board in March 1999.

These consultations take place in several stages. The General Conference decides to ask Member States to submit reports (Art. VIII of UNESCO's Constitution, Art. 7 of the *Convention against Discrimination in Education* and Art. 7 of the *Convention on Technical and Vocational Education*), whereupon questionnaires are prepared and sent out to Member States, which are given a deadline for replying. Replies are analysed and collated by the UNESCO Secretariat. These documents are then examined by the Committee on Conventions and Recommendations, which draws up its own report and transmits it to the Executive Board. The latter examines all the documents and transmits them to the General Conference, accompanied by its own comments. The General Conference sets out its observations, recommendations and decisions in a resolution and, if necessary, a general report. The United Nations, the National Commissions and any other authorities specified by the General Conference will then receive the report from the General Conference and, where appropriate, that of the Committee on Conventions and Recommendations and even those of the States.

Monitoring Measures

Under existing procedures UNESCO's standard-setting work is accompanied by measures to monitor Member States' application of all the instruments adopted by the Organisation irrespective of their legal status. UNESCO recently conducted a sixth Consultation of Member States on application of the *Convention* and *Recommendation against Discrimination in*

Education. That Consultation, like those before it, was based on the obligation of States Parties to the Convention to submit periodic reports, giving UNESCO information on the legislative and regulatory provisions they have adopted and other action they have taken to apply the Convention, including steps to frame and develop national policy, together with any obstacles encountered in applying the Convention.

At its 156th session in May/June 1999 the Executive Board examined the reports and responses received in the course of the sixth Consultation. This Consultation enabled the Organisation to examine the measures taken or encouraged on specific issues such as basic education for women and girls, persons belonging to minorities, refugees and indigenous people. Thus, some Member States "have plans or policy statements to guide their treatment of persons belonging to minorities and appoint special committees or ministerial branches to oversee policy and implementation". The Consultation also revealed specific measures to advance multi-cultural education: "Many Member States which have a large multi-cultural population develop and implement special governmental programmes promoting equality of opportunity and treatment of persons belonging to minorities, including creation of special funds and necessary social and cultural awareness programmes which are reflected in school curricula and administrations".

After examining in 1999 the reports and replies received for the sixth Consultation, the Executive Board took a decision that was endorsed by the General Conference of UNESCO in a resolution. That resolution invited the "Director-General to strengthen UNESCO's action against discrimination in education in order to ensure the widest possible democratisation of education and to study, with a view to the seventh consultation and in cooperation with the United Nations, the possibility of creating a coherent mechanism for reporting on and monitoring the right to education as it is set down in various United Nations conventions on human rights".

In this connection, one may mention the *International Covenant on Economic, Social and Cultural Rights*, and in particular its detailed provisions concerning the right to education (Arts. 13 and 14). Those provisions extend to all levels of education and their scope is broadest in the field of international law on human rights. The Committee on Economic, Social and Cultural Rights, as a supervisory body, is responsible for monitoring implementation of the International Covenant on Economic,

Social and Cultural Rights in the States Parties. It examines the national reports submitted regularly by these States and maintains a dialogue with them in order to ensure the most effective implementation of the rights enshrined in the International Covenant. Following such analysis, it draws up a report containing its recommendations and suggestions for the purpose in its concluding observations.

In order to help States Parties to the International Covenant to prepare their national reports, the Committee in 1999 drew up a *General Comment* on the right to education (Art. 13 of the International Covenant). The *General Comment* recognises the importance of UNESCO's standard-setting instruments on the right to education, in particular the *Convention against Discrimination in Education*– which establishes the principle of nondiscrimination and equal treatment—together with the *World Declaration on Education for All*, which defines "basic learning needs" (Art. 1) while recommending basic education for all. Thus, according to the General Comment, the normative content of the right to education embodied in Article 13 of the International Covenant and that of UNESCO's standard-setting instruments are mutually reinforcing. Moreover, the idea of the right to basic education for all as an essential building block for any individual, social or sustainable developments akin to that in the *General Comment*: "Education is both a human right in itself and an indispensable means of realising other human rights."

Three levels or categories of obligation devolving on States Parties to the Covenant—the obligation to respect the right to education, to protect it and to fulfil it —are also characteristic of UNESCO's approach in this field. Enhanced collaboration between the Committee and UNESCO would enable to realise UNESCO's fundamental objective in the field of education—to achieve universal recognition and effective enforcement of the right to education—which has become more topical than ever. It is all the more urgent to defend education as a "common good".

Collaboration with the Committee on Economic, Social and Cultural Rights and with the Office of the High Commissioner for Human Rights to study "the possibility of creating a coherent mechanism for reporting on and monitoring the right to education" would be instrumental in more effective application of international instruments covering the right to education. In such initiatives, a key role is played by UNESCO's Committee on Conventions and Recommendations. Given the expertise of the Committee on Economic, Social and Cultural Rights, its collaboration would also be valuable for implementing the *Dakar Framework for Action*, especially with regard to its legal implications. It was no doubt with this in mind that, during the debate at the 159th session of the Executive Board on the Report by the Director-General on the outcome and implications for UNESCO of the Dakar World Education Forum in May 2000, a number of Member States stressed the importance of collaborating with the Committee.

The *Convention on Technical and Vocational Education*, in its Article 7, provides that "the Contracting States shall specify, in periodic reports submitted to the General Conference of the United Nations Educational, Scientific and Cultural Organisation at the dates and in the form determined by it, the legislative provisions, regulations and other measures adopted by them to give effect to this *Convention*". Since few Member States (only 12) have ratified this Convention, UNESCO is doing its utmost to disseminate the substance of its articles to as many countries and institutions as possible. To this end, a number of the Convention's articles will be incorporated in the Revised Recommendation now being updated, in order to provide best approach to the new challenges faced today by technical and vocational education.

In this connection, UNESCO's work on follow-up to the *Recommendations* adopted by the Second International Congress on Technical and Vocational Education in Seoul is also relevant. To follow up these recommendations—on the theme "Lifelong learning and training: a bridge to the future"– the Director-General of UNESCO submitted to the UNESCO General Conference at its 30th session in November 1999 a document entitled "Establishment of an international long-term programme for the development of technical and vocational education following the second International Congress on Technical and Vocational Education, Seoul, Republic of Korea, April 1999". This programme aims to strengthen "technical and vocational education and training (TVET) as an integral component of lifelong learning, orienting TVET for sustainable development and providing TVET for all".

Adopted by the General Conference at its 30th session in November 1999, 30 C/Resolution 9 on "Establishment of an international long-term programme for the development of technical and vocational education", recognised "that the recommendations of the Congress will form the basis for UNESCO's new global strategy for technical and vocational education and training (TVET) in the first decade of the twenty-first century". The resolution also requested the Director-General of UNESCO "to urge Member States to support a variety of TVET activities envisaged in the recommendations of the Congress".

As part of the follow-up to the *Recommendations* from the Second International Congress on Technical and Vocational Education, UNESCO is carrying out a consultation with a view to updating the *Revised Recommendation concerning Technical and Vocational Education* while bearing in mind a vision of technical and vocational education and training for the twenty-first century. Moreover, an agreement between UNESCO and the Government of the Federal Republic of Germany on the establishment of a UNESCO International Centre for Technical and Vocational Education and Training was signed on 12 July 2000.

As the United Nations agency responsible for education, UNESCO must make decision-makers aware that teacher training has to be improved in order to meet special educational needs. The Organisation must ensure that the question of special educational needs is systematically addressed in all bodies discussing education for all. From this point of view, the *World Declaration on Education for All: Meeting Basic Learning Needs* is highly significant since it has provided a new vision for education. In its Preamble the Declaration recognises "the necessity to give to present and coming generations an expanded vision of, and a renewed commitment to, basic education to address the scale and complexity of the challenge [providing basic education for all]". The authors of the Declaration have expressed their determination to "act jointly" to achieve the objectives that it sets out, asserting that "education is a fundamental right for all people, women and men, of all ages, throughout our world".

UNESCO made all efforts, by mobilising the international community, to ensure implementation of the *World Declaration on Education for All.* In the perspective of the World Education Forum, this endeavour resulted in the establishment of six regional frameworks for action: "Education for All—A Framework for Action in sub-Saharan Africa: Education for African Renaissance in the Twenty-First Century"; "Asia and Pacific Regional Framework for Action: Guiding Principles, Specific Goals and Targets for 2015"; "Education for All in the Arab States—Renewing the Commitment: The Arab Framework for Action to Ensure Basic Learning Needs in the Arab States in the Years 2000-2010"; "Regional Framework for Action: Europe and North America"; "Education for All in the Americas: Regional Framework of Action"; and the "*Receive Declaration of the E-9 Countries*". In adopting the Receive Declaration, the Ministers and representatives of the nine high-population countries (E-9) reaffirmed their joint commitment "to sustain, intensify and accelerate" their efforts to achieve the goal of education for all. A continuous sharing of knowledge and experience could make a visible contribution towards more efficient implementation of national policies on education for all, especially in the field of literacy.

We can see from the Education for All assessment presented at the *World Education Forum* that considerable progress was made in the course of the 1990s. However, the international community is facing enormous challenges at the beginning of this century and new millennium: a quarter of the world still remains on the sidelines—some 113 million children, 60% of them girls, have no access to primary education, and at least 880 million adults, the majority of whom are women, are illiterate. In fact, despite an expansion in the education system, the disparities observed in access and quality are on an unprecedented scale.

To meet these challenges, the Dakar Framework for Action—Education for All: *Meeting Our Collective Commitments*, adopted at the World Education Forum, expresses the commitment of the entire international community. Some 1,100 participants from 164 countries and from a wide variety of backgrounds—teachers, ministers, decision-makers, academics, policy-makers, political activists and heads of major international organisations—reaffirmed the right to basic education for all at the World Education Forum.

The Dakar *Framework for Action* sets out six goals for achieving basic education for all by 2015. UNESCO will readjust its education programme to focus on the Dakar results and priorities. As coordinator, UNESCO has a key role in the follow-up to the World Education Forum: providing leadership through partnership, ensuring that measures provide impetus for the follow-up, and the process as a whole, is co-ordinated for meeting countries' needs as effectively as possible, in particular for countries experiencing difficulties.

The strategy for implementing the *Dakar Framework for Action* consists in requesting all States to develop national plans of action—or to strengthen those already existing—by 2002 at the latest. These plans should be integrated into a wider poverty reduction and development framework and should be developed through more transparent and democratic processes, involving stockholders, especially peoples' representatives, community leaders, parents, learners, non-governmental organisations (NGOs) and civil society. The plans will address problems associated with the chronic under-financing of basic education by establishing budget priorities that reflect a commitment to achieving EFA goals and targets at the earliest possible date, and no later than 2015. They will also set out clear strategies for overcoming the special problems facing those currently excluded from educational opportunities, with a clear commitment to girls' education and gender equity. The plans will give substance and form to the goals and strategies set out in the Dakar Framework for Action, and to the commitments made during international conferences organised successively in the 1990s. Regional activities to support national strategies will be based on strengthened regional and sub-regional organisations, networks and initiatives. Implementation of the preceding goals and strategies will require national, regional and international mechanisms to be galvanised immediately. The heart of EFA activity lies at national level.

The introduction of national action plans requires a crucial input from UNESCO, in particular so as to achieve better synchronisation, with all the agencies already present on the ground, of measures of practical support to countries in the preparation and implementation of the plans.

In this respect, it must be pointed out that the Framework Agreement between UNESCO and UNICEF on Collaboration in the Field of Education, of 9 February 1999, sets out the main areas of collaboration on the basis of the commitments and interests shared by the two organisations. Consultations between them on the follow-up to the *Dakar Framework for Action* focused on their respective strengths: "UNESCO, with its mandate to take on a leading, normative role" is well placed to "promote policy discussions around basic education; set standards for principles of action and indicators of assessment; engage in high-level advocacy; strengthen partnerships with other EFA actors, particularly to support capacity-building and policy formulation at the regional and national level; provide access to state-of-the-art knowledge about educational theory and practice by drawing on its well-established links with the academic and research community, as well as on its own experience from innovative action-research-oriented pilot activities." UNESCO will play a "normative role regarding conceptual development and policy formulation for upstream activities.

The *Dakar Framework for Action* stipulates that "political will and stronger national leadership are needed for the effective and successful implementation of national plans in each of the countries concerned". The international community acknowledges that many countries currently lack the resources to achieve education for all within an acceptable time frame. New financial resources, preferably in the form of grants and concession assistance, must therefore be mobilised by bilateral and multilateral funding agencies, including the World Bank and regional development banks, and the private sector. The participants in the World Education Forum affirmed that "no countries seriously committed to education for all will be thwarted in their achievement of this goal by a lack of resources".

Supporting that affirmation, the Heads of State and Government of the G 8 stated at the Summit held in Okinawa in July 2000 that "Every child deserves a good education. But in some developing countries access to education is limited, [in] particular for females and the socially vulnerable". They declared that without accelerated progress in the field of basic education, "poverty reduction will not be achieved and inequalities between countries and within societies will widen". "We reaffirm our commitment that no government seriously committed to achieving education for all will be thwarted in this achievement by lack of resources".

The implementation of the *Dakar Framework for Action* is a matter for inter-agency collaboration. As lead agency in this international movement, UNESCO is responsible for coordinating actions taken to follow up the collective commitments made at the World Education Forum. The field of international cooperation must be expanded, by involving not only UNESCO's four official partners in the Education for All movement—the World Bank, UNFPA, UNDP and UNICEF—but also other multilateral agencies, such as ILO, FAO and WHO in the follow-up to the *Dakar Framework for Action*. UNESCO also acknowledges the importance of adding to the debate on the rationalisation of financial flows for funding basic education, in cooperation with the Development Assistance Committee (DAC) of the Organisation for Economic Co-operation and Development.

UNESCO will continue its mandated role in coordinating EFA partners and maintaining their collaborative momentum, working closely with other organisations. In line with this, the Director-General of UNESCO will convene annually a small, flexible, high-level group which will serve as a lever for political commitment and technical and financial resource mobilisation. It will also provide an opportunity to hold the global community to account for commitments made in Dakar. It will be composed of top-level leaders from governments and civil society of developing and developed countries, and from development agencies. UNESCO therefore proposes establishing an *informal high-level group* of some 20 to 25 people: representatives of developing countries, donor countries funding basic education and multilateral aid agencies. The group will be convened by the Director-General to coordinate all Dakar follow-up activities. At the operational level, UNESCO has already set up a *working group on education for all*, with a more technical slant, which met in November 2000 at the Organisation's Headquarters in connection with the implementation of activities developed as part of the follow-up to the World Education Forum, and more particularly to coordinate various inter-agency initiatives.

Even nonbinding standard-setting instruments adopted by UNESCO carry follow-up mechanisms—for instance, the *Salamanca Statement* has its own Framework for Action, which stipulates that "legislation should recognise the principle of equality of opportunity for children, youth and adults with disabilities in primary, secondary and tertiary education carried out, in so far as possible, in integrated settings". The Statement urged all governments to adopt as a matter of law or policy the principle of inclusive education, enrolling all children in regular schools. The guidelines for action at the national level are highlighted, with emphasis being laid on the attainment of equal opportunities, a necessary prerequisite for combating the exclusion of women and the disabled, preparing for adult life and ensuring access by girls to education based on gender equality, and for the enjoyment and exercise of human rights.

The follow-up to the *Declaration* and *Integrated Framework of Action on Education for Peace, Human Rights and Democracy* is ensured through the Permanent System of Reporting on education for peace, human rights, democracy, international understanding and tolerance. In that connection, the Director-General of UNESCO sent a letter and questionnaire to Member States requesting their national reports. The reports should deal with the period since the adoption of the Declaration and Integrated Framework of Action, that is, from the beginning of 1995 to 2000. They should aim to show general trends and innovative practical measures and will be used as the basis for UNESCO's strategies and activities.

The *Declaration on Race and Racial Prejudice* provides that Member States should communicate to the Director-General of UNESCO "all necessary information concerning the steps they have taken to give effect to the principles set forth in the Declaration". Pursuant to the resolution adopted by the General Conference at its 20th session on the implementation of the Declaration, UNESCO prepared a comprehensive report on the world situation in the fields covered by the Declaration. In the field of education, several countries have taken steps to ensure equality in education, to promote human rights education in schools and the fight against racism, or to encourage human rights training for adults in professional circles. Normative actions concerning the *Convention* and *Recommendation against Discrimination in Education* have also contributed to implementation of the *Declaration on Race and Racial Prejudice.*

The Recommendation concerning the Status of Higher-Education Teaching Personnel contains provisions relating to the monitoring of its implementation in Member States—Part X of the Recommendation is entitled "Utilisation and implementation". This states that "Member States and higher education institutions should take all feasible steps to apply the provisions spelled out above to give effect, within their respective territories, to the principles set forth in this Recommendation". The application of this *Recommendation* highlights the importance of cooperation between the agencies of the United Nations system. The mandate of the Joint ILO/ UNESCO Committee of Experts on the Application of the *Recommendations concerning Teaching Personnel* (CEART) has been extended to cover responsibility for monitoring the application of the Recommendation. This monitoring also covers the *Dakar Framework for Action*, to the extent it contains the pledge to enhance "the status, morale and professionalism of teachers". The work of CEART concerns teachers' initial and in-service training and their skills, and specific strategies on how key provisions of the Recommendations could be used to assist ILO and UNESCO in helping Member States meet their commitments to follow up the World Education Forum and the World Conference on Higher Education. CEART indicated that, by setting up large websites, ILO and UNESCO now offer a useful framework for promoting the ILO/UNESCO Recommendation and the 1997 UNESCO Recommendation.

Much remains to be done, in line with the report of the 1997 session of the Joint Committee, to promote equal opportunities for teachers and resolve problems arising in that respect, in response to the weakening of the status of teachers. It is relevant to recall that the *Dakar Framework for Action* asked teachers to accept major responsibility with regard to reforms aiming to achicvc thc goal of cducation for all. Teachers are essential players in promoting quality education.

Since 1997, the Committee has examined four new allegations raising highly diverse questions connected with the ILO/UNESCO Recommendation, and made recommendations to the competent bodies of ILO and UNESCO.

At its seventh session, held at ILO in Geneva from 11 to 15 September 2000, the Committee discussed the idea of drawing up guidelines for Member States on teacher training programmes, with the aim of encouraging the competent ministries to include in such programmes a small number of definitions from the two Recommendations, in particular about the rights and responsibilities of teachers and their participation in decision-making, so as to publicise and apply their provisions. The Committee recommended that, together with ILO, UNESCO draw up international guidelines for Member States on the establishment of teacher-training programmes.

In addition, every year since 1997, ILO and UNESCO have worked together to promote the celebration of World Teachers' Day. The executive heads of ILO, UNESCO, UNDP and UNICEF issued a joint message on World Teachers' Day, entitled "World Teachers' Day 2000: Expanding Horizons".

The *Hamburg Declaration on Adult Learning* and the *Agenda for the Future* set out the aims, strategies and commitments for adult learning. The authors of the Declaration solemnly declared that "all parties will closely follow up the implementation of this Declaration and the Agenda for the Future. One of the key actions to implement the Agenda is the launch of International Adult Learners' Week, which is a valuable complement to International Literacy Day. The Week was launched at Expo 2000 in Hanover on 8 September 2000, International Literacy Day.

Many sub-regional and regional meetings have been held as part of the follow-up to the Hamburg Declaration. They foresee the creation of networks to introduce new approaches in adult education and integrate literacy into the broader perspective of adult education. Moreover, they underscore the importance of the new role of International Adult Learners' Week and the need for national adult education plans, while supporting innovative policies. The emphasis has been laid on putting the Hamburg Declaration into practice. The follow-up meetings dealt with the issue of adult access to basic education and the close relationship between community basic education and sustainable development. The problem of integrating education in the expanded concept of adult education and the question of new partnerships between States and civil society were also considered.

These mobilising activities show that "effective lifelong learning can help address basic skills needs in literacy, widen participation in and promote access to learning, reduce inequality, improve employability, and contribute to community development and to social inclusion", as noted in Resolution 11 adopted by the UNESCO General Conference at its 30th session, November 1999.

As part of the follow-up to the World Conference on Higher Education, 350 focal points were designated by Member States to stimulate and co-ordinate various initiatives. In a globalising world, higher education has taken on particular significance, as in today's knowledge-based society, a critical question is that those with knowledge have an edge over those without. It is therefore a matter of urgency to promote the concept of lifelong education. Some themes, such as access to education, should be prioritised. The principle of merit-based access to higher education, endorsed by the *World Declaration on Higher Education for the Twenty-First Century*, is closely linked to the follow-up to the *Dakar Framework for Action*. In the decennial review of education for all, the participants reaffirmed their commitment to basic education but also stressed lifelong education for all as a response to the challenges imposed by the knowledge-based society. Access is a priority issue. UNESCO endeavours to promote access to higher education through a new programme of activities in conjunction with various partners.

The Third International Conference of Ministers and Senior Officials responsible for Physical Education and Sport (MINEPS III), held in Punta del East (Uruguay) in December 1999, was a key action in the follow-up to the *International Charter on Physical Education and Sport*. The Recommendations of Commission II of the Conference were on "Physical education and sport, an integral part and fundamental element of the right to education and the process of continuing education".

Considering that "physical education and sport is a human right", the Recommendations recall the "principles enshrined in the *International Charter on Physical Education and Sport*", and invite "the Director-General of UNESCO, with the cooperation of existing and future regional and national bodies and networks as well as specialists on the subject, to draw up a world traditional games and sports policy, leading eventually to an international charter on traditional games and sports, to be followed by a midterm and a long-term plan of action". By the Declaration of Punta del East, adopted at MINEPS III on 3 December 1999, the Ministers "endorse the Berlin Agenda for Action adopted by the World Summit on Physical Education in 1999 and encourage Member States to ensure that sport and physical education are incorporated in school programmes or, as a minimum, that their legal requirements with respect to physical education programmes in school curricula are being met".

The Advisory Committee on Education for Peace, Human Rights, Democracy, International Understanding and Tolerance has also played a role in monitoring the implementation of UNESCO's standard-setting instruments in the field of education through its recommendations and suggestions on the right to education. In view of the increasing number of children living in poor, illiterate families, the Committee "considered the question of promoting equal opportunity and access to basic education for all to be of the highest importance". It emphasised the key role of human rights education for democracy and the importance of civics education. It is undeniably the right to education which, inasmuch as it is a human right, constitutes one of the fundamentals of any democratic society. Today there is growing inequality, both between States and within individual countries, presenting a major challenge to the international community. In the future, it is our duty to take up that challenge by creating the conditions for an education of "learning to care and learning to share".

Beyond the individual will of Member States to apply the various international instruments to which they have committed themselves, there is a more global, promising will on the part of those same States to achieve common objectives that cannot be achieved without international cooperation. Indeed, it may be recalled that, at the Summit of Heads of State and Government of the G-8, held in Okinawa from 21-23 July 2000, it was stated that "Every child deserves a good education. But in some developing countries access to education is limited, [in] particular for females and the socially vulnerable". The participants declared that without accelerated progress in the field of basic education, "poverty reduction will not be achieved and inequalities between countries and within societies will widen [...]. We reaffirm our commitment that no government seriously committed to achieving education for all will be thwarted in this achievement by lack of resources".

References

Best, Francine. *Education, Culture, Human Rights, and International Understanding: The Promotion of Humanistic, Ethical, and Cultural Values in Education.* Paris: UNESCO, 1990.

Education for All 2000 Assessment, submitted by countries to the World Education Forum, Dakar, April 2000.

Jean Piaget, "The right to education in the modern world" in *Freedom and Culture*, compiled by UNESCO, Wingate, London, pp. 69-116.

Jean Debiesse, "The Right to Free and Compulsory Education" in the *UNESCO Courier*, July-August 1951, p. 14.

World Education Report 2000 – The Right to Education: Towards Education for All Throughout Life, UNESCO Publishing, Paris, 2000.

3

Primary Education as a Fundamental Right

'Everyone has the right to education' – according to Article 26 of the Universal Declaration of Human Rights.

In the quest to achieve Education for All, states must prioritise free and compulsory primary education. It is a fundamental right that cannot be forfeited. It is a litmus test for the individual to assess his or her government's commitments to fundamental rights, as well as those of the international community. The right to education is unique in that it empowers the individual to exercise other civil, political, economic, social and cultural rights, attaining a life of dignity, while ensuring a brighter future for all, free from want and from fear.

Primary education must be inclusive and accessible to all, in law as well as in fact. No provider of public education may discriminate on the grounds of gender, ethnicity, language, religion, opinion, disability, or social and economic status.

UNESCO works to make primary education accessible for all, as well as to ensure full retention and completion, forming the grounds for a further promotion of children's cognitive, creative and emotional development.

Achieving Universal Primary Education

The second United Nations Millennium Development Goal is to achieve Universal Primary Education, more specifically, to "ensure that by 2015, children everywhere, boys and girls alike will be able to complete a full course of primary schooling." Currently, there are more than 75 million children around the world of primary school age who are not in school. The majority of these children are in regions of sub-Saharan Africa and South Asia and within these countries, girls are at the greatest disadvantage in receiving access to education at the primary school age. Since the Millennium Development Goals were launched, many developing countries, such as China, Chile, Cuba, Singapore and Sri Lanka, have successfully completed a campaign towards universal primary education.

There has been great progress achieved since 1999 in the achievement of the millennium development goal (MDG). UNESCO has found that :

- number of children enrolled in primary schools worldwide rose by more than 40 million between 1999 and 2007
- net primary enrollment in sub-Saharan Africa rose from 58% to 74% over the same period
- international aid commitments to basic education almost doubled from $2.1 billion in 2002 to $4.1 billion in 2007

However, despite all these important achievements, the world is currently not on course to achieve its target of universal primary education (UPE) by 2015. Currently, 56 million children could still be out of school in 2015 and girls will still lag behind boys in school enrollment and attendance. Sub-Saharan Africa is particularly affected as over a quarter of its children of primary school age were out of school in 2007. It is estimated that there is a $16.2 billion annual external financing gap between available domestic resources and what is needed to achieve the basic education goals in low income countries, with current aid levels addressing only 15% of that gap and resources are all too often not provided to those countries who need it most and the amounts pledged not fully honored. Difficulties faced by donors in the sphere of achieving UPE, highlighted by researchers at the Overseas Development Institute, include:

- failings in aid architecture (though the Paris Declaration and FTI initiatives represent significant improvements)
- the evidence-based case for further investment in basic education has not been made strongly enough
- recipient governments are reluctant to borrow funds for the recurrent costs education entails.

FACTORS CONTRIBUTING TO LACK OF ACCESS AND POOR ATTENDANCE

Location

Location contributes to a child's lack of access and attendance to primary education. In certain areas of the world it is more difficult for children to get to school. For example; in high-altitude areas of India, severe weather conditions for more than 7 months of the year make school attendance erratic and force children to remain at home.

In these remote locations, insufficient school funds contribute to low attendance rates by creating undesirable and unsafe learning environments. In 1996, the General Accounting Office (GAO) reported that poor conditions existed in many rural areas; one out of every two rural schools had at least one inadequate structural or mechanical feature. In these situations where regular school attendance is rare, a low population contributes to the problem. In other locations, large numbers are often the cause of low attendance rates.

Due to population growth, many urban schools have expanded their boundaries making school transportation more complicated. "For over 50 years the U.S. has been shifting away from small, neighborhood schools to larger schools in lower density areas. Rates of children walking and biking to school have declined significantly over this period". There is evidence to prove that the distance to and from school contributes a child's attendance, or lack thereof. In a study done investigating the relation between location (distance) and school attendance in Mali, about half the villages reported that the school was too far away, causing students not to enroll.

There is still speculation as to whether primary schools are more accessible in rural or urban areas because situations differ depending on geographic location. In a study done examining the correlation between location and school attendance in Argentina and Panama, researchers found that urban residence was positively correlated with school attendance, but another study in a Louisiana school district found that schools with the lowest attendance rates were in metropolitan areas.

More research needs to be done to determine geography's specific effects on attendance, but no matter where you live, there is evidence that location will contribute to a child's access and attendance to education.

Gender

Gender contributes to a child's lack of access and attendance to education. Although it may not be as an obvious a problem today, gender equality in education has been an issue for a long time. Many investments in girls' education in the 1900s addressed the widespread lack of access to primary education in developing countries.

There is currently a gender discrepancy in education. In 25 countries the proportion of boys enrolling in secondary school is higher than girls by 10% or more, and in five; India, Nepal, Togo, Turkey and Yemen, the gap exceeds 20%. Enrollment is low for both boys and girls in sub-Saharan Africa, with rates of just 27% and 22%. Girls trail respectively behind. It is generally believed that girls are often discouraged from attending primary schooling, especially in less developed countries for religious and cultural reasons, but there is little evidence available to support this association. However, there is evidence to prove that the disparity of gender in education is real. Today some 78% of girls drop out of school, compared with 48% of boys. A child's gender continues to contribute to access and attendance today.

Cost

Costs contribute to a child's lack of access and attendance to primary education. High opportunity costs are often influential in the decision to attend school. For example; an estimated 121 million children of primary-school age are being kept out of school to work in the fields or at home (UNICEF). For many families in developing countries the economic benefits of no primary schooling are enough to offset the opportunity cost of attending.

Besides the opportunity costs associated with education, school fees can be very expensive, especially for poor households. In rural China, families dedicate as much as a third of their income to school fees. Sometimes, the cost gets too expensive and families can't support their children's education anymore, although the statistics disagree. "China has 108.6 million primary school students, with a 1 percent dropout rate, but experts doubt these figures because the dropout rates in rural areas appear much higher".Although the relationship between school fees and attendance still isn't perfectly clear, there is evidence to prove that cost is a factor that contributes to a child's access and attendance to primary education.

Language

In developing countries throughout the world the educational context is characterized not by monolingual settings, but rather multilingual situations. Often children are asked to enroll in a primary school where the Medium of Instruction (MI) is not her home language, but rather the language of the government, or another dominant society . Studies throughout the world demonstrate the importance of the MI in determining a child's educational attainment. According to Mehrotra (1988) "In a situation where the parents are illiterate..., if the medium of instruction in school is a language that is not spoken at home the problems of learning in an environment characterized by poverty are compounded, and the chances of drop-out increase correspondingly. In this context, the experience of the high- achievers has been unequivocal: the mother tongue was used as the medium of instruction at the primary level in all cases. ... There is much research which shows that students learn to read more quickly when taught in their mother tongue. Second, students who have learned to read in their mother tongue learn to read in a second language more quickly than do those who are first taught to read in the second language. Third, in terms of academic learning skills as well, students taught to read in their mother tongue acquire such skills more quickly".

Normative Action for Universalising Primary Education

The right to primary education, free of charge, is established by international instruments, notably UNESCO's Convention against Discrimination in Education, Articles 13 and 14 of the International Covenant on Economic, Social and Cultural Rights and Article 28(1) of the Convention on the Rights of the Child. Article 4 (a) of the *Convention against Discrimination in Education* and Article 13(2) (a) of the International Covenant recognise clearly the right of everyone to primary education, free of charge. Article 14 of the International Covenant lays down State obligations for a detailed plan of action for the progressive implementation of the right to compulsory education free of charge for all. These obligations are similar to the political commitments made under the *Dakar Framework for Action* regarding the national EFA action plan.

In spite of this normative framework, primary schooling is in fact not free in many developing countries and universal free primary education is still far from being a reality. Moreover, school fees imposed are contrary to the international normative framework and incompatible with international legal obligations.

Normative action for universalising access to primary education that is free of charge for all therefore needs be intensified, laying special emphasis on the *minimum core obligations* of States. This must be central to the endeavour to achieve EFA, and needs to be widely publicised. The right to education must figure prominently, for example, with respect to the World Bank/ UNICEF School Fee Abolition Initiative and in all advocacy for the realisation of the right to free primary education.

Nature and Scope of State obligations

The United Nations Committee on Economic, Social and Cultural Rights (CESCR) has interpreted the right to compulsory primary education free of charge for all in its General Comment No. 11 on plans of action for primary education (Article 14 of the Covenant and General Comment No. 13 on the right to education (Article 13 of the Covenant) as well as in its Concluding Observations (COBs) on numerous State Party reports submitted under Articles 16 and 17 of the Covenant. As General Comment No. 11 states, the nature of this requirement for primary education free of charge is *unequivocal*. As regards the nature of the obligations of States Parties under Article 13(2)(a), General Comment No. 13 states that the obligation to provide primary education for all is an immediate and *core obligation* of these States. Article 13 of the Covenant enjoins upon State Parties to the International Covenant to "priorities the introduction of compulsory, free primary education".

States are duty bound to respect and fulfil their *core obligation*. As CESCR has stated, they must ensure equal access to primary education for all children of school age residing in their territory, including non-nationals and irrespective of their legal status. Any denial of the right to free primary education on the basis of nationality or statelessness and/or legal residence status is therefore incompatible with international obligations under Articles 13(2)(a) and 2(2) of the International Covenant. The same goes for children of migrant workers and of minority groups.

As formulated in Article 13(2)(a), primary education has two distinctive features: it is "compulsory" and "available free to all". Compulsory schooling means that neither parents, nor guardians, nor the State are entitled to treat as optional the decision as to whether the child should have access to primary education. Similarly, the prohibition of gender discrimination in access to education, required also by Articles 2 and 3 of the Covenant, is further underlined by this requirement. It should be emphasised, however, that the education offered must bc adcquate in quality, relevant to the child and promote the realisation of the child's other rights. In order to ensure universal primary school attendance, States Parties are obliged to set the minimum working age at no less than 15 years.

The obligation under Article 14 of the Covenant to adopt a detailed plan of action for the progressive implementation of the principle of compulsory education free of charge for all is a *continuous obligation.* Accordingly, States Parties are under a continuous obligation to report on the measures taken under existing plans of action, improve such plans and, to that effect, set appropriate indicators and benchmarks in their periodic reports to the Committee. National plans of action should address both the accessibility and quality of primary education. To a certain extent, these issues were already covered in the EFA reports of States.

Right to Free Primary Education

UNESCO attaches high importance to the State obligations for free primary education. UNESCO's Medium-Term Strategy states that "advancing the right to education as enshrined in the Universal Declaration of Human Rights is central to UNESCO's mission. Free, compulsory and universal primary education for all is among the most clearly defined of these rights, which governments have a duty and responsibility to make a reality". Central to these reflections is the concern to reach the un-reached children belonging to cultural and linguistic minorities, children from socially and economically marginalised groups, children in geographically remote areas and in particular children from poor households, who are deprived of any means to bear the cost of primary education.

Governments are expected to follow up on the recommendations made by the High-Level Group on EFA. In the first Recommendation of the Communique issued at the second meeting of the High-Level Group on EFA, the Ministers of Education stated that "as next steps, we particularly recommend that: governments in the South must ensure that free and compulsory primary education is a right reflected in national legislation and in practice". Similar recommendations were made at the third meeting of the High-Level Group on EFA organised in New Delhi (India) in November

2003. The action agenda in the Communique issued after the meeting contains, *inter alia*, commitments by the Ministers to "enacting national legislation to enforce children's right to free and compulsory quality education, prevent and progressively eliminate child labour, and prohibit early marriage". The EFA Global Monitoring Reports provide information as regards realisation of the right to primary education, including statistical information on duration for compulsory education in different countries.

Monitoring the implementation of the right to free primary education is an important part of UNESCO's normative action. Member States have the obligation to take measures for implementing the Convention against Discrimination in Education and provide information on the progress with respect, *inter alia*, to ensuring universal access to primary education. The Guidelines for preparation of reports for the seventh consultation of Member States on measures taken to implement the Convention contain detailed provisions for this purpose, with emphasis on EFA and with particular concern for disadvantaged and marginalised groups, especially children from poor households.

Legal Parameters of Free Education

The requirement that primary education be available *free* for all has been interpreted by the CESCR as guaranteeing the availability of primary education without charge to the child, parents or guardians. Fees imposed by the government, local authorities or the school as well as other direct costs constitute disincentives to the enjoyment of the right and may jeopardise its realisation. They are also often highly regressive in effect and must be eliminated. Their elimination is a matter that must be addressed by the required plan of action.

States Parties are thus obliged to eliminate all school-related fees so as to make compulsory primary education truly free for all children. While direct costs such as school fees imposed by the government, local authorities or schools run counter to international obligations and must be eliminated, indirect costs such as expenses for schoolbooks, uniforms or travel to and from school may be permissible. Currently, the heaviest charges on a family's budget come from the indirect costs, notably for parents' compulsory contributions. Indirect costs, such as compulsory levies on parents, or the obligation to wear a relatively expensive school uniform, must be eliminated. Other indirect costs may be permissible, subject to the examination by CESCR on a case-by-case basis. States should adopt special measures to alleviate the negative effects of indirect costs on children from poorer households. Such measures include the free provision of textbooks and school transport, as well as scholarships and other financial subsidies for financially disadvantaged children. To the extent that school uniforms are compulsory, they must be provided free of charge to children from poorer households. The free provision of midday meals is a best practice in providing incentives for parents to send their children to school.

An important question as regards the entitlement to receive free primary education is how to alleviate the effect of indirect costs on poorer households. This requires special measures for providing financial and other assistance. States Parties should include information on any indirect costs related to primary education in their periodic reports to CESCR and target disadvantaged and marginalised children and their families in the plans of action that they adopt under Article 14 of the Covenant and as a follow-up to the World Education Forum. Compensatory measures for disadvantages due to family economic circumstances and various forms of financial aid for schooling are important to enable families of modest economic circumstances to support more easily the education of their children.

The variety of schooling costs and complexity of situations in some countries suggest that there is an imperative need for a methodology to define what is commonly understood as 'schooling costs', as well as a system of classification for these costs. The international community's efforts should focus on abolishing direct costs and minimising indirect costs. In this respect, it is important to note that Articles 3 and 4 of UNESCO's Convention against Discrimination in Education offer the necessary guidelines for this purpose by indicating the measures to be taken in the matter of school fees, the granting of scholarships and other forms of assistance, etc.

Many developing countries are adopting incentives such as provisions for textbooks, day-school meals and transport, especially for children from disadvantaged and marginalised groups, and in particular from poor households. Such practices are exemplary and deserve to be encouraged. They make it attractive for children to attend school and are significant in mitigating school dropouts. Moreover, in countries with severe resource constraints and widespread poverty, inequalities in educational opportunity are often more pronounced and have required States to adopt many different kinds of compensatory measures.

PRINCIPLE OF NONDISCRIMINATION AND EQUAL ACCESS TO EDUCATION

Making education free is not, however, the only way of making it accessible: nondiscrimination is no less essential, since it enables those from disadvantaged or vulnerable categories to benefit equally from the right to education. There is an even greater obstacle to overcome here, as there are not only economic factors at play but also cultural and sociological constraints that cannot be overlooked and are difficult to circumvent.

The principle of *nondiscrimination* and *equal access* to education as a right, expressed in the Convention against Discrimination in Education and stipulated in Articles 2(2) and 3 of the International Covenant, is an important dimension of the right to primary education for all. Primary education must be accessible to all, especially the most vulnerable groups, *in law and in fact*, without discrimination on any of the prohibited grounds. States Parties to the International Covenant are obliged to remove gender stereotyping, which impedes access to primary education by girls. In addition, any disparities in school enrolment rates between girls and boys and between rural and urban areas must be eliminated. States Parties must ensure equal access to primary education for all children of school age residing in their territory.

As regards "Nondiscrimination and equality of opportunity, including minority language education and equal opportunities for boys and girls; special measures in favour of disadvantaged and marginalised individuals and groups, including the poor", articles 2(2) and 13(2)(a) of the Covenant require States Parties to the Covenant to adopt temporary special measures to ensure the equal enjoyment of the right to free primary education by all, including girls, children from poorer households, children with disabilities and minority and refugee children. Minority children in some countries are segregated in separate schools or remedial classes and excluded from mainstream education; refugee children are often excluded by law from free primary education altogether. Examples of special measures are the establishment of mobile schools and creating adequate opportunities for distance learning to accommodate children living in remote rural areas.

While Article 5(1)(c) of the Convention against Discrimination in Education recognises the right of members of national minorities to their own educational activities, including the use or the teaching of their own language, this right is not explicitly recognised in the Covenant. However, in its concluding observations, CESCR had repeatedly recommended that States Parties ensure, to the extent possible, that children belonging to linguistic minorities have adequate opportunities to receive instruction in or of their native language at school. In line with Article 14(2) of the European Framework Convention for the Protection of National Minorities, this right could be made subject to certain qualifications such as numerical thresholds or "sufficient demand".

Principle of Equity and Positive Measures

Removal of all *educational disparities* is a major challenge. Certain categories suffer from exclusion or discrimination, such as girls and women and underserved groups (street children, working children, rural and remote population, nomads and migrant workers, indigenous peoples, ethnic, racial and linguistic minorities, refugees, displaced persons and people under occupation, and the disabled requiring special attention), even if the achievement of equity entails positive discrimination or granting priorities to certain groups.

The CESCR has clarified that the adoption of *temporary special measures* intended to bring about *de facto* equality for men and women and for disadvantaged groups is not incompatible with the right to nondiscrimination and equal access to free primary education, as long as such measures do not lead to the maintenance of unequal or separate standards for different groups, and provided that they are not continued after the objectives for which they were taken have been achieved. In its concluding observations, the CESCR has, for example, recommended that States Parties: upgrade schooling programmes for indigenous and migrant children, child workers and children belonging to other disadvantaged and marginalised groups, in particular girls; take effective measures to promote school attendance by Roman children and children belonging to other minority groups as well as refugee and internally displaced children, by increasing subsidies, scholarships and the number of teachers instructing in minority languages; promote equal access by Roman children to primary education, e. g. Through the grant of scholarships and the reimbursement of expenses for schoolbooks and of travel expenses to attend school; and closely monitor school attendance by Roman children. In order to alleviate the effects of indirect costs on poorer households, States Parties should provide financial and other assistance to enable children from poorer households, including child heads of household, to exercise the right to primary education. Similarly, minority and indigenous children and their families may be entitled to temporary special measures, including scholarships and financial subsidies such as reimbursement of expenses for schoolbooks and of travel expenses.

Educational Rights of Children Belonging to Minorities

The right of minority and indigenous children to receive *instruction in* or of their native *minority or indigenous languages* arguably forms part of the right to primary education, subject to certain qualifications. Accordingly, CESCR has recommended that States Parties ensure, "to the extent possible", that children belonging to minority linguistic groups have an opportunity to learn their mother tongue, including regional dialects, at school and take all possible measures to ensure that the teaching of indigenous languages in schools is increased. For this purpose, States Parties should: ensure that there are an adequate number of schools and teachers instructing minority or indigenous languages; develop adequate learning materials; and allocate sufficient budgetary resources to bilingual and multi-cultural education.

Children belonging to minorities or indigenous communities are entitled to have *equal opportunities* to receive instruction in or of their mother tongue; any distinction between different minority and indigenous groups must be justified by reasonable and objective criteria. Despite the trend towards requiring instruction in or of the main minority languages within a State Party, CESCR clearly *rejects* the establishment of *separate schools* for children belonging to different ethnic groups and asks States Parties to teach *one overarching curriculum* to all classes, irrespective of ethnicity. It goes without saying that such curricula should provide for instruction in the official language of States Parties.

The rights of national minorities are protected for carrying out their own educational activities in accordance with Article 5, paragraph 1(c), of the Convention against Discrimination in Education, which reflects the principle of respect for cultural diversity. Education of ethnic and linguistic minorities is indeed a complex issue. In today's societies, which are increasingly becoming multi-cultural and multi-ethnic, there is need for a better understanding of the right to (primary) education and learning in the mother tongue.

Right to Standard and Quality of Education

The need to provide primary education of good quality was stressed at the World Education Forum, and this is of critical importance in the context of EFA. The education offered must be adequate in quality, relevant to the child and promote the realisation of the child's other rights. Abolishing costs allows a large number of children to attend school but is not a sufficient measure for them to remain within the education system. Governments must take complementary measures in order to ensure, for instance, teachers' recruitment and professional training, provisions for textbooks, school maintenance and development expenditure for quality education.

The obligation to provide primary education free of charge is inextricably linked with the obligation to ensure quality education, as established by the Convention against Discrimination in Education. The term "education" in the Convention is defined as including "access to education, the *standard and quality of education*, and the conditions under which it is given" (Article 1(2)). Further, the Convention lays down the obligation for the States Parties "to ensure that the standards of education are equivalent in all public educational institutions of the same level, and that the conditions relating to the *quality* of the education provided are also equivalent" (Article 4(b), emphasis added). The importance attached to quality education is also expressed in the Recommendation concerning the Status of Teachers, which provides that "as an educational objective, no State should be satisfied with mere quantity, but should seek also to *improve quality*" (Article 10(g)). Poor standards of education in public schools and the phenomenal expansion of private educational institutions in many developing countries raise the fundamental question of preserving quality education—both in public and private schools. In line with the Recommendation concerning the Status of Teachers, which "applies to *all teachers in both private and public schools*", it is crucial to valorise the teaching profession.

The work of CESCR is helpful in understanding *quality* and *content*. Primary *education* must comply with "minimum educational standards" to be established and effectively monitored by States Parties, be culturally appropriate and of good quality (General Comment No. 13, para. 6(c)), and conform to the educational objectives set out in Article 13(1) of the Covenant. As stated by CESCR in its concluding observations, States Parties are obliged to ensure that educational standards in public schools do not fall behind those in private schools. Domestically competitive salaries and the adequate status and working conditions of qualified teachers, as well as a sufficient quantity of teachers and functioning educational facilities, are among the preconditions for ensuring the quality of primary education.

The argument that school fees may be necessary to ensure the quality of primary education is unacceptable: it is the obligation of States to ensure that the quality of education does not suffer from its free-of-charge character. In fact, imposing fees may lead to the further exclusion of socially and culturally marginalised groups, in particular children from poor families who are unable to pay the fees and remain deprived of education.

Financing Free Primary Education

Governments are primarily responsible for ensuring that access to primary education is universality and not denied to any child. It is incumbent upon them to mobilise resources for this purpose. In order for a State Party to the International Covenant to be able to attribute its failure to meet its core obligations under Article 13(2)(a) to a lack of available resources, it must demonstrate that every effort has been made to use all resources that are at its disposition in an effort to satisfy, as a matter of priority, these core obligations.

A State Party cannot escape the unequivocal obligation to adopt a plan of action, required under Article 14 of the International Covenant, on the grounds that the necessary resources are not available. If the obligation could be avoided in this way, there would be no justification for the unique requirement contained in Article 14 of the International Covenant, which applies, almost by definition, to situations characterised by inadequate financial resources. By the same token, and for the same reason, the reference to "international assistance and cooperation" in Article 2. 1 and to "international action" in Article 23 of the Covenant are of particular relevance in this situation. Where a State Party is clearly lacking in the financial resources and/or expertise required to "work out and adopt" a detailed plan, the international community has a clear obligation to assist.

Several questions must be reflected on as regards the need to develop a legal framework for free primary education for all, especially in those countries which are lagging behind in achieving EFA goals: what are the provisions, if any, for financing such education in a country's constitution? What kind of legal framework for financing primary or basic education is being put in place as part of developments in national legislation and education policy, along with national budget priorities, to enable governments to raise the necessary resources for ensuring universal access to primary education free of charge?

Preserving Public Interest in Education

The concept of education as a public good underlines the normative framework for the right to education. Reflections on this concept are crucial in developing and applying national legal frameworks for education. This could be considered in the context of globalisation, which carries with it the danger of creating a marketplace in knowledge that excludes the poor and the disadvantaged. UNESCO's Medium-Term Strategy for 2002-2007, which recognises the importance of policy dialogue for advancing the right to education, provides that "UNESCO will further seek to engage Member States and new educational providers in a dialogue highlighting education as a public good and encourage all actors in the field of education to pay due regard in their undertakings to the need for equity, inclusion and social cohesion in today's societies".

School Feeding Programs

Education is a crucial factor in ending global poverty. With education, employment opportunities are broadened, income levels are increased and maternal and child health is improved.

In areas where access, attendance and quality of education have seen improvements, there has also been a slow in the spread of HIV/AIDS and an increase in the healthiness of the community in general. In fact, children of educated mothers are 50% more likely to live past the age of five. Not only does education improve individual and familial health, but it also improves the health of a community. In countries with solid education systems in place, there are lower crime rates, greater economic growth and improved social services.

"There are approximately 300 million chronically hungry children in the world. One hundred million of them do not attend school, and two thirds of those not attending school are girls. World Food Programme's school feeding formula is simple: food attracts hungry children to school. An education broadens their options, helping to lift them out of poverty." –World Food Programme

One successful method to ensuring that children attend school on a regular basis is through school feeding programs. Many different organizations fund school feeding programs, among them the World Food Programme and the World Bank. The idea of a school feeding program is that children are provided with meals at school with the expectation that they will attend school regularly. School feeding programs have proven a huge success because not only do the attendance rates increase, but in areas where food is scarce and malnutrition is extensive, the food that children are receiving at school can prove to be a critical source of nutrition. School meals have led to improved concentration and performance of children in school. Another aspect of school feeding programs is take home rations. When economic reasons, the need to care for the elderly or a family member suffering from HIV, or cultural beliefs keep a parent from sending their child (especially a female child) to school, these take home rations provide incentives to sending their children to school rather than to work

Current Efforts

Global Campaign for Education

This organization promotes education as a basic human right. It motivates people and groups to put public pressure on governments and the international community in order to assure that all children are provided with free, compulsory public education. It brings together major NGOs and Teachers Unions in over 120 countries to work in solidarity towards their vision of universal primary education.

Right to Education Project

The Right to Education Project aims to promote social mobilisation and legal accountability, looking to focus on the legal challenges to the right to education. To ensure continued relevance and engagement with activists and the academic community the Project also undertakes comparative research to advance an understanding of the right to education.

Role of UNICEF

UNICEF believes that in treating education as a basic human right, it will address the basic inequalities in our society, especially gender inequalities. It focuses on the most disadvantaged children through a range of innovative programs and initiatives. In working with local, national and international partners, UNICEF's work is contributing to the realization of the 2nd millennium development goal by 2015.

Oxfam International

This organization is a confederation of 12 organizations that are dedicated to reducing poverty and eliminating injustices in the world. Oxfam works on a grassroots level in countries around the world to ensure that all people have access to the basic human rights, including education.

Save the Children

This organization advocates education as a way for individuals to escape poverty. They are running a campaign entitled "Rewrite the Future" to encouraging American citizens, in positions of power and wealth, to take action against the injustices in education systems around the world. Save the Children also operates education programs in 30 countries all over the world.

Peace Corps

This United States government organization has volunteers on the ground in 75 countries. Many of the volunteers are working as teachers in rural areas or working to promote and improve access to education in the areas in which they are stationed.

United Nations Educational Scientific and Cultural Organization

UNESCO works to improve education through projects, advice, capacity-building and networking. UNESCO's Education for All Campaign by 2015 is the driving force in UNESCO's work in the field of education at the moment.

World Bank

This organization provides financial and technical assistance to developing countries. Loans and grants from the World Bank provide much of the funding for educational projects around the world, including but not limited to school feeding programs.

Child Aid

Child Aid conducts school- and library-based reading programs in over 50 indigenous villages in Guatemala, where literacy rates are lower than anywhere in Latin America. Through its Reading for Life program it trains teachers and librarians, creates and improves community libraries and delivers tens of thousands of children's books annually.

World Food Program

This organization provides food relief in areas that need it most and is one of the major funders of school feeding programs.

Food and Agriculture Organization of the United Nations

This organization runs a campaign entitled Education for Rural People in which they work to ensure education for rural people as the key to reduction of poverty, food security and sustainable development.

Global Alliance for Improved Nutrition (GAIN)

This organization is a hub for organizations committed to ending vitamin and mineral deficiencies. GAIN works with other international organizations, governments and the private sector to implement large-scale food fortification programs as well as targeted ones including school feeding projects aimed at the most at risk of malnutrition. Home Page

Fast Track Initiative (FTI)

The Fast Track Initiative (FTI) was launched in 2002. It was designed as a major initiative to help countries achieve the Millennium Development Goal (MDG) of Universal Primary Education (UPE) by 2015. It was endorsed by the Development Committee of the World Bank as a 'process that would provide quick and incremental technical and financial support to countries that have policies but are not on track to attain Universal Primary Completion by 2015'.

Building Tomorrow

This Indianapolis, IN based social-profit empowers young people to support their peers in sub-Saharan Africa by raising funds and awareness for school infrastructure projects. They have built seven primary schools in Uganda since their inception in 2005 and are working to support the UN Millenium Development Goal of Universal Primary Education.

Teach for America

The mission of Teach for America is to address the inadequacies in the

United States education system by placing highly qualified college graduates into under resourced schools for a two-year period in an attempt transform these leaders into lifelong advocates of education reform in the United States.

Our Education

This is a campaign to empower young people in the United States to stand up and speak out against the inadequacies in the United States education system and to demand change through political activism.

Breakthrough Collaborative

This organization empowers high potential middle school students from lower income communities to excel in school and at the same time inspires motivated high school and college students to pursue careers in education. It is a six week summer enrichment program where "students teach students" run in more than 30 sites all over the United States.

References

Douglas A. Sylva. *The United Nations Children's Fund: Women or Children First?* Diss. Catholic Family and Human Rights Institute, 2003. New York, New York, 2003.

Dowd, Amy Jo; Greer, Heather. *Girls' Education: Community Approaches to Access and Quality. Strong Beginnings.* Westport: Save the Children Federation, Inc., 2001.

Geissinger, Helen. "Girls' Access to Education in a Developing Country." *International Review of Education.* V43 n5-6 (1999): 423-38. EBSCOhost. 15 Nov. 2006

Mehrotra, S. (1998): Education for All: Policy Lessons From High-Achieving Countries:UNICEF Staff Working Papers, New York, UNICEF.

4

Right to Lifelong Learning

Debates about education generally focus on school education or, at most, school and vocational education. They generally focus on children or, at most, children at school and young people in their first years after school. The educational needs of adults rarely receive attention and, where they do, they are considered only in the context of training or re-training for employment. The need for education and the right to education extend far beyond schools and children. Adults too have needs and rights. They are the focus of our discussion today.

Adults have educational rights because they have educational needs. Often people in western societies assume that, because our countries have an extensive school system with near universal enrolment, children become adults who are literate and numerate, equipped to participate in their world and personally fulfilled. This is so for most but not for all. The compulsory mass education systems of the last century have certainly produced the best educated populations ever but they have not yet ensured that everyone has the knowledge, information and skills required for each person to reach his or her fullest potential as a person and a citizen.

Since its beginning, the United Nations have expressed their conviction that education is one of the basic pillars on which modern societies should lean. Over the last six decades, UNESCO has organized five international conferences expressly devoted to Adult Education. Great progress towards the comprehension of the universal right to lifelong education were performed in each one of them.

Lifelong Learning: Moving beyond Education for All

Over the past two decades, the world has experienced profound changes. A rapid globalisation process has resulted in a highly connected world, with economic and political power more concentrated than ever. Many old structural problems have further deteriorated or become more evident to public awareness, while new ones have emerged. Technology has undergone impressive leaps, bringing with it new possibilities as well as new threats. All these developments have major consequences on people's lives around the world, as well as on education and learning systems.

However, the education field continues to revolve around the traditional "education reform" mentality. More money and resources devoted to doing basically more of the same. Top-down policies and measures. "Improving the quality of education" instead of revisiting it. Quantities predominating over qualities. Education understood mainly or solely as *school* education. Access, retention and completion rates as main (school) education indicators. Tests aimed at evaluating how much information students are able to digest and retrieve. Weak attention to learning, easily confused with testing and school achievement. Overburdened curricula attempting to capture as much content as possible. And so on and so forth.

All this is apparent not only at the national but also at the international level. World platforms such asEducation for All (EFA), coordinated by UNESCO, are not tuned with LIfelong Learning (LLL) the new emerging paradigm, adopted over the past few years by many countries in the North, especially in Europe, and promoted by many international agencies, UNESCO being one of them.

The Education for All (EFA) world initiative was launched in 1990 (Jomtien, Thailand) and ratified in 2000 (Dakar, Senegal). In Dakar, a new deadline was established (2015) given the fact that the six EFA goals were not accomplished 2000. The goals remained six but were slightly modified (Box 1).

EFA goals replicate the conventional education mentality and do not facilitate a holistic understanding of education and of learning throughout life. This is because, among reasons,

- EFA goals are a list. Each goal is treated and measured separately. The linkages between them are not apparent. EFA's traditional and ongoing focus on Goal 2 – children's primary education – reflects and replicates

Box 1. Education for All goals (1990-2000-2015)

Jomtien: 1990-2000	*Dakar: 2000-2015*
1.Expansion of early childhood care and development activities, including family and community interventions, especially for poor, disadvantaged and disabled children.	1. Expanding and improving comprehensive early childhood care and education, especially for the most vulnerable and disadvantaged children.
2. Universal access to, and completion of, primary education (or whatever higher level of education is considered as "basic") by the year 2000.	2. Ensuring that by 2015 all children, particularly girls, children in difficult circumstances and those belonging to ethnic minorities, have access to and complete free and compulsory primary education of good quality.
3. Improvement in learning achievement such that an agreed percentage of an appropriate age cohort (e.g. 80% of 14 year olds) attains or surpasses a defined level of necessary learning achievement.	3. Ensuring that the learning needs of all young people and adults are met through equitable access to appropriate learning and life skills programmes.
4. Reduction in the adult illiteracy rate (the appropriate age cohort to be determined in each country) to, say, one-half its 1990 level by the year 2000, with sufficient emphasis on female literacy to significantly reduce the current disparity between the male and female illiteracy rates.	4. Achieving a 50 per cent improvement in levels of adult literacy by 2015, especially for women, and equitable access to basic and continuing education for all adults.
5. Expansion of provision of basic education and training in other essential skills required by youth and adults, with programme effectiveness assessed in terms of behavioural changes and impacts on health, employment and productivity.	5. Eliminating gender disparities in primary and secondary education by 2015, with a focus on ensuring girls' full and equal access to and achievement in basic education of good quality.
6. Increased acquisition by individuals and families of the knowledge, skills and values required for better living and sound and sustainable development, made available through all educational channels including the mass media, other forms of modern and traditional communication, and social action, with effectiveness assessed in terms of behavioural change.	6. Improving all aspects of the quality of education and ensuring excellence of all so that recognised and measurable learning outcomes are achieved by all, especially in literacy, numeracy and essential life skills.

the false historical "option" between child and adult education, and the neglect of early childhood care and education, despite well-known rhetoric on the subject. In fact, the EFA Development Index (EDI), created in 2003 to monitor EFA developments in countries, includes only four EFA goals, leaving out Goal 1 (early childhood care and education) and Goal 3 (youth/adult basic education).

- EFA goals are organised by age – early childhood (Goal 1), school age (Goal 2), youth and adults (Goals 3 and 4), in the Dakar list – without articulation between them. Learners' segmentation according to age reflects the conventional education mentality that is behind the segmentation of education policies, goals and institutions. Focus on age contributes to losing sight of social learning organisations like the family and the community, and has institutionalised the false "option" between children's education and adult education, whereby children and adults have to compete for their right to education, especially in circumstances of multiple needs and scarce resources such as those that characterise countries in the South. EFA Goal 6 formulated in Jomtien in 1990, which referred to family education and public information ("Increased acquisition by individuals and families of the knowledge, skills and values required for better living and sound and sustainable development...") was eliminated in Dakar in 2000.
- EFA goals adhere to the traditional formal/non-formal dichotomy, leaving out *informal* learning, fundamental and expanding throughout the world given among others the expansion of life and of modern information and communication technologies (ICTs). The three-tier category (formal/non-formal/informal education) long used in the education field shows the centrality of *formal*education, with all other categories defined as *non-* or *in-*. In fact, the revised International Standard Classification of Education (ISCED 1997) does not include informal education, currently acknowledged as *informal learning* (incidental or random learning) given the absence of an organised education activity.
- EFA goals continue to view *literacy* in isolation, as a separate area and goal, without acknowledging that literacy is a basic learning need of the population and thus part of *basic education.*
- EFA goals adopt "*basic education*" as the main organising concept – not *lifelong learning*. The Jomtien conference spoke of an "expanded

vision of basic education", an education aimed at "meeting the basic learning needs of the population", in and out of the school system. However, the mission of education is not only *meeting basic* learning needs, but also *expanding them and generating* new learning needs along the process.

Box 2. Education: Formal and non-formal

Education: "Within the framework of ISCED, the term education is taken to comprise all deliberate and systematic activities designed to meet learning needs. This includes what in some countries is referred to as cultural activities or training. Whatever the name given to it, education is understood to involve organized and sustained communication designed to bring about learning. The key words in this formulation are to be understood as follows:

— COMMUNICATION: a relationship between two or more persons involving the transfer of information (messages, ideas, knowledge, strategies, etc.). Communication may be verbal or non-verbal, direct/face-to-face or indirect/remote, and may involve a wide variety of channels and media.

— LEARNING: any improvement in behaviour, information, knowledge, understanding, attitude, values or skills.

— ORGANIZED: planned in a pattern or sequence with explicit or implicit aims. It involves a providing agency (person or persons or body) that sets up the learning environment and a method of teaching through which the communication is organized. The method is typically someone who is engaged in communicating or releasing knowledge and skills with a view to bringing about learning, but it can also be indirect/inanimate e.g. a piece of computer software, a film, or tape, etc.

— SUSTAINED: intended to mean that the learning experience has the elements of duration and continuity. No minimum duration is stipulated, but appropriate minima will be stated in the operational manual.

Formal education (or initial education or regular school and university education): "Education provided in the system of schools, colleges, universities and other formal educational institutions that normally constitutes a continuous 'ladder' of full-time education for children and young people, generally beginning at age five to seven and continuing up to 20 or 25 years old. In some countries, the upper parts of this 'ladder' are constituted by organized programmes of joint part-time employment and part-time participation in the regular school and university system: such programmes have come to be known as the 'dual system' or equivalent terms in these countries.

Non-formal education: "Any organized and sustained educational activities that do not correspond exactly to the above definition of formal education. Non-formal education may therefore take place both within and outside educational institutions, and cater to persons of all ages. Depending on country contexts, it may cover educational programmes to impart adult literacy, basic education for out-of-school children, life-skills, work-skills, and general culture. Non-formal education programmes do not necessarily follow the 'ladder' system, and may have differing duration".

"Education, for the purposes of ISCED, excludes communication that is not designed to bring about learning. It also excludes various forms of learning that are not organized. Thus, while all education involves learning, many forms of learning are not regarded as education. For example, incidental or random learning which occurs as a by-product of another event, such as something that crystallizes during the course of a meeting, is excluded because it is not organized i.e. does not result from a planned intervention designed to bring about learning."

From Education to Learning and from Lifelong Education to Lifelong Learning

The shift of focus from *education* to *learning*, and from *lifelong education* to *lifelong learning*, has been on the table at least since the 1970s. However, and although *learning* has in fact become a much repeated word, with a multitude of labels, disregard for effective *learning* continues as well the long-entrenched confusion between *education* and *learning*. It is generally assumed that *learning* is always the result of some sort of *teaching*, and that teaching results automatically in learning.

The Fifth International Conference on Adult Education (CONFINTEA V), held in Hamburg in 1997, called for such transit, ending up with the *Hamburg Declaration on Adult Learning.* However, few understood and adopted such change of focus in the 12 years between CONFINTEA V andCONFINTEA VI.

Lifelong Learning and the Right to Education

Lifelong learning is activated today as the key organising principle for education and training systems, and for the building of the "knowledge society".

Lifelong learning acknowledges essentially two inter-related facts: (a) learning is life*long* (not confined to a particular period in life, "from the womb to the tomb"); and (b) learning is life*wide* (not confined to school but taking place everywhere: home, community, playground, workplace, sports yard, mass media, through play, conversation, debate, reading, writing, teaching, problem solving, social participation, social service, travel, use of ICTs, and so on).

On the other hand, one can relate the "emphasis on learning" to two different dimensions:

- ensuring that education (whether formal or non-formal) results in effective learning
- ensuring relevant learning opportunities beyond the school system

Thus, the right to education can no longer be understood as the right to access the school system (and eventually complete a certain number of years of schooling). The right to education implies essentially the right to learn and to learn throughout life. The state has an obligation to ensure equal learning opportunities for all, within and beyond the school system, at all ages.

Lifelong learning can be related to various concepts:

- Learning throughout life
- Learning to live
- Life is the curriculum
- Learning to learn
- Learning families
- Learning communities
- Learning societies.

Advances in neuroscience research are contributing to a better understanding of learning, and of learning throughout life, at various ages and stages. The belief that learning occurs and can occur at any age is confirmed by such research, thus providing scientific support to the claim that *school age*should not be confused with *learning age*. Now we know that the brain is mature between the mid-20s and the 30s, and that the mature brain can focus better and is capable of deeper and more complex learning. Also, the adult brain is capable of learning new tasks and being shaped by new experiences. Cognitive decline with age is avoidable if the brain is kept active, curious, in a permanent state of learning.

What Lifelong Learning is Not

Lifelong Learning is not only about *adults* – as many people and organisations continue to use it. Lifelong Learning is not equivalent to adult education or adult learning; it is *lifelong*, "from the womb to the tomb", thus embracing children, youth and adults across the life span. Curiously, some countries in Latin American and the Caribbean that have adopted the Lifelong Learning terminology include it as an additional category or section within Ministries of Education or other ministries, as if it were separate from the rest (Torres, 2009). UNESCO itself has contributed to such confusions. The former UNESCO Institute for Education (UIE), based in Hamburg, traditionally devoted to adult education and responsible for organising the International Conference on Adult Education (CONFINTEA), was renamed UNESCO Institute for Lifelong Learning (UIL). EFA goal 3 – "Ensuring that the learning needs of all young people and adults are met through equitable access to appropriate learning and life-skills programmes" – is the only one labelled "lifelong learning" in UNESCO's documents and website.

The LIfelong Learning paradigm has so had far little impact in countries in the South. Many countries, especially in Africa and Asia, are still struggling with access and the completion of children's primary education and high adult illiteracy rates. Most of them struggle with quality issues at all levels of the education system. Generally, *education* continues to be associated with *school education*, and learning with school assessment. The picture of learning within and outside the school system is still distant and considered a luxury for many governments, social organisations and international agencies engaged with education in the South. International platforms such as EFA and theMillennium Development Goals (MDGs) contribute in fact to the reinforcement of such trends.

There are also legitimate concerns *vis-à-vis* the Lifelong Learning paradigm as adopted and developed by countries in the North, mainly as a strategy for human resource development. Many fear thatLifelong Learning and its "focus on learning" may be a way to further neglect teaching and teachers, and to disengage governments from their commitment to ensure the right to education, by leaving learning in the hands of people, as their own individual responsibility. However, lifelong learning does not need to be reduced to an economic strategy; it does not imply abandoning teaching but rather strengthening it and acknowledging educators' own learning needs; it does not have to be associated with individual learning, but as the possibility to combine social and personal learning in different contexts and moments; and it does not have to conflict with the right to education. On the contrary, the right to education expands beyond access and becomes the right to learn.

It is true that Lifelong Learning is an agenda proposed and adopted by countries in the North, whose contexts and perspectives differ considerably from those in the South. Thus there is the need to define Lifelong Learning from the perspective of the South, and of the diversity of situations and cultures characterising each region and country.

Building Learning Societies

Adopting Lifelong Learning as a paradigm is not just about introducing minor adjustments to education structures, systems and policies. It implies a major revolution of traditional education and learning cultures:

- revisit the school-centred education culture that continues to view the school as the only education and learning system
- acknowledge and articulate the various learning systems, to ensure necessary coordination and synergy at both local and national level
- understand education/training, face-to-face/distance, formal/non-formal/informal as part of a continuum
- ensure effective learning within the school system, beyond tests measuring "school achievement"
- recognise previous knowledge and know-how as a key transectoral component of education and training policies
- rethink age as a central factor to organise education/training systems and opportunities
- abandon prejudices about age and learning, open up to new scientific evidence confirming that learning is an ageless endeavour
- accept literacy as a lifelong learning process rather than as a learning period
- go beyond the book as the single reading object that continues to define "reading habits", and accept the wide variety that today characterises the reading world
- incorporate the screen as a new reading and writing device for all ages
- promote and support peer- and inter-generational learning at home, in school, at the community, at work, everywhere.
- envisage education and learning beyond classrooms and closed spaces, while ensuring outdoors learning, contact with nature, people, real-life situations
- combine all means and media available to make learning happen, through multimedia strategies

- acknowledge the importance not only of "modern" technologies but also of "traditional" ones massively available and still poorly utilised (radio, TV, blackboard, tape recorders, and others)
- take advantage of distance education/learning opportunities, through all available means, better if combined with face-to-face contact
- diversify policies and strategies to accommodate the specific needs and desires of specific communities, groups and individuals
- think education and learning not only in terms of isolated individuals who contribute to statistics, but also in social terms (groups, communities, networks, organisations)
- build learning families, with the help of specific policies and strategies aimed at enhancing the cultural and educational capital of the family as a whole
- build learning communities, in urban and rural areas, so that all members – children, young people, adults – are engaged in learning activities, and all local resources are utilised, with community and local development in mind
- work towards a culture of collaboration that promotes collective access to, and use of, resources, rather than "each one have one" (each school a library, each student a computer, each person a cell phone, and so on).

The real challenge is building a learning society – families, communities and societies that learn – a goal far more complex, democratic and egalitarian than building an information society.

Fundamental Education and Adults

The term 'fundamental education' has largely gone out of use today, at least in international debate and discussion about education, but at the time when the Universal Declaration of Human Rights was drawn up, it was more in vogue. It was included in the Declaration specifically in order to recognise the right to education for illiterate adults and others who had not had the opportunity when they were young to receive a full elementary education.

The term first came into use internationally when it was adopted by the Preparatory Commission of UNESCO in 1946. This Commission, composed of representatives from the various countries involved in establishing UNESCO, was charged with drawing up a proposed plan of work for the Organisation to be submitted to UNESCO's first General Conference in November-December 1946. Among other things, the Commission's proposals included provision for work in the field of 'Fundamental Education', which was put forward as one of UNESCO's primary fields of interest.

Where half the people of the world are denied the elementary freedom which consists in the ability to read and write, there lacks something of the basic unity and basic justice which the United Nations are pledged together to further. Fundamental Education is only part of the wider and fuller human understanding to which UNESCO is dedicated, but it is an essential part. There was some uncertainty at that time over what exactly was meant by 'fundamental education', especially as this term did not correspond to any of the terms then in use in most countries to describe a particular level or part of their education systems, but there was general agreement that it meant an education that would provide for the acquisition of literacy and the other essential skills, knowledge and values needed for full participation in society. It was preferred to other cognate terms which were circulating then, such as 'Mass Education', 'Popular Education' and 'Basic Education'. 'Mass Education' for example, was specifically rejected because it 'evoked unpleasant connotations of educational methods which paid insufficient attention to individual differences'.

The content at least of 'fundamental education' was conceived not very differently from that of 'basic education' half a century later, the main differences being the emphasis of 'fundamental education' on the 'pressing needs and problems of the community', and that of 'basic education' on preparation for 'lifelong learning'. The latter notion was not current in the 1940s. 'Fundamental education' was regarded as a kind of 'minimum' or 'basic amount' of education that each community or society needed to provide for everyone; the question of access to, or preparation for education beyond this 'minimum' was mostly left to one side.

From an operational standpoint, in terms of 'means and methods' of implementation, 'fundamental education' was broadly interpreted as community education (adult literacy programmes, agricultural and health education, and so on). In some formulations of the community education approach, it was suggested that primary schooling could serve as 'one firm institutional basis for fundamental education', along with community centres. This later developed into the idea of 'community education centres' providing primary schooling as well as adult literacy and other non-formal adult education programmes. At that time, some experience of the community education approach had been accumulated in certain countries such as Brazil, India and Mexico, but there was little real understanding internationally of how to go about implementing this approach on a scale that could seriously respond to the 'fundamental education' needs of the vast rural population of Africa, Asia and Latin America which had never experienced any formal education. At the grassroots level, the approach presupposed a certain degree of community initiative and responsibility, as well as the capacity of communities to mobilise the necessary material and human resources for education, whether for formal education such as primary schools, or for non-formal education such as agricultural extension and health education. In much of Africa and Asia in the 1940s and 1950s, and also to a large extent in Latin America, significant advances in the provision of 'fundamental education' at the community level could hardly be made without the injection of substantial financial and/or material and human resources from outside the community, and this was not a major priority for most governments at that time.

Still, those who drew up the Universal Declaration of Human Rights were arguably less concerned with the precise form that 'fundamental education' should take than with the problem it was intended to address, namely, the millions of illiterate adults and others in the world who had not previously had an opportunity for modern education, whether formal or non-formal. How this problem could best be tackled was essentially a practical and not a theoretical matter: it would depend on the efforts undertaken—and the experience thus gained—by individual countries, whatever the label these efforts went under.

Adult Education and Literacy

The notion of 'fundamental education' remained current internationally for only a decade or so, while its concern with literacy was absorbed into an expanded concept of 'adult education'.

At first, 'fundamental education' and 'adult education' were regarded as two different aspects of 'popular education'. In the majority of countries then Member States of UNESCO, 'adult education' was an older and more well-established concept than 'fundamental education', but it was mainly concerned with the learning needs of adults who had already received an elementary education and wanted 'further' or 'continuing' education. Thus, at the first International Conference on Adult Education it was agreed that illiteracy should be treated 'as part of the fundamental education field, closely related to but distinguishable from adult education'.

However, this narrow interpretation of 'adult education' could hardly be sustained in those parts of the world where a majority of adults were illiterate. Thus, in the following years, the international focus of adult education gradually widened to include literacy and the learning needs of adults who had not previously received any formal education. As a result, little room was left for a separate concept of 'fundamental education'.

In 1960 the Second International Conference on Adult Education, held in Montreal, Canada, proposed that regional seminars be organised for countries in Latin America, Asia and Africa 'having common problems in regard to Adult Education in general, and illiteracy in particular'. In 1972 the Third International Conference on Adult Education, which was convened in Tokyo, Japan, went even further, declaring flatly that 'Literacy is a cornerstone of adult education'.

More than any other factor, the advent of a large number of countries to independence in the late 1950s and early 1960s was probably decisive in shifting international concern away from the notion of 'fundamental education', in its broad 'community education' sense, to what was coming to be considered as the key problem that 'fundamental education' needed to address: the eradication of illiteracy. Since literacy is quintessentially something that is gained by the learner, this shift was the earliest sign of that larger shift of emphasis from 'education' to 'learning' which eventually culminated, many years later, in international consensus on the priority of 'meeting basic learning needs'.

Eradication of Illiteracy

Pressures for international action to help eradicate illiteracy built up soon after the Universal Declaration of Human Rights was proclaimed. The United Nations was particularly concerned over the situation in colonial territories. In 1950, the General Assembly called upon UNESCO 'to communicate. Full information on measures for suppressing illiteracy which could be applied with satisfactory results in Non-Self-Governing Territories, and to communicate annually to the United Nations an account of these measures'.

In the course of the 1950s, illiteracy acquired preeminent status among indicators of the denial of the right to education. By the early 1960s, its eradication had become a national priority in probably a majority of the newly independent and other developing countries. The challenge was to translate this priority into effective action.

Functional Literacy

At that time, international understanding of the various factors that needed to be taken into account in devising effective approaches to the promotion of literacy was still limited. Certain countries had carried out large-scale literacy campaigns before the Second World War, and there had been community education campaigns in a number of colonial territories after the war, but aside from these, a comprehensive body of international experience that could be drawn upon simply did not exist.

A critical uncertainty was whether the ease of acquiring literacy varied from one language to another. In order to throw some light on this question, UNESCO's 'fundamental education' programme had included, among other activities, an international study of the teaching of reading and writing, the conclusions of which greatly influenced subsequent international action for the promotion of literacy. Two conclusions in particular were especially influential: (1) that 'the basic attitudes and skills involved in reading are the same in all languages', and (2) that the only meaningful standard of literacy is a functional one.

The first of these conclusions helped to pave the way for increased international co-operation in promoting literacy, although the study's concentration on reading and writing in the mother tongue left a significant gap that was not fully appreciated at the time: literacy in a second language. This has since come to be recognised as a key problem in much of Africa and in many parts of Latin America and Asia, where, in the absence of sufficient learning materials in the mother tongue, literacy in a second language is often the only literacy that learners can realistically aspire to.

The second conclusion eventually led to the adoption, in the following decade, of a 'functional literacy' approach in the design of literacy programmes and projects. It also called into question the continued usefulness of the then-international standard definition of a 'literate' person as someone 'who can with understanding both read and write a short simple statement on his everyday life'.

World Illiteracy

Other work by UNESCO in the 1950s, notably in the area of statistics, also significantly influenced subsequent national and international efforts to eradicate illiteracy. The earliest statistical estimates of the worldwide extent of illiteracy were published by UNESCO in 1957. These estimates were based on an extensive review of national censuses and other surveys going back in some cases to the beginning of the century. An important finding of the comparative analysis of national censuses was the great variety of questions utilised in the questionnaires to identify persons who were either 'literate' or 'illiterate'. In some countries, for example Italy, the question was simply whether the person could read, whereas in others it was whether the person could both read and write. Some countries specified a level or standard of reading and/or writing, for example India, and Turkey. Canada carefully formulated its census instructions so as to allow for the special situation of blind persons. There still are differences between countries today in the questions utilised by national censuses to identify literacy/ illiteracy, but a comprehensive analysis of current international practices is lacking.

This early work by UNESCO on world literacy data contributed greatly to international appreciation of the sheer scale of the challenge to eradicate illiteracy. Taking 'ability to read and write' as the criterion of literacy, and after making as much allowance as possible for differences between countries in their census definitions, it emerged that in around half the countries in the world in 1950, half or more of the adult population were estimated to be illiterate.

The great majority of such countries were located in Africa and Asia. In Africa, only in Lesotho and Mauritius were more than half the adults estimated to be literate. In Asia, among the larger countries or territories, only in Hong Kong, Israel, Japan, Myanmar, Philippines, Sri Lanka and Thailand were more than half the adults estimated to be literate. In Latin America the situation was somewhat better with more than half the adult population estimated to be literate in Argentina, Chile, Colombia, Cuba, Ecuador, Mexico, Paraguay, Puerto Rico, Uruguay and Venezuela.

An important finding of the historical analysis was that the world's illiterate population appeared to be steadily increasing even as the illiteracy rate was decreasing, which broadly indicated that the expansion of educational opportunities was not keeping up with population growth. This phenomenon had been suspected at the time, but had not up to then been clearly demonstrated statistically at the global level, although it was known to be the case in certain countries. In Brazil, for example, the 1950 census showed an illiterate population of 15. 3 million persons aged 15 years old and over, amounting to 51 per cent of the total population in that age-group, whereas in the previous census the corresponding figures were 13. 3 million and 56 per cent. Other countries with good historical census data where the same phenomenon could be observed included Egypt, India, Mexico, Portugal, Sri Lanka, Turkey and Venezuela. Looking forward, it would not be until the late 1980s that the world's illiterate population would eventually peak. Thus, for forty years after the Universal Declaration of Human Rights was proclaimed, the absolute number of persons in the world with no meaningful experience of the right to education was actually to increase.

Alternative Strategies

Two general conclusions for educational policy were drawn from the findings above. The first was the need to step up national efforts to reach out to the increasing number of illiterate adults, and the second was the need to accelerate access to elementary education for the younger generation so as to 'cut off the problem at its base', as was stated at the time.

Many countries expanded their literacy activities in the 1960s. Internationally, two competing views emerged concerning the appropriate strategy. One view, based largely on the prewar experience of the former USSR, stressed the 'national campaign' approach. However, national political, economic, social and cultural circumstances varied so much that this type of approach could not easily be replicated. In any case, critics charged that this approach too often resulted in people just acquiring a superficial level of literacy that could contribute little to the society's overall development. Putting 'the struggle against illiteracy' on a 'war footing', they argued, could not dispense with the need for a sound methodology based on a thorough understanding of what would induce illiterate persons to make the effort to learn to read and write.

Thus, there emerged by the mid-1960s the idea of the 'selective approach' closely linked to the notion of 'functional literacy'. People are not 'made' literate, proponents of this approach contended, but make themselves literate when they have the motivation and incentives to do so. In other words, they learn when literacy meets their 'learning needs', although this term was not widely used at the time. Next, it was argued that in place of the 'national campaign', efforts to promote literacy should be focused intensively on organised sections of society where motivation for literacy is strongest and where opportunities exist for using education to raise the level of living and accelerate development. This was taken to mean that literacy programmes needed to be closely integrated with socioeconomic development programmes, while literacy instruction needed to be combined with the provision of relevant information and vocational training tailored to the learner's specific socioeconomic situation within the broader development context. The term 'work-oriented adult literacy training' was used at the time to describe this approach.

These ideas came to the fore internationally at the World Congress of Ministers of Education on the Eradication of Illiteracy held in Teheran in September 1965, and they provided the basic rationale for what was to become the largest ever internationally-sponsored programme specifically focused on eradicating adult illiteracy: the Experimental World Literacy Programme (EWLP) launched in 1966 by UNESCO and the United Nations Development Programme (UNDP).

Experimental World Literacy Programme (EWLP)

This programme was to be a watershed in international co-operation for the eradication of illiteracy. EWLP was 'experimental' in the sense that it embraced a number of national pilot projects aiming to try out the 'selective approach' focused on 'functional' literacy, and in particular to test and demonstrate literacy's economic and social 'returns'.

The hopes and expectations originally associated with EWLP were high. The 1960s marked the United Nations' first 'Development Decade', and EWLP was widely regarded at the time as a breakthrough in international recognition of the role of education in development. Among other things, EWLP was expected to provide valuable information on the relationship of literacy to social and economic development, produce a considerable impact on economic development in the countries where projects were to be conducted and prepare the way for an eventual World Campaign for the Eradication of Mass Illiteracy. Altogether, eleven countries participated directly in EWLP before the programme was phased out in the mid-1970s: Algeria, Ecuador, Ethiopia, Guinea, India, Iran, Madagascar, Mali, Sudan, the Syrian Arab Republic and the United Republic of Tanzania. A number of other countries adopted similar approaches to those of EWLP.

By virtue of its sheer size and complexity, as much as by the ideas associated with it, EWLP attracted worldwide interest. At the time of the programme's full operation, around 1971, a total of nearly a quarter of a million adults were enrolled in the various national EWLP projects, and a vast amount of original instructional materials were developed. In contributing directly to expanding the capabilities of large numbers of relatively poor people, EWLP was highly successful. However, the ambitious hopes of achieving a methodological 'breakthrough' that could justify the launching of a World Campaign were never realised. The differences between the various projects in organisation, target population, pedagogical objectives and methods were more pronounced that the similarities, and a well-defined model 'work-oriented' adult literacy methodology that could be applied on a global scale never emerged.

Promoted mainly as a technical solution to problems of 'socioeconomic development' rather than simply as a transfer of resources to help implement a human right, EWLP was fated to disappoint almost as soon as it started. From the outset, due to the very nature of literacy work—compared, say, to the construction of a new road or power station—it was never really possible for EWLP to demonstrate the social and economic 'returns' that would satisfy orthodox investment criteria. Thus, the whole idea of a World Campaign to eradicate illiteracy fizzled out and has never since been revived.

The international discussion and debate over the purposes and means of promoting literacy that flourished in the aftermath of EWLP maintained a broad consensus in favour of the concept of 'functional literacy', but this concept became increasingly accepted as relevant to a wider range of activities than just work and employment. Moreover, notwithstanding the international interest surrounding EWLP, many countries continued to mount mass campaigns for the eradication of illiteracy throughout the 1970s, e. g Algeria, Brazil, Burma (now Myanmar), Cameroon, China, Colombia, Ethiopia, Guatemala, Guinea, Indonesia, Jamaica, Mexico, Peru, Somalia, Thailand, United Republic of Tanzania and Zambia, among others. The success of many of these campaigns and the diversity of approaches followed, further challenged the idea of a single 'model' approach as originally envisaged by EWLP.

It was at this time, in the aftermath of EWLP, that the Brazilian educator Paulo Freire's ideas concerning literacy became influential internationally. For Freire, the process of acquiring literacy, i. e. Learning to read and write, was necessarily accompanied by the learner's increasing consciousness of his/her existential situation and of the possibility of acting independently to change it, a process which he termed 'concentration', and which today would more likely be called 'empowerment'. In that perspective, literacy programmes necessarily had a 'political', and not merely technical-pedagogic, dimension.

Freire's ideas were influential in opening the way to an appreciation of the many uses of literacy beyond those relating to work and employment which had been given so much emphasis in EWLP: uses ranging from the exercise of civil and political rights to the upbringing of children, from reading for pleasure and enjoyment to reading for self-instruction or spiritual enlightenment. Learning to read and write, many advocates urged, was a crucial step in the process of learning to learn.

Thus, the notion of 'functional literacy' was gradually pointed towards a more inclusive concept, that of 'learning needs', under which literacy could be accommodated both on its own account and as a necessary condition for satisfying many other 'learning needs'. By the mid-1980s, the idea of illiterate adults and others who lacked formal education having a 'right to learn' had entered international discussion and debate. The Fourth International Conference on Adult Education, for example, felt moved to declare that 'recognition of the right to learn is now more than ever a major challenge for humanity'.

At this time, elementary education, whether formal or non-formal, was increasingly coming to be regarded as a process that should be designed to meet 'basic learning needs'. From this point, it was only a short step towards the demands of the World Conference on Education for All that society should aim to satisfy the 'basic learning needs' of everyone, whether children, youth or adults.

Secular Trends

Trends in world literacy have reinforced the shift above towards the more inclusive concept of 'learning needs'. Throughout the 1970s and 1980s the earliest decades for which UNESCO has continuous time series estimates—illiteracy rates in the world's less developed regions steadily declined. This trend continued into the 1990s. In a growing number of countries, illiteracy as such, at least by the traditional measure of being unable to read and write a short simple statement about one's everyday life, was no longer the characteristic educational condition of the majority of the adult population. Thus, whereas half the countries in the world had estimated adult illiteracy rates of over 50 per cent in 1950, only twenty-three countries are estimated to have such high rates today. A majority of countries in the world today have estimated illiteracy rates of below 10 per cent; in these countries and many others with low illiteracy rates, implementation of the right to education for adults represents a more complex challenge than was the case fifty years ago.

Nevertheless, illiteracy is still the characteristic educational condition of large numbers of adults in the world's less developed regions, and the numbers are estimated to be increasing in most of these regions, although at progressively slower rates. In Eastern Asia/Ocean, a longstanding national literacy campaign in China appears to have been decisive in bringing the number down. In the other regions, the expansion of elementary education, which has mainly been responsible for bringing down the overall rates of illiteracy, has not so far managed to stem the flow of 'new recruits' to the existing population of illiterate adults.

Moreover, despite the progress made over the past few decades in reducing world literacy inequalities, whether these refer to differences in literacy rates between males and females or between the major regions of the world, the majority of illiterate adults in the less developed regions of the world still are females and there still are regions where the majority of adult females themselves are estimated to be illiterate. In every region with the exception of Latin America and the Caribbean, females account for a growing percentage of all illiterate adults. The percentage will continue to grow if girls are not given equal access to primary schooling.

Besides its growing concentration among women, world illiteracy is also increasingly concentrated geographically in Southern Asia and the least developed countries in sub-Saharan Africa. Of the twenty-three countries with estimated adult illiteracy rates higher than 50 per cent today, fifteen are located in sub-Saharan Africa and five in Southern Asia. The three large Southern Asia countries, Bangladesh, India and Pakistan, are together estimated to account for nearly half (45 per cent) of the world's illiterate adults today, compared to around one-third in 1970. Yet, notwithstanding that there is still a vast number of illiterate adults in the world, growing numbers of the world's adults have received some formal education and have acquired some simple literacy skills. Even in those countries with the largest numbers of illiterate adults, listed in the worlds a whole, over the same period, the increase in the number of literate adults is estimated at 1,926 million, compared to an estimated increase of 17 million in the number of illiterate adults.

Undoubtedly many of the 'literate' adults to which these statistics refer have acquired only rudimentary literacy skills. Most will have received only primary education, often of dubious quality, and some will have dropped out of school before completing their primary school studies. Thus it is uncertain what percentage of the world's adults can be classified as functionally literate in their respective societies. Recent surveys carried out in some of the Organisation for Economic Cooperation and Development (OECD) countries suggest that up to 20 per cent of adults in these countries can be regarded as functionally illiterate. In the less developed regions of the world, the figure is unlikely to be lower.

In a global perspective, therefore, implementation of the right to education for adults has become less a question of literacy in the traditional sense—although this indicator is still useful for the purposes of identifying the most flagrant instances of denial of the right to education—than a question of access to relevant 'learning opportunities', i. e. Opportunities for the world's adults to satisfy their 'basic learning needs'.

In so far as such 'learning opportunities' are embraced by the original notion of 'fundamental education', they arguably should be provided 'free' to all adults who wish to profit from them. This question, though, is bound up with the larger question, considered below, of whether 'basic education' generally should be provided free.

Expanding Vision of Educational Opportunity

While coming to represent an expanded vision of 'elementary and fundamental education', the concept of 'basic education' has at the same time come to form part of a larger vision that extends beyond that of 'meeting basic learning needs'. The Declaration adopted by the World Conference on Education for All proclaims that 'Basic education is the foundation for lifelong learning'. Thus, in place of the view which prevailed in most countries in the years before the Universal Declaration of Human Rights was adopted, that elementary education is something complete in itself provided to the great majority of children who will go to work at an early age, while a minority are prepared for secondary and eventually higher studies, there has emerged the view that elementary education is just the first phase of a continuous process that can and ought to extend through everyone's lifetime.

The adoption of 'lifelong education' and 'lifelong learning' as guiding principles of educational policy, both in countries that are currently able to provide extensive education and learning opportunities, and in those that are still struggling to eradicate illiteracy and get all children into primary school, represents a commitment to the democratisation of education that is limited only by the resources available for its implementation. Enrolment at the secondary and tertiary levels of education taken together account for nearly half of the total enrolment in the world's formal education systems today, compared to barely one-fifth at the time when the Universal Declaration of Human Rights was proclaimed.

Although the ideas of 'lifelong education' and 'lifelong learning' have old philosophical roots and can be traced back historically to the earliest efforts to promote universal education, it is unlikely that they would have achieved their current status in educational policies if recent trends and developments in the wider political, economic, social and cultural context had not also been favourable. Both 'lifelong education' and 'lifelong learning' have come to represent in different ways the expectations that societies now have of education and of the scope that should be provided for every individual to develop his or her potential.

Lifelong Education

International interest in the concept of 'lifelong education' was first aroused in the 1960s by discussion and debate within UNESCO concerning the future development of adult education. International cooperation in adult education at that time was complicated by the fact that the challenges facing adult education varied so greatly among countries: in many of the newly independent countries the majority of adults were illiterate, which was not within the recent experience of countries where adult education programmes had long been established.

Moreover, among the latter there were many different approaches to adult education, ranging from the Folk High Schools of the Scandinavian countries to 'workers' education' in the former USSR, 'further education' in the United Kingdom, 'continuing education' in the United States and Canada, and *education popular* in France. Other than the adult target group itself, there did not exist at that time a unifying principle or concept of adult education that could provide adult educators working in different national circumstances and traditions with a common ideal or purpose, nor one that could settle the question of adult education's status vis-a-vis the regular mainstream education system, to which in most countries adult education was usually regarded as an appendage and very much as a 'poor relation'.

Prompted in part by the Second World Conference on Adult Education, which recommended, among other things, that governments should 'regard adult education not as an addition, but as an integral part of their national systems of education', UNESCO's General Conference at its 12th Session two years later took up the matter and went one step further, inviting Member States 'to regard the various forms of out of-school and adult education as an integral part of any educational system, so that *all men and women, throughout their lives*, may have the opportunities for pursuing education conducive alike to their individual advancement and to their active participation in civic life and in the social and economic development of their country'.

At the international level, this invitation was the genesis of the idea of 'lifelong education', for it was soon realised, as one of the leading protagonists recalled later, that the design of any coherent overall strategy for the development of out-of-school and adult education would need to consider education as a whole, as well as the succession and interrelation of its various stages over the life-cycle.

The discussion and debate that ensued both within UNESCO and in the wider intellectual community was eventually absorbed later in the decade into a broader international discussion and debate over the future of education generally, culminating in the setting up in 1971 of the International Commission on the Development of Education. The Commission's report brought the idea of 'lifelong education' to the attention of a wide international audience.

The Commission put forward a vision of what it called 'the Learning Society', and recommended as the 'Guiding principle for educational policies' that 'Every individual must be in a position to keep learning throughout his [or her] life'. It added: 'The idea of lifelong education is the keystone of the learning society'. In the Commission's vision: The lifelong concept covers all aspects of education, embracing everything in it, with the whole being more than the sum of its parts. There is no such thing as a separate 'permanent' part of education which is not lifelong. In other words, lifelong education is not an educational system but the principle on which the overall organisation of a system is founded, and which should accordingly underlie the development of each of its component parts.

For the Commission, therefore, 'learning throughout... Life' and 'lifelong education' were complementary concepts, the latter being essentially a precondition for the realisation of the former. However, the Commission did not specifically attempt to situate its vision in the context of the Universal Declaration of Human Rights, apart from taking note of the fact that the application of the right to education 'continues to be hampered in many places by conditions similar to those prevailing at the time it was first expressed'.

Lifelong Learning

Meeting shortly after the Faure Commission's report was published, the Third World Conference on Adult Education specifically evoked the Universal Declaration of Human Rights in declaring its belief that 'the right of individuals to education, their right to learn and to go on learning, is to be considered on the same basis as their other fundamental rights, such as the right to health and to hygiene, the right to security, the right to all forms of civil liberty, etc. '

This was the first time that the idea of a 'right to learn and to go on learning' was expressed by an international conference, although it was formulated as synonymous with 'the right of individuals to education', not as an additional, separate right. In fact, in the years immediately following the publication of the Faure Commission's report, 'lifelong education' and 'lifelong learning' were usually considered together as a single overall concept, as for example in the Recommendation on the Development of Adult Education adopted by the General Conference of UNESCO in 1976.

By the end of the 1980s, the idea of a 'right to learn' distinct from that of the 'right to education' had gained ground, with the Fourth International Conference on Adult Education, for example, adopting a Declaration on the 'right to learn' that did not actually mention the 'right to education' at all. However, the balance was restored at the Fifth International Conference on Adult Education, with the Conference declaring that 'The recognition of *the right to education and the right to learn* throughout life is more than ever a necessity'.

Since the early 1990s, the trend in educational policies towards a learning-centred view of education generally, and of adult education in particular, has been especially marked in some OECD countries. As far back as the early 1970s, policy-makers in these countries had shared the doubts of the Faure Commission concerning the viability of continued 'linear expansion' of the formal system of full-time education, and in addition were skeptical towards the possibility of further expansion being fully financed by governments. By the end of the 1990s, the idea of public financing of educational opportunities beyond the period of compulsory education had given way in these countries to the idea of shared responsibility or 'partnership' between government, employers and learners themselves.

In France, to take one example, the financing of participants in 'recurrent' or continuing education programmes provided in higher education establishments under the control of the Ministry of National Education in 1996 was accounted for to the extent of 40 per cent from public funds, 40 per cent by employers and 20 per cent by the participants themselves. With different percentages according to national circumstances, this tripartite distribution of responsibility for the financing of 'lifelong education' has increasingly become the norm in the industrial countries.

In these countries, therefore, the 'right to lifelong learning' has run into the quite basic question of 'Who should pay?' In regard to regular mainstream secondary and higher education at least, this is answered by Article 13, paragraph 2 of the International Covenant on Economic, Social and Cultural Rights, which requires 'the progressive introduction of free education'. The 'introduction of free education' in respect to secondary education is also mentioned in Article 28 paragraph 1(b) of the Convention on the Rights of the Child. However, in regard to continuing education for adults at the secondary and tertiary levels, the position with respect to the international treaties is not as straightforward. This kind of education was not anticipated in the Universal Declaration of Human Rights or in any of the international treaties, and States apparently do not feel under an obligation to ensure that such education shall be provided 'free'. In so far as the 'right to lifelong learning' is understood to include a 'right' to continuing education, it would seem in practice to amount to little more than the 'right' of any citizen to participate, at his or her own expense, in the market for goods and services generally, with more or less encouragement from public funds depending on the situation in individual countries.

The Hamburg Declaration on Adult Learning

The Hamburg Declaration on Adult Learning was adopted by the Fifth International Conference on Adult Education held in Hamburg, 14-18 July 1997.

The fulltext of the Declaration is given below:

1. We, the participants in the Fifth International Conference on Adult Education, meeting in the Free and Hanseatic City of Hamburg, reaffirm that only human-centred development and a participatory society based on the full respect of human rights will lead to sustainable and equitable development. The informed and effective participation of men and women in every sphere of life is needed if humanity is to survive and to meet the challenges of the future.

2. Adult education thus becomes more than a right; it is a key to the twenty-first century. It is both a consequence of active citizenship and a condition for full participation in society. It is a powerful concept for fostering ecologically sustainable development, for promoting democracy, justice, gender equity, and scientific, social and economic development, and for building a world in which violent conflict is replaced by dialogue and a culture of peace based on justice. Adult learning can shape identity and give meaning to life. Learning throughout life implies a rethinking of content to reflect such factors as age, gender equality, disability, language, culture and economic disparities.

3. Adult education denotes the entire body of ongoing learning processes, formal or otherwise, whereby people regarded as adults by the society to which they belong develop their abilities, enrich their knowledge, and improve their technical or professional qualifications or turn them in a new direction to meet their own needs and those of their society. Adult learning encompasses both formal and continuing education, non-formal learning and the spectrum of informal and incidental learning available in a multicultural learning society, where theory- and practice-based approaches are recognized.

4. Though the content of adult learning and of education for children and adolescents will vary according to the economic, social, environmental and cultural context, and the needs of the people in the societies in which they take place, both are necessary elements of a new vision of education in which learning becomes truly lifelong. The perspective of learning

throughout life commands such complementarity and continuity. The potential contribution of adult and continuing education to the creation of an informed and tolerant citizenry, economic and social development, the promotion of literacy, the alleviation of poverty and the preservation of the environment is enormous and should, therefore, be built upon.

5. The objectives of youth and adult education, viewed as a lifelong process, are to develop the autonomy and the sense of responsibility of people and communities, to reinforce the capacity to deal with the transformations taking place in the economy, in culture and in society as a whole, and to promote coexistence, tolerance and the informed and creative participation of citizens in their communities, in short to enable people and communities to take control of their destiny and society in order to face the challenges ahead. It is essential that approaches to adult learning be based on people's own heritage, culture, values and prior experiences and that the diverse ways in which these approaches are implemented enable and encourage every citizen to be actively involved and to have a voice.

6. This Conference recognizes the diversity of political, economic and social systems and governmental structures among Member States. In accordance with that diversity and to ensure full respect for human rights and fundamental freedoms, this Conference acknowledges that the particular circumstances of Member States will determine the measures governments may introduce to further the spirit of our objectives.

7. The representatives of governments and organizations participating in the Fifth International Conference on Adult Education have decided to explore together the potential and the future of adult learning, broadly and dynamically conceived within a framework of lifelong learning.

8. During the present decade, adult learning has undergone substantial changes and experienced enormous growth in scope and scale. In the knowledge-based societies that are emerging around the world, adult and continuing education have become an imperative in the community and at the workplace. New demands from society and working life raise expectations requiring each and every individual to continue renewing knowledge and skills throughout the whole of his or her life. At the heart of this transformation is a new role for the state and the emergence of expanded partnerships devoted to adult learning within civil society. The state remains the essential vehicle for ensuring the right to education for all, particularly for the most vulnerable groups of society, such as minorities

and indigenous peoples, and for providing an overall policy framework. Within the new partnership emerging between the public, the private and the community sectors, the role of the state is shifting. It is not only a provider of adult education services but also an adviser, a funder, and a monitoring and evaluation agency. Governments and social partners must take the necessary measures to support individuals in expressing their educational needs and aspirations, and in gaining access to educational opportunities throughout their lives. Within governments, adult education is not confined to ministries of education; all ministries are engaged in promoting adult learning, and interministerial co-operation is essential. Moreover, employers, unions, non-governmental and community organizations, and indigenous people's and women's groups are involved and have a responsibility to interact and create opportunities for lifelong learning, with provision for recognition and accreditation.

9. Basic education for all means that people, whatever their age, have an opportunity, individually and collectively, to realize their potential. It is not only a right, it is also a duty and a responsibility both to others and to society as a whole. It is essential that the recognition of the right to education throughout life should be accompanied by measures to create the conditions required to exercise this right. The challenges of the twenty-first century cannot be met by governments, organizations or institutions alone; the energy, imagination and genius of people and their full, free and vigorous participation in every aspect of life are also needed. Youth and adult learning is one of the principal means of significantly increasing creativity and productivity, in the widest sense of those terms, and these in turn are indispensable to meeting the complex and interrelated problems of a world beset by accelerating change and growing complexity and risk.

10. The new concept of youth and adult education presents a challenge to existing practices because it calls for effective networking within the formal and non-formal systems, and for innovation and more creativity and flexibility. Such challenges should be met by new approaches to adult education within the concept of learning throughout life. Promoting learning, using mass media and local publicity, and offering impartial guidance are responsibilities for governments, social partners and providers. The ultimate goal should be the creation of a learning society committed to social justice and general well-being.

11. *Adult literacy*. Literacy, broadly conceived as the basic knowledge and skills needed by all in a rapidly changing world, is a fundamental human right. In every society literacy is a necessary skill in itself and one of the foundations of other life skills. There are millions, the majority of whom are women, who lack opportunities to learn or who have insufficient skills to be able to assert this right. The challenge is to enable them to do so. This will often imply the creation of preconditions for learning through awareness-raising and empowerment. Literacy is also a catalyst for participation in social, cultural, political and economic activities, and for learning throughout life. We therefore commit ourselves to ensuring opportunities for all to acquire and maintain literacy skills, and to create in all Member States a literate environment to support oral culture. The provision of learning opportunities for all, including the unreached and the excluded, is the most urgent concern. The Conference welcomes the initiative for a literacy decade in honour of Paulo Freire, to begin in 1998.

12. *Recognition of the right to education and the right to learn* throughout life is more than ever a necessity; it is the right to read and write, the right to question and analyse, the right to have access to resources, and to develop and practise individual and collective skills and competences.

13. *Women's integration and empowerment*. Women have a right to equal opportunities; society, in turn, depends on their full contribution in all fields of work and aspects of life. Youth and adult learning policies should be responsive to local cultures and give priority to expanding educational opportunities for all women, while respecting their diversity and eliminating prejudices and stereotypes that both limit their access to youth and adult education and restrict the benefits they derive from them. Any attempts to restrict women's right to literacy, education and training must be considered unacceptable. Practices and measures should be taken to counter them.

14. *Culture of peace and education for citizenship and democracy*. One of the foremost challenges of our age is to eliminate the culture of violence and to construct a culture of peace based on justice and tolerance within which dialogue, mutual recognition and negotiation will replace violence, in homes and communities, within nations and between countries.

15. *Diversity and equality*. Adult learning should reflect the richness of cultural diversity and respect traditional and indigenous peoples' knowledge and systems of learning; the right to learn in the mother tongue should be respected and implemented. Adult education faces an acute

challenge in preserving and documenting the oral wisdom of minority groups, indigenous peoples and nomadic peoples. In turn, intercultural education should encourage learning between and about different cultures in support of peace, human rights and fundamental freedoms, democracy, justice, liberty, coexistence and diversity.

16. *Health.* Health is a basic human right. Investments in education are investments in health. Lifelong learning can contribute substantially to the promotion of health and the prevention of disease. Adult education offers significant opportunities to provide relevant, equitable and sustainable access to health knowledge.

17. *Environmental sustainability.* Education for environmental sustainability should be a lifelong learning process which recognizes that ecological problems exist within a socio-economic, political and cultural context. A sustainable future cannot be achieved without addressing the relationship between environmental problems and current development paradigms. Adult environmental education can play an important role in sensitizing and mobilizing communities and decision-makers towards sustained environmental action.

18. *Indigenous education and culture.* Indigenous peoples and nomadic peoples have the right of access to all levels and forms of education provided by the state. However, they are not to be denied the right to enjoy their own culture, or to use their own languages. Education for indigenous peoples and nomadic peoples should be linguistically and culturally appropriate to their needs and should facilitate access to further education and training.

19. *Transformation of the economy.* Globalization, changes in production patterns, rising unemployment and the difficulty of ensuring secure livelihoods call for more active labour policies and increased investment in developing the necessary skills to enable men and women to participate in the labour market and income-generating activities.

20. *Access to information.* The development of the new information and communication technologies brings with it new risks of social and occupational exclusion for groups of individuals and even businesses which are unable to adapt to this context. One of the roles of adult education in the future should therefore be to limit these risks of exclusion so that the information society does not lose sight of the human dimension.

21. *The ageing population.* There are now more older people in the world in relation to the total population than ever before, and the proportion is still rising. These older adults have much to contribute to the development of society. Therefore, it is important that they have the opportunity to learn on equal terms and in appropriate ways. Their skills and abilities should be recognized, valued and made use of.

22. In line with the Salamanca Statement, integration and access for people with disabilities should be promoted. Disabled persons have the right to equitable learning opportunities which recognize and respond to their educational needs and goals, and in which appropriate learning technology matches their special learning needs.

23. We must act with the utmost urgency to increase and guarantee national and international investment in youth and adult learning, and the commitment of private and community resources to them. The Agenda for the Future which we have adopted here is designed to achieve this end.

24. We call upon UNESCO as the United Nations lead agency in the field of education to play the leading role in promoting adult education as an integral part of a system of learning and to mobilize the support of all partners, particularly those within the United Nations system, in order to give priority to implementing the Agenda for the Future and to facilitating provision of the services needed for reinforcing international co-ordination and co-operation.

25. We urge UNESCO to encourage Member States to adopt policies and legislation that are favourable to and accommodate people with disabilities in educational programmes, as well as being sensitive to cultural, linguistic, gender and economic diversity.

26. We solemnly declare that all parties will closely follow up the implementation of this Declaration and the Agenda for the Future, clearly distinguishing their respective responsibilities and complementing and co-operating with one another. We are determined to ensure that lifelong learning will become a more significant reality in the early twenty-first century. To that end, we commit ourselves to promoting the culture of learning through the "one hour a day for learning" movement and the development of a United Nations Week of Adult Learning.

27. We, gathered together in Hamburg, convinced of the necessity of adult learning, pledge that all men and women shall be provided with the

opportunity to learn throughout their lives. To that end, we will forge extended alliances to mobilize and share resources in order to make adult learning a joy, a tool, a right and a shared responsibility.

References

Aspin, David N. & Chapman, Judith D. (2007) "Lifelong Learning Concepts and Conceptions" in: David N. Aspin, ed.: *Philosophical Perspectives on Lifelong Learning*, Springer. ISBN 1-4020-6192-7

Blaschke, Lisa Marie. "Heutagogy and Lifelong Learning: A Review of Heutagogical Practice and Self-Determined Learning". *The International Review of Research in Open and Distance Learning.* Athabasca University. Retrieved 24 November 2012.

Commission of the European Communities: "Adult learning: It is never too late to learn". COM(2006) 614 final. Brussels, 23.10.2006.

Department of Education and Science (2000). Learning for Life: White Paper on Adult Education. Dublin: Stationery Office.http://eric.ed.gov/PDFS/ED471201.pdf]

Fischer, Gerhard (2000). "Lifelong Learning - More than Training" in *Journal of Interactive Learning Research,* Volume 11 issue 3/4 pp 265-294.

Whyte, Cassandra B/ (2002). "Great Expectations for Higher Education". Speech at Higher Education Round Table Event. Oxford, England.

5

Human Rights-based Approach to Education For All

The goal of a human rights-based approach to education is simple: to assure every child a quality education that respects and promotes her or his right to dignity and optimum development. Achieving this goal is, however, enormously more complex.

The right to education is high on the agenda of the international community. It is affirmed in numerous human rights treaties and recognized by governments as pivotal in the pursuit of development and social transformation. This recognition is exemplified in the international goals, strategies and targets that have been set during the past 20 years. The Education for All goals were established at Jomtien (Thailand) in 1990 and reaffirmed at the 2000 World Education Forum in Dakar (Senegal). In the Millennium Development Goals, established in 2000, the world's governments committed to achieving universal access to free, quality and compulsory primary education by 2015. In 'A World Fit for Children', the outcome document from the United Nations General Assembly Special Session on Children in 2002, governments reaffirmed these commitments and agreed to a range of strategies and actions to achieve them. More ambitious targets have been established in many regions. Countries in Latin America and the Caribbean, for example, are increasingly making school attendance compulsory for children of pre-primary age. These various strategies have had an effect: In 1948, when education was recognized as a human right, only a minority of the world's children had access to any formal education; now a majority of them go to school, and participation in formal education beyond the elementary stages has increased.

However, the progress made to date is far from adequate. UNESCO statistics on enrolment indicate that 77 million children in 2004 were still not enrolled in school. According to UNICEF sources this figure may be as high as 90 million children for 2005–2006 in terms of school attendance figures from household surveys. In many regions, girls lag far behind. In other regions, there is a growing problem of underachievement by boys. Poverty is a key factor impeding enrolment, primary and secondary completion, and learning outcomes, and children from ethnic minority and indigenous communities consistently underachieve. The evidence indicates that, on current trajectories, the international targets for access will not be met. The challenges to the achievement of quality in education are even greater. Most international attention has been focused on helping children get into school. What happens once they are there, and the nature of the education they receive, has been afforded far less emphasis. As a consequence, even if they go to school, huge numbers of children experience a quality of education that is extremely poor, leaving them without the skills and knowledge they need to lift themselves out of poverty. The failure of such schooling to fulfil human rights is illustrated by national test data from a number of countries including Bangladesh, Brazil, Ghana, Pakistan, the Philippines and Zambia. These show a majority of primary school leavers to be achieving well below their countries' minimum performance standards, with results in some cases being "only marginally better than for children who have not completed school."

Although there are notable and creative exceptions to the rule, there is growing recognition that the approaches adopted to achieve the goals of universal access and quality education are inadequate. There has been a failure to acknowledge the complexity of the barriers impeding children's access to school, to listen to the concerns expressed by children themselves concerning their education, to build a culture of education in which all children are equally respected and valued, to engage parents and local communities in supporting education, to embrace a holistic approach to education, to address children's rights in education or to embed schools as vibrant centres for community action and social development. Energy has been focused too narrowly on enrolment, without sufficient attention to attendance, completion and attainment, or to the processes through which those outcomes can be achieved.

Many international agencies have, therefore, increasingly turned to a human rights-based approach. As early as 1997, as part of the United Nations Programme for Reform, the UN Secretary-General called on all entities of the UN system to bring human rights into the mainstream of their activities and programmes. The outcome was the UN Statement of Common Understanding, which integrates international human rights into plans, strategies and policies associated with development programmes. The rights-based approach focuses on the inalienable human rights of each individual, as expressed in UN instruments, and on governments' obligation to fulfil, respect and protect those internationally defined human rights. In so doing, it aims to support and empower individuals and communities to claim their rights. In addition, a distinctive feature of this approach is that it requires an equal commitment to both process and outcomes.

Adopting a rights-based approach to education is not a panacea. It does pose some challenges – for example, the need to balance the claims of different rights holders and address potential tensions between the realization of different rights or between rights and responsibilities. Nevertheless, consistent adherence to its core principles can help meet the education goals of governments, parents and children. It demands the creation of strategies to reach all children, including the most marginalized. It empowers communities, parents and other stakeholders to claim their rights, insist that these be fully implemented and, when necessary, seek their enforcement in national courts.

Education As a Human Right

Education has been formally recognized as a human right since the adoption of the Universal Declaration of Human Rights in 1948. This has since been affirmed in numerous global human rights treaties, including the United Nations Educational, Scientific and Cultural Organization (UNESCO) Convention against Discrimination in Education (1960), the International Covenant on Economic, Social and Cultural Rights (1966) and the Convention on the Elimination of All Forms of Discrimination against Women (1981). These treaties establish an entitlement to free, compulsory primary education for all children; an obligation to develop secondary education, supported by measures to render it accessible to all children, as well as equitable access to higher education; and a responsibility to provide basic education for individuals who have not completed primary education.

Furthermore, they affirm that the aim of education is to promote personal development, strengthen respect for human rights and freedoms, enable individuals to participate effectively in a free society, and promote understanding, friendship and tolerance. The right to education has long been recognized as encompassing not only access to educational provision, but also the obligation to eliminate discrimination at all levels of the educational system, to set minimum standards and to improve quality. In addition, education is necessary for the fulfilment of any other civil, political, economic or social right.

The United Nations Convention on the Rights of the Child (1989) further strengthens and broadens the concept of the right to education, in particular through the obligation to consider in its implementation the Convention's four core principles: non-discrimination; the best interests of the child; the right to life, survival and development of the child to the maximum extent possible; and the right of children to express their views in all matters affecting them and for their views to be given due weight in accordance with their age and maturity. These underlying principles make clear a strong commitment to ensuring that children are recognized as active agents in their own learning and that education is designed to promote and respect their rights and needs. The Convention elaborates an understanding of the right to education in terms of universality, participation, respect and inclusion. This approach is exemplified both in the text itself and in its interpretation by the Committee on the Rights of the Child, the international body established to monitor governments' progress in implementing child rights.

Beyond the formal obligations undertaken by governments in ratifying these human rights treaties, a number of global conferences have affirmed the right to education. Although lacking the legally binding force of the treaties, these conferences have introduced an additional impetus for action, together with elaborated commitments and time frames for their attainment. The World Conference on Education for All (1990) set the goal of universal primary education for the year 2000, a goal not met but subsequently reaffirmed for 2015 at the World Education Forum in 2000. This Forum also committed to an expansion and improvement of early childhood care and education, the elimination of gender disparities in education and the improvement of quality in education.

In addition, the international community and leading development institutions have agreed to the Millennium Development Goals, expressed in the Millennium Declaration, which commit them to ensuring that all girls and boys complete a full course of primary education and that gender disparity is eliminated at all levels of education by 2015. More recently, the 'International Conference on the Right to Basic Education as a Fundamental Human Right and the Legal Framework for Its Financing' (Jakarta, Indonesia, 2–4 December 2005) adopted the Jakarta Declaration. This emphasizes that the right to education is an internationally recognized right in its interrelationship with the right to development, and that the legal and constitutional protection of this right is indispensable to its full realization.

Human Rights-Based Approaches to Development

An increasing emphasis has been placed in recent years on rights-based approaches to development. In part, this shift has been the result of growing recognition that needs-based or service-delivery approaches have failed to substantially reduce poverty. One significant limitation of these approaches has been that they are often undertaken by authorities who may not be sensitive to the needs of the poor. It is also felt that combining human rights, development and activism can be more effective than any single approach.

As part of the UN Programme for Reform launched in 1997, the UN Secretary-General called on all entities of the UN system to mainstream human rights into their activities and programmes. This led to an inter-agency process of negotiation, resulting in the adoption of a UN Statement of Common Understanding that has been accepted by the UN Development Group.

The statement provides a conceptual, analytical and methodological framework for identifying, planning, designing and monitoring development activities based on international human rights standards. Essentially, it integrates the norms, standards and principles of international human rights into the entire process of development programming, including plans, strategies and policies. It seeks to create greater awareness among governments and other relevant institutions of their obligations to fulfil, respect and protect human rights and to support and empower individuals and communities to claim their rights.

The Principles that Inform a Rights-based Approach

- *Universality and inalienability:* Human rights are universal and inalienable, the entitlement of all people everywhere in the world. An individual cannot voluntarily give them up. Nor can others take them away. As stated in article 1 of the Universal Declaration of Human Rights, "All human beings are born free and equal in dignity and rights."
- *Indivisibility:* Human rights are indivisible. Whether civil, cultural, economic, political or social, they are all inherent to the dignity of every person. Consequently, they all have equal status as rights and cannot be ranked in a hierarchy.
- *Interdependence and interrelatedness*: The realization of one right often depends, wholly or in part, on the realization of others. For example, realization of the right to health may depend on realization of the right to information.
- *Equality and non-discrimination*: All individuals are equal as human beings, and by virtue of the inherent dignity of each person, are entitled to their rights without discrimination of any kind. A rights-based approach requires a particular focus on addressing discrimination and inequality. Safeguards need to be included in development instruments to protect the rights and well-being of marginalized groups. As far as possible, data need to be disaggregated – for example, by sex, religion, ethnicity, language and disability – in order to give visibility to potentially vulnerable populations. Furthermore, all development decisions, policies and initiatives, while seeking to empower local participants, are also expressly required to guard against reinforcing power imbalances or contributing to the creation of new ones.
- *Participation and inclusion:* Every person and all peoples are entitled to active, free and meaningful participation in, contribution to and enjoyment of civil, economic, social, cultural and political development, through which human rights and fundamental freedoms can be enjoyed.
- *Empowerment:* Empowerment is the process by which people's capabilities to demand and use their human rights grow. They are empowered to claim their rights rather than simply wait for policies, legislation or the provision of services. Initiatives should be focused

on building the capacities of individuals and communities to hold those responsible to account. The goal is to give people the power and capabilities to change their own lives, improve their own communities and influence their own destinies.

- *Accountability and respect for the rule of law:* A rights-based approach seeks to raise levels of accountability in the development process by identifying 'rights holders' and corresponding 'duty bearers' and to enhance the capacities of those duty bearers to meet their obligations. These include both positive obligations to protect, promote and fulfil human rights, as well as negative obligations to abstain from rights violations. In addition to governments, a wide range of other actors should also carry responsibilities for the realization of human rights, including individuals, local organizations and authorities, the private sector, the media, donors, development partners and international institutions. The international community also carries obligations to provide effective cooperation in response to the shortages of resources and capacities in developing countries. A rights-based approach requires the development of laws, administrative procedures, and practices and mechanisms to ensure the fulfilment of entitlements, as well as opportunities to address denials and violations. It also calls for the translation of universal standards into locally determined benchmarks for measuring progress and enhancing accountability.

Adopting a Rights-Based Approach to Education

Needs-based development approaches to education have, to date, failed to achieve the Education for All goals. Because it is inclusive and provides a common language for partnership, a rights-based approach – although certainly not without tensions and challenges – has the potential to contribute to the attainment of the goals of governments, parents and children. Girls' right to education, for example, can be achieved more effectively if measures are also implemented to address their rights to freedom from discrimination, protection from exploitative labour, physical violence and sexual abuse, and access to an adequate standard of living. Equally, the right to education is instrumental in the realization of other rights. Research indicates, for example, that one additional year of schooling for 1,000 women helps prevent two maternal deaths.

A rights-based approach can contribute significant added value:

- *It promotes social cohesion, integration and stability:* Human rights promote democracy and social progress. Even where children have access to school, a poor quality of education can contribute to disaffection. A rights-based approach to education, which emphasizes quality, can encourage the development of school environments in which children know their views are valued. It includes a focus on respect for families and the values of the society in which they are living. It can also promote understanding of other cultures and peoples, contributing to intercultural dialogue and respect for the richness of cultural and linguistic diversity, and the right to participate in cultural life. In this way, it can serve to strengthen social cohesion.
- *It builds respect for peace and non-violent conflict resolution:* A rights-based approach to education is founded on principles of peace and non-violent conflict resolution. In achieving this goal, schools and communities must create learning environments that eliminate all forms of physical, sexual or humiliating punishment by teachers and challenge all forms of bullying and aggression among students. In other words, they must promote and build a culture of non-violent conflict resolution. The lessons children learn from school-based experiences in this regard can have far-reaching consequences for the wider society.
- *It contributes to positive social transformation:* A rights-based approach to education that embodies human rights education empowers children and other stakeholders and represents a major building block in efforts to achieve social transformation towards rights-respecting societies and social justice.
- *It is more cost-effective and sustainable*: Treating children with dignity and respect – and building inclusive, participatory and accountable education systems that respond directly to the expressed concerns of all stakeholders – will serve to improve educational outcomes. In too many schools, the failure to adapt to the needs of children, particularly working children, results in high levels of dropout and repeated grades. Children themselves cite violence and abuse, discriminatory attitudes, an irrelevant curriculum and poor teaching quality as major contributory factors in the inability to learn effectively and in subsequent dropout. In addition, health issues can diminish the ability of a child to

commence and continue schooling, and for all children, especially girls, an inclusive education can reduce the risk of HIV infection. A rights-based approach is therefore not only cost-effective and economically beneficial but also more sustainable.

- *It produces better outcomes for economic development:* A rights-based approach to education can be entirely consistent with the broader agenda of governments to produce an economically viable workforce. Measures to promote universal access to education and overcome discrimination against girls, children with disabilities, working children, children in rural communities, and minority and indigenous children will serve to widen the economic base of society, thus strengthening a country's economic capability.
- *It builds capacity:* By focusing on capacity-building and empowerment, a rights-based approach to education harnesses and develops the capacities of governments to fulfil their obligations and of individuals to claim their rights and entitlements.

Applying a Rights-Based Approach to Policy and Programming

The UN Statement of Common Understanding elaborates what is understood to be a rights-based approach to development cooperation and development programming. It emphasizes that all programmes of development cooperation, policies and technical assistance should further the realization of human rights, and therefore that human rights principles and standards should guide all phases of the programming process. The following elements are necessary, specific and unique to a rights-based approach and can be used for policy and programming in the education sector:

- Assessment and analysis identify the claims of human rights in education and the corresponding obligations of governments, as well as the immediate, underlying and structural causes of the non-realization of rights.
- Programmes assess the capacity of individuals to claim their rights and of governments to fulfil their obligations. Strategies are then developed to build those capacities.
- Programmes monitor and evaluate both the outcomes and processes, guided by human rights standards and principles.

- Programming is informed by the recommendations of international human rights bodies and mechanisms.

In addition, many elements of good programming practice are essential within a rights-based approach. Overall, then, the required steps are:

- Situation assessment and analysis.
- Assessing capacity for implementation.
- Programme planning, design and implementation.
- Monitoring and evaluation.

Situation Assessment and Analysis

Whereas a development approach to situation analysis addresses risks, power, stakeholders, root causes and gender, a rights-based approach to programming is informed by reference to the full range of relevant human rights – including any guidance provided by treaty bodies through General Comments and their concluding observations in relation to education. It also necessitates the following dimensions:

- *Analysis of the legislative, policy and practice environment:* It is not sufficient that legislation is in place. Too often, legislation exists but is not implemented. Inadequate resources, lack of capacities in terms of the wherewithal to implement policy, lack of public demand and low levels of information, awareness and training render it ineffective, and there are no means of redress if the rights it introduces are not respected.
- *A focus on primary responsibility of governments:* In education, governments bear the primary responsibility to, for example, provide schools, train teachers, develop the curriculum, monitor standards, eliminate discrimination and promote equal opportunity of access. Other key players – such as local authorities, schools, parents and communities – also have responsibilities, although in some cases their capacities to fulfil these are necessarily dependent on the government meeting its primary responsibilities.
- *Applying the four central principles of the Convention on the Rights of the Child:* Non-discrimination, best interests of the child, the right to life, survival and development, and the right to express views and have them given due weight must be a focus throughout the analysis.

- *Analysis of rights violations and denials:* It is essential that this analysis includes the immediate, underlying and structural causes of violations and is extended to access to education, quality in education and respect for children's rights within education.
- *A focus on the poorest and most vulnerable*: These groups are usually the most disempowered and at greatest risk of violation or denial of their rights.
- *A participatory approach*: This enables the input of a range of stakeholders – including parents, teachers, religious leaders, community groups and children – into the analysis and provides opportunities to feed back on its conclusions. Children's perspectives are indispensable. Whenever possible, the views of girls and boys of different ages, in and out of school, with and without disabilities, and from different ethnic groups, geographic locations and socio-economic situations should be taken into account.
- *Disaggregated data:* To ensure the visibility of all groups of children in relation to enrolment, attendance, completion, attainment in education and other pertinent factors, it is crucial that data are disaggregated by sex, disability, race, ethnic or social origin, economic status, religion, language, geographic location and other status.

Assessing Capacity for Implementation

A rights-based approach to education policy and programming places a particular focus on assessing the capacity of both rights holders to claim their rights and governments and public authorities to fulfil their obligations. The process should involve plans and activities to increase the capacity of individuals to support the implementation of education priorities.

Capacities of rights holders to claim rights

In order to claim rights, people need to know what their rights are and how they are being addressed, how decisions are made and by whom, and what mechanisms, if any, exist to seek redress in cases of violations. If teachers are persistently absent or fail to teach, parents and the community need to know that their children have the right to education and that they should join together to demand the resolution of such problems. They need opportunities for access to policymakers and the media. They may also need support in analysing how their rights are being denied and how to argue their case for change. Efforts also need to be made to build opportunities for children to claim their rights. There is a growing body of tools and strategies for promoting children's access to the media, policymakers and politicians, as well as evidence of the capacity for effective child advocacy. Empowering rights holders to claim their rights requires a range of strategies, including information, advocacy, capacity-building, parent networking, peer support and technical assistance.

Capacities of government and public authorities to fulfil obligations

Assessment of the capacities of government and public authorities to meet their obligations with regard to educational rights is key. Obstacles to complying with responsibilities may derive from:

- Lack of resources – financial (tax base or budget priorities) or human (skills and institutional capacity).
- Lack of authority – legal, moral, spiritual or cultural.
- Lack of responsibility – refusing to accept obligations and demonstrating no political commitment to doing so.
- Lack of coordination between levels and sectors.
- Lack of knowledge – for example, illiterate parents may not know that they have an obligation to send their children to school.

The analysis will indicate the strategies necessary to achieve change. For example, in order to assess parents' capacities to fulfil their obligation to send their children to school, States need to analyse the real costs associated with schooling. The absence of school fees may be insufficient to eliminate the economic burden on parents; school uniforms, equipment and transportation, as well as the loss of domestic support or the earnings of a child, need to be included in the analysis when developing policies aimed at universal education. In situations of crisis, conflict and transition, the obstacles are likely to be particularly acute. However, it is possible to build capacity and commitment to sustain or restore access to education even in war-torn environments.

Programme planning, design and implementation

A rights-based approach to programming recognizes that the process of development is as important as the outcome. Indeed, the process largely determines the type of outcome resulting from development activities. The principles that inform a rights-based approach outlined above should be taken into consideration in the planning, design and implementation of programmes. Although not all are new to development practice – participation and accountability, for example, are also characteristic of good programming – the added value of a rights-based approach is that such principles acquire moral and political force. This is important, given that the people who may benefit the most from the application of these principles, i.e., poor and marginalized groups, are not generally in a position to claim their rights.

Taking a rights-based approach to education will necessitate that:

- The programme engages with government in a constructive dialogue regarding its obligations, and how best it can fulfil these. This may require incentives and technical assistance, as well as capacity-building.
- Claims holders are involved in the assessment, decision-making and implementation of education provision.
- Evidence-based advocacy is used to increase the scale of impact through, for example, replication, legislative and policy change, and resource allocation.
- Civil society is involved in programme design and implementation to promote government accountability.
- Special attention is paid to the most marginalized and discriminated against groups. This approach involves going beyond addressing poorer communities to identify the most vulnerable people among the poor, for example, children with disabilities, children in low castes, internally displaced persons and children living with HIV. It then develops programming specifically to reach them.
- All programme activities are explicitly linked to human rights standards. Such standards set minimum guarantees for poor and disadvantaged groups. They also help identify where problems exist and what capacities and functions are required to address them. In the programming process, human rights standards can help define a comprehensive but targeted scope for development strategies that will yield more cost-effective results.

Monitoring and Evaluation

A rights-based approach to monitoring and evaluating education has implications, beyond those that would be addressed as good development practice, for both the process by which it is undertaken and the outcomes it seeks to measure. In terms of process, there is a need for greater transparency of information about education provision.

In addition, children and their communities need to be actively engaged as partners and involved in design, analysis, sharing of information and documentation. Their involvement empowers them and improves the quality of the information. Such monitoring and evaluation frameworks will help capture both the qualitative and quantitative indicators in respect of realizing the rights-based approach to education. In terms of outcomes, monitoring and evaluation needs to address:

- Changes in the lives of children to measure whether their education rights are better realized or no longer violated.
- Changes in legislation, policy, structures and practices and their impact on the realization of educational rights.
- Changes in relation to equity and non-discrimination in respect of access to education, the quality of that education and the experience of children within it. For example, have more marginalized children been reached and have discriminatory references in the curriculum been removed?
- Opportunities for participation and active citizenship of children, as well as other stakeholders, in schools and in the wider development of education policy.
- Changes in civil society and community capacity to support the rights-based approach – for example, through advocacy for improved education, active support for local schools, and ensuring the equal right of girls and boys.

Addressing Tensions in Fulfilling the Right to Education

A rights-based approach to programming is not a magic wand. It does not provide simple solutions to challenges that have proved intractable for many years. While providing a principled framework and a methodology for its application, it can also expose tensions, real or apparent, between different rights, among rights holders, and between rights and responsibilities.

Reconciling Conflicting Agendas for Education

In its General Comment on the aims of education, the Committee on the

Rights of the Child emphasized that the overarching aim must be to promote, support and protect "the human dignity innate in every child and his or her equal and inalienable rights" while taking into account the child's developmental needs and diverse evolving capacities. This is to be achieved through the holistic development of the full potential of the child, including a respect for human rights, an enhanced sense of identity and affiliation, and socialization with others and with the environment.

In practice, however, there are competing agendas for the aims of education systems. For governments, there are two major goals in funding education: to develop the economic workforce and potential future wealth; and to promote social cohesion, integration and a sense of national identity. Indeed, the development of mass education during the 20th century is recognized to have played an important role in promoting national integration and uniformity in both industrialized countries and the developing world. A rights-based understanding of education moves beyond the more traditional model of schooling, which has defined the education agenda very much from the perspective of the government by emphasizing training, human capital investment, and containment of young people and their socialization.

Parents, too, have demands of the education system. Most parents want it to equip their children for a successful life, and hence expect it to provide their children with the knowledge, skills and confidence that will help them gain employment and achieve economic success. They also look to schools to transmit their values, culture and language – in other words, they seek in the education system the reinforcement and promotion of their own beliefs.

A third constituency with demands on education is, of course, the child, for whom the goal is acquiring the capacities through which to fulfil her or his aspirations. Education also provides the opportunity for emotional development and friendship outside the family. It is the route through which economically and socially marginalized children can escape poverty and participate fully in their communities. It also plays a vital role in safeguarding children from exploitative and hazardous labour and sexual exploitation, promoting human rights and democracy, and protecting the environment.

There are, then, significant and sometimes competing expectations of the education system – from governments that are providing the legal and administrative framework and funding, from parents responsible for their children's upbringing and from children themselves as rights holders. Some expectations are common to all: economic success, reinforcement of values and social standing. However, the fact that governments are concerned with the wider society and parents with their individual child can and does create significant tensions in the education agenda. These tensions are acknowledged in international human rights law, which introduces the right of parents to educate their children according to their beliefs. It reflects the need to limit a government's power to impose its economic, political and religious agenda on children.

The UN Convention on the Rights of the Child introduces an additional perspective. It imposes limits not only on the state but also on parents. It insists that children's best interests must be a primary consideration in all matters affecting them, that their views must be given serious consideration and that the child's evolving capacities must be respected. In other words, the Convention affects the right of parents to freedom of choice in their child's education; parental rights to choose their children's education are not absolute and are seen to decline as children grow older. The rationale behind parental choice is not to legitimize a denial of their child's rights. Rather, it is to prevent any state monopoly of education and to protect educational pluralism. In the case of conflict between a parental choice and the best interests of the child, however, the child should always be the priority.

The right to education thus involves these three principal players: the state, the parent and the child. There is a triangular relationship between them, and in the development of rights-based education it is important to bear in mind that their differing objectives need to be reconciled. In addition, other actors with a significant contribution and responsibility include teachers, the local community, policymakers, the media and the private sector.

Balancing Rights and Responsibilities of Children

Human rights are not contingent on the exercise of responsibility. They are innate and universal. There is no requirement on the part of a child, for example, that she or he demonstrate a responsible attitude in order to 'earn' an entitlement to education. Nevertheless, there is a direct and complex relationship between rights and responsibilities, rooted in the reciprocal and mutual nature of human rights.

All children have a right to learn. This means they are entitled to an effective learning environment in multiple spaces, not just the school setting and at the primary level. It also implies that they have responsibilities to ensure their behaviour does not deny that right to other children. All children are entitled to express their views and have them given due weight. This involves listening as well as talking. It requires that children play a part in the creation of constructive spaces that promote mutual respect. And as teachers have responsibilities for children's rights, so children, too, have responsibilities towards teachers. The same principles of mutual respect apply between children and adults. The right to protection from violence extends to both children and adults, and places a responsibility on children to avoid the use of aggression or physical violence. While teachers bear responsibility for preparing lessons, teaching, grading work, maintaining positive classroom discipline and creating opportunities for children to express views, so children carry responsibilities for undertaking their work, collaborating with other children, keeping the classroom in order and, so far as it is within their means, arriving regularly and on time.

One of the most effective means of promoting children's understanding of the reciprocal basis of rights is to create an environment where their own rights are respected. Through this experience, they develop the capacities to exercise responsibility.

Tensions in the Implementation of a Rights-based Approach

In a rights-based approach to education, founded on principles of universality and equity, there are inevitable tensions that arise in the process of implementation. Some of these are associated with limits on resources and can only be addressed through a commitment to progressive realization. Some derive from insufficient understanding of the concept of rights or the potential strategies that can be adopted to resolve them. The rest of this chapter considers a number of these tensions. There are no straightforward solutions to many of them, but Chapters 3 and 4 provide some indications of approaches that can be taken to reconcile them, consistent with a commitment to the human rights of all.

Access and Quality

Where resources are scarce, the requirement to make education universally available can mean a reduction in the per capita funding for each child –

leading to higher teacher-student ratios, overcrowded classes, fewer materials and resources per class, and lower building standards – thereby sacrificing quality for access. In these circumstances, access to education is an overriding concern, and it is not acceptable to discriminate between groups of children and offer preferential treatment to some on the basis of resources. Yet, whenever possible, efforts need to be made to increase the budgetary allocation to ensure there is access to quality education for all children. A tendency to discriminate must be guarded against, and donors may need to ensure that funding is dedicated to the provision of education without discrimination on any grounds.

Equity and Efficiency

The approaches necessary to make schooling available for all children may be less efficient and cost-effective. Although it may be more expensive to develop small satellite schools in villages, for example, this may be the only way of encouraging parents to allow young girls to attend. It may be more economically efficient to place all children who do not speak the national language in a separate school, but doing so may deny them the right to an education on an equal basis with other children. It is important to consult with children, parents and communities to explore what will work most effectively in their environment. This will help build a sense of ownership and collaboration in finding solutions that will best strengthen access to education. There is little point in designing a cost-effective system that is rejected by the local community.

Universality and Diversity

The respect for difference and the right to be different in regard to cultural, linguistic and religious identity needs to be reconciled with the universal right to education as part of a broader set of human rights. Approaches to education provision that ensure universal education for all need to be undertaken with due regard for local and regional differences, particularly in regard to language and culture. Failure to do so implies a failure to reach out to all communities.

Priorities and Trade-offs

Scarce resources can lead to trade-offs, such as the decision to invest in primary education at the cost of limiting access to secondary education, or to postpone the development of educational opportunities for children with disabilities. Realistically, it is not possible for all governments to fulfil their obligations to ensure the right to education for all children immediately. However, where financial and human resources are limited, the principle of progressive realization requires governments to have a clear strategy and time frame for achieving the objective of universal access to primary and secondary education, and each action should be conducive to the full realization of the right to education for all.

Outcomes and Process

Pressure to achieve such targets as the Millennium Development Goals may lead to strategies that are designed to produce immediate results but fail to invest in long-term social change to sustain a genuine commitment to and capacity for meaningful education. For example, an increased number of school places and teachers may lead to higher levels of enrolment, only to result in increased drop-out rates because no accommodation has been made to children's particular circumstances. Ensuring attendance, completion and reasonable attainment in school involves consultations with children and parents; policies to address poverty; the development of more relevant curricula; and respect for children's rights in school, including the abolition of physical and humiliating punishments.

Emergency Responses in the Short and Longer Term

In emergencies, the immediate focus is inevitably on survival and the provision of food, water, shelter and medical treatment. For children, however, the immediate re-introduction of education is not only a right but can also be a vital resource in restoring normality, overcoming psychosocial trauma, building capacities for survival and providing structure out of chaos. There are a growing number of positive examples of programmes designed to provide immediate schooling in the aftermath of crises. Ensuring that a maximum number of children attend school under these difficult circumstances has to be balanced, however, with the parallel need to guarantee quality education in the short and longer term.

Teachers' and Children's Rights

It is sometimes argued by teachers that affording respect for the rights of children diminishes respect for their own rights. They may erroneously believe that prohibiting physical punishment or involving students in decisions diminishes their position or makes it more difficult to maintain discipline. This view derives from an assumption that rights represent a fixed quantity of entitlement and that giving more to one constituency necessarily deprives the other. It also derives from an authoritarian understanding of the teacher-child relationship. While respecting the rights of children does involve some transfer of power, this does not necessitate the loss of rights on the part of the teacher. In practice, without mutual respect, the pedagogic relationship is fragile. Creating a school environment in which children's rights are respected is more likely to enhance respect for the role of the teacher, although this outcome can only be achieved if teachers are appropriately supported and resourced.

Work and School

Controversy about the role of work in children's lives continues. There are tensions associated with the extent to which it, on the one hand, provides preparation for life, and on the other, impedes educational outcomes. There is no consensus as to whether there are forms of work that are acceptable and can be accommodated alongside the right to education – or whether all child work should be prohibited during the years of compulsory schooling. The Convention on the Rights of the Child makes clear that children must be protected from all forms of work that are harmful to their development or that interfere with their education. International Labour Organization (ILO) Convention 182 elaborates the worst forms of child labour and makes clear governments' obligations to protect all children from these areas of work. Governments need to introduce legislation and policies that guarantee these protections. It is also incumbent on governments to provide education that offers a viable alternative to employment in terms of its quality and relevance; to introduce policies that address the poverty and livelihood insecurity that force many children into work; and to make education sufficiently flexible and inclusive to allow those children to attend who have no choice but to work.

A Rights-Based Conceptual Framework for Education

The development of a human rights-based approach to education requires a framework that addresses the right of access to education, the right to quality education and respect for human rights in education. These dimensions are interdependent and interlinked, and a rights-based education necessitates the realization of all three.

The right to education requires a commitment to ensuring universal access, including taking all necessary measures to reach the most marginalized children. But getting children into schools is not enough; it is no guarantee of an education that enables individuals to achieve their economic and social objectives and to acquire the skills, knowledge, values and attitudes that bring about responsible and active citizenship. A study by the Southern and Eastern African Consortium for Monitoring Educational Quality (1995–1998), for example, measures primary school students' reading literacy against standards established by national reading experts and sixth-grade teachers. In four out of seven countries, fewer than half of sixth grade students achieved minimum competence in reading. Poor achievement is also evident in a study conducted by the *Programme d'Analyse des Systèmes Éducatifs de la CONFEMEN* (PASEC) in six French-speaking African countries in 1996–2001: Achievement levels were "low" in French or mathematics for up to 43 per cent of fifth grade pupils in all six countries, and more than 40 per cent of students in Senegal struggled to put several numbers with two decimal points in order. Achieving a quality education is also a challenge in industrialized nations. Recent studies show that large numbers of students in rich countries do not acquire the basic skills to be competent in today's world.

To ensure quality education in line with the Dakar Framework for Action (2002) and the aims of education elaborated by the Committee on the Rights of the Child, attention must be paid to the relevance of the curriculum, the role of teachers, and the nature and ethos of the learning environment. A rights-based approach necessitates a commitment to recognizing and respecting the human rights of children while they are in school – including respect for their identity, agency and integrity. This will contribute to increased retention rates and also makes the process of education empowering, participatory, transparent and accountable. In addition, children will continue to be excluded from education unless measures are taken to address their rights to freedom from discrimination, to an adequate standard of living and to meaningful participation. A quality education cannot be achieved without regard to children's right to health and well-being. Children cannot achieve their optimum development when they are subjected to humiliating punishment or physical abuse.

This conceptual framework highlights the need for a holistic approach to education, reflecting the universality and indivisibility of all human rights.

The following sections set out the central elements that therefore need to be addressed in each of the three dimensions mentioned above.

*1. **The right of access to education***	• Education throughout all stages of childhood and beyond • Availability and accessibility of education • Equality of opportunity
*2. **The right to quality***	• A broad, relevant and inclusive curriculum education • Rights-based learning and assessment • Child-friendly, safe & healthy environments
*3. **The right to respect***	• Respect for identity • Respect for participation rights • Respect for integrity in the learning environment

The Right of Access to Education

Obligations to ensure the right of access to education

- Provide free and compulsory primary education.
- Develop forms of secondary education that are available and accessible to everyone, and introduce measures to provide free education and financial assistance in cases of need.
- Provide higher education that is accessible on the basis of capacity by every appropriate means.
- Provide accessible educational and vocational information and guidance.
- Introduce measures to encourage regular attendance and reduce drop-out rates.
- Provide education on the basis of equal opportunity.
- Ensure respect for the right to education without discrimination of any kind on any grounds.
- Ensure an inclusive education system at all levels.
- Provide reasonable accommodation and support measures to ensure that children with disabilities have effective access to and receive education in a manner conducive to achieving the fullest possible social integration.

- Ensure an adequate standard of living for physical, mental, spiritual, moral and social development.
- Provide protection and assistance to ensure respect for the rights of children who are refugees or seeking asylum.
- Provide protection from economic exploitation and work that interferes with education.

The right of access to education comprises three elements: the provision of education throughout all stages of childhood and beyond, consistent with the Education for All goals; the provision of sufficient, accessible school places or learning opportunities; and equality of opportunity.

Education throughout all stages of childhood and beyond

Learning is a lifelong process. A rights-based approach to education seeks to build opportunities for children to achieve their optimum capacities throughout their childhood and beyond. It requires a life-cycle approach, investing in learning and ensuring effective transitions at each stage of the child's life.

Although the Convention on the Rights of the Child does not impose explicit obligations to provide early childhood education, the Committee on the Rights of the Child interprets the right to education as beginning at birth and as closely linked to the child's right to maximum development. It calls on governments to ensure that young children have access to programmes of health care and education designed to promote their well-being, and stresses that the right to optimum development implies the right to education during early childhood, with systematic and quality family involvement.

Quality education during the early years plays a vital part in promoting readiness for school and is also the best guarantee of promoting sustainable economic and social development, and attaining the Millennium Development Goals and the Education for All and A World Fit for Children goals. A study of children in Nepal shows that more than 95 per cent of children who had attended a non-formal preschool facility enrolled in primary school, where they also performed better than those who had not attended. Around 80 per cent of the first group passed grade one, compared to around 60 per cent of the group without preschool experience.

While human rights law affirms that every child is entitled to free, compulsory primary education, obligations in respect of secondary education are less emphatic. The duty is to encourage its development and make it available and accessible to every child, and free where possible. The weaker formulation does not reflect a lesser commitment to secondary education, but rather a recognition that it is currently beyond the resources of many countries to make it free and compulsory. Since these conventions were drafted, there has been an increasing recognition of the fundamental importance of secondary education.

Moreover, development does not cease at age 18. Education can and should take place throughout life consistent with the third goal of Education for All, which calls for meeting the learning needs of all young people and adults through access to learning and life skills programmes. Governments should support the achievement of a strong base for lifelong learning, through education directed towards responsible autonomy, self-directed learning and preparation for full citizenship.

Availability and accessibility of education

States have obligations to establish the legislative and policy framework, together with sufficient resources, to fulfil the right to education for every child. Each child must therefore be provided with an available school place or learning opportunity, together with appropriately qualified teachers and adequate and appropriate resources and equipment. The level of provision of primary education must be consistent with the numbers of children entitled to receive it.

All learning environments must be both physically and economically accessible for every child, including the most marginalized. It is important to recognize that a school that is accessible to one child may not be accessible to another. Schools must be within safe physical reach or accessible through technology (for example, access to a 'distance learning' programme). They must also be affordable to all.

Equality of opportunity

Every child has an equal right to attend school. Making schools accessible and available is an important first step in fulfilling this right but not sufficient to ensure its realization. Equality of opportunity can only be achieved by removing barriers in the community and in schools.

Even where schools exist, economic, social and cultural factors – including gender, disability, AIDS, household poverty, ethnicity, minority status, orphanhood and child labour – often interlink to keep children out of school. Governments have obligations to develop legislation, policies and support services to remove barriers in the family and community that impede children's access to school.

Schools can directly or indirectly impede the access of some children, for example, through reflecting a male-dominated culture, pervading patterns of violence and sexual abuse or prevailing societal norms, such as caste bias. Negative teacher attitudes towards girls, biases in the curriculum, lack of female teachers and role models, and lack of adequate access to hygiene and sanitation can also inhibit enrolment and contribute to poor attainment and high drop-out levels. Schools may refuse to accept children with disabilities or AIDS. Inflexibility in school systems may exclude many working children. Governments should take action to ensure the provision of education that is both inclusive and non-discriminatory and that is adapted to ensure the equal opportunity of every child to attend.

The Right to Quality Education

Obligations to ensure the right to quality education

- Develop children's personalities, talents, and mental and physical abilities to their fullest potential.
- Promote respect for human rights and fundamental freedoms, and prepare children for a responsible life in a spirit of peace, tolerance, equality and friendship.
- Promote respect for the child's, his or her parents' and others' cultural identity, language and values.
- Promote respect for the natural environment.
- Ensure the child's access to information from a diversity of sources.
- Ensure that the best interests of children are a primary consideration.
- Promote respect for the evolving capacities of children in the exercise of their rights.
- Respect the right of children to rest, leisure, play, recreation, and participation in arts and culture.

The Dakar Framework for Action commits nations to the provision of primary education of good quality and to improving all aspects of educational quality. Although there is no single definition of 'quality', most attempts to define it incorporate two fundamental perspectives. First, cognitive development is a primary objective of education, with the effectiveness of education measured against its success in achieving this objective. Second, education must promote creative and emotional development, supporting the objectives of peace, citizenship and security, fostering equality and passing global and local cultural values down to future generations.

These perspectives have been integrated into the aims of education set out in the Convention on the Rights of the Child, which formulates a philosophy of respect for children as individuals, recognizing each child as "unique – in characteristics, interests, abilities and needs." It sets out a framework of obligations to provide education that promotes children's optimum development. Article 29 implies "the need for education to be child-centred, child-friendly and empowering, and it highlights the need for educational processes to be based on the very principles it enunciates." Every child has a right to an education that empowers him or her by developing life skills, learning and other capacities, self-esteem and self-confidence. The provision of a quality education demands attention to the content of the curriculum, the nature of the teaching and the quality of the learning environment. It implies a need for the creation of flexible, effective and respectful learning environments that are responsive to the needs of all children.

A broad, relevant and inclusive curriculum

Common guidance is provided in all the key human rights treaties for the development of the curriculum, indicating an underlying global consensus on the content and scope necessary for a rights-based education.

The curriculum must enable every child to acquire the core academic curriculum and basic cognitive skills, together with essential life skills that equip children to face life challenges, make well-balanced decisions and develop a healthy lifestyle, good social relationships, critical thinking and the capacity for non-violent conflict resolution. It must develop respect for human rights and fundamental freedoms, and promote respect for different cultures and values and for the natural environment. The Committee on the Rights of the Child stipulates that the curriculum, both in early childhood provision and in school, "must be of direct relevance to the child's social, cultural, environmental and economic context, and to his or her present and future needs and take full account of the child's evolving capacities"

The curriculum must be inclusive and tailored to the needs of children in different or difficult circumstances. All teaching and learning materials should be free from gender stereotypes and from harmful or negative representations of any ethnic or indigenous groups. To enable all children with disabilities to fulfil their potential, provision must be made to enable them to, for example, learn Braille, orientation or sign language.

Rights-based learning and assessment

The way in which children are provided with the opportunity to learn is as important as what they learn. Traditional models of schooling that silence children and perceive them as passive recipients are not consistent with a rights-based approach to learning.

There should be respect for the agency of children and young people, who should be recognized as active contributors to their own learning, rather than passive recipients of education. There should also be respect for the evolving and differing capacities of children, together with recognition that children do not acquire skills and knowledge at fixed or predetermined ages. Teaching and learning must involve a variety of interactive methodologies to create stimulating and participatory environments. Rather than simply transmitting knowledge, educators involved in creating or strengthening learning opportunities should facilitate participatory learning. Learning environments should be child friendly and conducive to the optimum development of children's capacities.

Assessment of learning achievement is vital. Testing enables schools to identify learning needs and develop targeted initiatives to provide support to individual children. Analysis of results enables governments to assess whether they are achieving their educational objectives and to adjust policy and resources accordingly. Dissemination of results is a necessary aspect of accountability and transparency in education and facilitates discussions on the quality of education. At the same time, a commitment to realizing children's rights to their optimum capacities implies the need for sensitive and constructive methods of appraising and monitoring children's' work that take account of their differing abilities and do not discriminate against those with particular learning needs.

A child-friendly, safe and healthy environment

The obligation to give primacy to the best interests of children and to ensure their optimum development requires that learning environments are welcoming, gender sensitive, healthy, safe and protective. Although situations of extreme poverty, emergency and conflict may often impede this, children should never be expected to attend schools where the environment is detrimental to their health and well-being. Schools should take measures to contribute towards children's health and well-being, taking into account the differing needs of children. This will necessitate measures to ensure that obstacles to health and safety are removed – for example, consideration as to the location of schools, travel to and from school, factors that might cause illness or accidents in the classroom or playgrounds, and appropriate facilities for girls. It also requires the proactive provision of facilities, services and policies to promote the health and safety of children and the active participation of the local community. A healthy environment also needs to provide safe and stimulating opportunities for play and recreation.

The Right to Respect in the Learning Environment

Obligations to respect children's rights in the learning environment

- Respect every child equally without discrimination on any grounds.
- Teach respect for human rights and fundamental freedoms, for difference and for life in a society where there is understanding, peace, tolerance, equality and friendship.
- Give primary consideration to the best interests of the child.
- Respect the evolving capacities of the child.
- Respect the right of children to express their views on all matters of concern to them and have those views given due weight in accordance with children's age and maturity.
- Recognize the right to freedom of expression, religion, conscience, thought and assembly.
- Respect the privacy of children.
- Take all appropriate measures to ensure that school discipline is administered in a manner consistent with the child's dignity and all other rights in the Convention on the Rights of the Child.
- Protect children from all forms of physical violence, injury or abuse, neglect or negligence, maltreatment or exploitation, including sexual abuse.

Human rights are inalienable. In other words, they are inherent in each human being. Accordingly, they must be respected in all learning environments. The right to education must be understood as incorporating respect for children's identity, their right to express their views on all matters of concern to them, and their physical and personal integrity.

Respect for identity

UNESCO's Convention against Discrimination in Education (1960) protects the educational rights of national minorities. Depending on the educational policy of each State, it establishes the right to use or be taught in one's own language, provided this does not exclude minorities from understanding the language and culture of the community as a whole and that it is not provided at a lower standard than the one generally provided. The Convention on the Protection and Promotion of Diversity in Cultural Expressions (2005) introduces obligations to respect cultural diversity, including through educational programmes.

In addition, article 30 of the Convention on the Rights of the Child stresses the right of children to enjoy their own culture, practice their own religion and use their own language. International human rights law also requires States to respect the freedom of parents to decide the kind of education they would like for their child. Governments are entitled to determine which religion, if any, should be taught in schools, as well as the medium of instruction for schools. And finally, the Convention on the Rights of the Child, in its recognition of the right of children to express their views on all matters of concern to them and to have those views given due weight, introduces a further dimension to the issue of choice and freedom in education provision. Thus, it is in the arena of these cultural rights that the tensions discussed in Chapter 1 between children, parents and governments in respect of education are often most sharply drawn.

There is no simple solution to these tensions, nor any one correct approach. Whatever approach is adopted, however, governments have obligations to ensure that children do not experience discrimination, that respect is afforded to their culture and religion, and that every effort is made to prevent social exclusion and educational disadvantage as a consequence of speaking a minority language. In determining the most appropriate system for addressing respect for identity, a rights-based approach requires that children, families and communities are consulted and involved. And if relevant obligations are not being fulfilled, mechanisms should be in place to challenge schools, education authorities and the government.

Respect for participation rights

Article 12 of the Convention on the Rights of the Child establishes that children are entitled to express their views on all matters of concern to them and to have these given due weight in accordance with their age and maturity. This principle of participation is affirmed by other rights to freedom of expression, religion and association. These rights apply to all aspects of their education and have profound implications for the status of children throughout the education system. Participation rights do not simply extend to the pedagogic relationships in the classroom but also across the school and in the development of legislation and policy. The Committee on the Rights of the Child has frequently recommended that governments take steps to encourage greater participation by children in schools. Children can also play an important role in advocating for the realization of their rights. Governments need to introduce legislation and policy to establish and support these rights at all levels in the education system.

Respect for integrity

The Convention demands not only that children are protected from all forms of violence but also that school discipline is administered in a manner consistent with the child's dignity. However, frequent and severe violence, including emotional abuse and humiliation in school, remains widespread in countries throughout the world. The Committee on the Rights of the Child has consistently argued that such punishments constitute a violation of the rights of the child and a denial of children's integrity. Much violence is also perpetrated by children against children and children against teachers, and it is equally important to challenge such behaviour.

Physical and other forms of humiliating and abusive treatment are not only a violation of the child's right to protection from violence, but also highly counterproductive to learning. Children cite violence as a significant factor contributing to school dropout. Furthermore, it diminishes self-esteem and promotes the message that violence is acceptable. Many factors contribute to the continued use of violence towards children in schools, including:

- Social and legal acceptance of violence against children.

- Lack of adequate training for teachers, resulting in poor classroom management and a consequent breakdown of discipline.
- Lack of knowledge of the benefits associated with positive discipline and how to promote it.
- A failure to understand the harmful impact of physical punishment.
- Lack of understanding of the different ways in which children learn, and the fact that children will differ in their development and their capacities to understand.

Action must be taken to address all these barriers and to achieve rights-respecting educational environments in which all forms of physical and humiliating punishments are prohibited and a commitment to non-violent conflict resolution is promoted.

Rights-based Education Through Sector-Wide Approaches

Over the past decade of international assistance to education, Sector-Wide Approaches (SWAps) have become the dominant approach, intended to accelerate progress on the MDGs and EFA goals. There is no single definition of a SWAp; rather, it has been increasingly recognised that a SWAp is a partnership process rather than a rigidly-defined funding mechanism. In essence, a SWAp can be seen simply as an approach to support the education system to work as a coherent system that is able to achieve its goals. Referring to a SWAp thus implies both the coherent, long-term plan and programme for the education sector and a modality of financial assistance and technical support that enables governments, with the support of the wider society, to create and sustain such a system.

In theory, there is neither an explicit linkage, nor a contradiction, between a SWAp and a rights-based approach in education. Nevertheless, there are potential significant benefits in linking the two. SWAps are intended to bring about a coherent approach to the sector, which creates the potential for addressing the complex and interlinked factors of inequality and social exclusion in a more effective way. SWAps in education seek to accelerate progress towards both international and national goals, but in many countries the 100 per cent UPC target, let alone wider goals, will not be reached without a deeper understanding of the barriers that leave some children excluded, or not learning effectively. SWAps emphasise longer-term and more supportive partnerships between governments, civil society and international development partners. This provides new opportunities for achieving deep change in attitudes, practices and ways of working for all partners involved.

It is clear that many children in South Asia do not yet enjoy their right to a good quality education, in a supportive, protective context free of discrimination. The interactions between poverty, gender inequality and social exclusion are reflected in marked disparities in educational demand and access, between the most advantaged and disadvantaged groups and individuals.

Development of Sector-wide Approaches

Over the past decade there have been substantial changes in the way in which educational development is conceptualised and how international assistance to the sector is managed. From the mid-1990s there began a trend away from traditional project approaches. The new concept at that time was of a 'Sector Investment Programme' (SIP). These aimed to support governments in planning coherently for the whole sector within the context of an overarching, realistic and coasted policy framework, backed by concurrent attention to macroeconomic stabilisation and public service reform. Funding was to be provided flexibly as a part of government budgets, with governments and ministries of education able to make choices about resource allocation. Financial procedures were to be harmonised and monitoring at sector and programme level integrated, to meet diverse reporting needs. Donors would give up their control over specific project interventions, but gain participation as 'Development Partners' in education policy dialogue and broader budget framework negotiations.

However, as implementation has got underway, it has been realised that 'one size does not fit all'. Neither governments nor international partners in any context have been able to implement a SIP as originally conceived. It has been accepted that national and local realities are the proper starting point for any sector programme. Therefore, over time, the term 'Sector-Wide Approach' (SWAp) has been adopted in preference to 'SIP', to describe what is more of a direction, process and ethos than a rigid blueprint or narrowly-defined funding mechanism. While the term 'SWAp' is strictly speaking something of a misnomer, in that the modality is often applied to a subsector, there is nevertheless a sufficiently widely shared understanding of the characteristics of a SWAp for it to be a useful term. A summary of these characteristics put forward by ODI provides a useful working definition.

In South Asia, programmes are not yet 'pure' SWAps. Sri Lanka most closely resembles the theoretical model of a SWAp, while Bangladesh has many characteristics of a giant project, with funding being pooled through the ADB. Nepal has a core document which outlines aspirations, funded by a pool of seven donors giving sector budget support according to an annual plan, with many large and small projects operating in parallel, outside the framework. However Nepal, in its proposed School Sector Reform, due to begin mid-2009, is moving much closer to a more comprehensive education sector plan.

Fast Track Initiative on EFA

The EFA Goals developed at the World Conference on EFA and strengthened and reaffirming at the World Education Forum do not constitute an international rights commitment per se, but do acknowledge that education is a right. Goals 2 and 5 (in modified form) are also Millennium Development Goals (MDGs).

Increasingly, education sector level support through SWAps is set within the context of support to Poverty Reduction Strategy Programmes (PRSPs) that seek to chart an overall path towards achievement of the MDGs and to guide progress in the relevant sectors, and coasted in Medium Term Expenditure Frameworks (MTEFs). Related to these overall changes in aid modality, most donor agencies have now committed to a harmonisation agenda set out in the Paris Declaration on Aid Effectiveness.

The Education for All—Fast Track Initiative (EFA-FTI) 'was launched in 2002 as a global partnership between donor and developing countries to ensure accelerated progress towards the Millennium Development Goal of universal basic education by 2015. All low-income countries that demonstrate serious commitment to achieve universal primary completion can receive support from FTI. FTI is built on mutual commitments. Partner countries have put primary education at the forefront of their domestic efforts and develop sound national education plans. Donors provide coordinated and increased financial and technical support in a transparent and predictable manner. FTI is a global education partnership that aims to support and promote:

— Sound education plans

— Better coordination

— Country-led programs

— Predictable aid
— Measurable results & best practices'

Potential of SWAps

Accelerating the realisation of education rights

SWAps were developed as a pragmatic mechanism for more effective development assistance. Whilst they are gradually being linked more explicitly to poverty reduction frameworks and achieving the EFA goals, they do not of themselves imply a rights based or inclusive approach. However, it is often being discovered in practice that even the narrowly-defined MDG will not be achieved without attention to wider rights and social exclusion issues. It is also being realised that SWAps have a strong potential to support a more rights-based approach.

Implications for education systems and SWAps

In countries where there are complex patterns of social exclusion, combined with a number of the access and quality issues illustrated above, the challenges for the education system and SWAp are considerable. It is the responsibility of the duty bearers to develop a system of education that addresses the 'demand' and socialite' barriers, to ensure that the system helps to break down (rather than inadvertently creating) barriers to access and to learning and in addition actively protects and promotes children's education-related and wider rights. The system needs to reach:

— Those who have never enrolled, many of whom are from the 'extreme poor', live in remote areas, in areas disrupted by conflict and/or in life situations that make them 'hard to reach'.
— Those who have been 'pulled out' of school because of poverty, conflict, early marriage, the need or desire to work (some then becoming 'hard to reach' as a result).
— Those whose schooling has been disrupted due to a sudden onset emergency.
— Those who have been, or are at risk of being, 'pushed out' of school because of discrimination, boredom or non-learning due to poor 'quality' in the widest sense.
— Those who are at risk of not learning because of irregular attendance patterns due to family circumstances such as economic needs or the

need to care for a sick relative or younger child, and girls beyond puberty who for cultural reasons as well as provision of adequate facilities do not attend during their menstruation time.

— Schools that are not yet delivering a good quality and rights-realising education, many of which are located in the poorest and more vulnerable communities.

— Children who have differentiated learning needs within classes and schools.

— All schools and education programmes in the country (including those outside the state sector), to ensure that rights are upheld and no child suffers discrimination within the system.

Many education SWAps and large programmes are organised around three goals related to 'access, quality and management', including components such as school construction, textbooks, teacher training and fee elimination, usually with an accompanying component of capacity building. A consideration of the many factors explored above that constrain the realisation of children's educational rights suggests that this approach is likely to need considerable unpacking' (exploring in more depth and detail). In addition to the common emphasis on general 'pro-poor' policies, it is likely that there will need to be attention to addressing attitudinal barriers, targeting for equity and ensuring sufficient focus on the hidden and hard to reach' children whose rights are the furthest from being realised.

Importance of Rights-based Approach

Although planning for education supposedly includes all children, research and data shows us that many children have neither access to education (including transition between levels), nor equal opportunities to learn when in a school or system.

The rights of many children to an education are not realised in this situation. Girls, rural children and children from poor households are less likely to attend primary school than boys, urban children and children from wealthier households. At the secondary level of education these disparities are even greater.

Until recently, data on access to education was often not disaggregated beyond gender, in spite of occasional studies conducted by concerned agencies. Household surveys, such as the MICS surveys by UNICEF, are particularly useful in this context because they collect detailed data on the characteristics of the population, including data on groups that are excluded. In addition, some countries are collecting data related to marginalised groups; for example, India collects data on scheduled castes and tribes while Nepal disaggregation according to gender, Dalits (low caste) and Janajatis. Later in this guide there is a discussion on a recently-developed composite Education Parity Index, by which the progress of disparity reduction in an education system can be measured in relation to the access of marginalised groups to education. In a rights-based approach, this index would sit alongside the overall progress towards Education for All and the MDGs.

Children have rights to learning and development, which apply to all 0–18 year old at all times. Children begin learning from birth and learn through everything that they do and experience, whether or not this learning is planned or intended.

However, given the complex demands of the modern world, there is also a specifically defined right to education as a planned programme of learning, usually in the form of 'schooling'. The exact age to which this right applies varies slightly between countries, but is usually from around 5–7 up to age 17–18.

There are rights to, in and through education. All children, equally, have the right to education; namely to access, attend and complete a full cycle of education, regardless of any differentiating factor, including gender, economic situation, class, caste, ethnicity, linguistic identity, personal abilities or talents, or having a disability or special need.

The right to education has no meaning unless 'education' implies an effective process that results in learning and development. Thus children also have rights in education, namely that the education is of good quality, in the widest sense. The educational process (methodology) must take account of children's age, stage of development, linguistic and cultural background and individual abilities. The content (curriculum) must be broad and balanced, relevant to the child's sociocultural background, and prepare each child not only for future employment but, more fundamentally, for living a fulfilled life and contributing to a peaceful, tolerant and environmentally sustainable community and society. Schools must not discriminate against any child and must also actively uphold children's protection rights, including freedom from abuse, humiliation or violence.

Children also have rights through education. Good quality education, by its very nature, has a rather special role as a vehicle for advancing and promoting wider rights and reducing discrimination and exclusion. An education in which children are actively learning (rather than passively absorbing what they are told) gives children skills such as expressing their views, listening to and working with others, reading with an open and critical mind, showing curiosity and taking responsibility. All of these, as well as opening up opportunities for meaningful and dignified employment, promote their rights to participation and citizenship, both now and in the future. Education is also a key vehicle for child protection, health promotion and developing a wide range of skills for life and livelihoods.

Rights Principles and Concepts

As countries, organisations and institutions have attempted to put their rights commitments into practice, a set of concepts and principles has developed to support this process. These are discussed here in relation to their implications for education

— Education-related rights are universal. All children of the relevant age of schooling in a particular country have a right to education. Quality education is the right of each child, regardless of whether or not there is any perceived socioeconomic benefit to society of educating him/her. Children also hold education rights regardless of their legal status, for example if they are migrants or refugees or if their birth has not been registered. Targets for educational enrolment and completion must therefore be 100 per cent rather than being content with reaching 95 per cent, for example.

— Education rights are inalienable and indivisible. All human rights have equal status and cannot be ranked in order of importance. Human rights cannot be taken away from any child, for any reason. For example, a girl does not lose her right to education because she has become pregnant or has married. Children do not lose their right to education because they have infringed the law, or for any reason live away from their families.

— Rights are interrelated. Achieving one right usually helps to achieve other rights, and this is especially the case with education. However, the right to education should never be pursued at the expense of children's other rights to safety, protection, to live with their families, or to language, culture and identity. This implies ensuring that strategies for access, quality and child protection/welfare work together, avoiding an over-focus on ensuring school enrolment and attendance without regard to the actual experience of children in school.

— Education rights must be applied without discrimination. No child should be denied their right to an education on the basis of their economic status, gender, social status, caste, disability or any other reason. In practice, this often implies much more than a passive 'equal treatment', but a strong emphasis on actively reducing exclusion and discrimination for those children who are most marginalised and disadvantaged in education.

— Education rights can be thought of in terms of 'rights holders' and 'duty bearers'. All people are both rights holders and duty bearers. In an education system, the key rights holders are all children in the country, who have rights to quality education provision whether or not they are currently within the system. The key duty bearers are all of those who are responsible for delivering that education, for example parents, teachers, head teachers, parents, administrators and Ministers of Education.

— Children, parents and communities have a right to participate in decisions about education. All people are empowered to claim their rights, rather than simply waiting for policies, legislation or the provision of services. Education should enhance children's capacity to participate in their wider community and society, both now and in the future. A rights-based approach requires the development of laws, administrative procedures and practices to ensure the realisation of entitlements, as well as mechanisms to enable people to address violations.

— Education rights can be achieved through progressive realisation. It is impossible to realise every right immediately. Governments may need to make short-term priorities that appear to give preference to certain children more than others, if this is the most effective way of reaching all children as quickly as possible. Plans and strategies should set an end-point for when all children will be in school with benchmarks along the way for reaching that goal, if necessary allocating additional funds for the 'last 10 per cent' who are the hardest to reach with quality education.

The following sections explore the reasons why so many children—and especially girls—are unable to attend school even at primary level. That is, why they are prevented from realising their right to education. While there are many and varied reasons, it is important to be aware that many children do not just fall into a single category, but suffer 'multiple disparities'. Thus, for example, many children belong to marginalised groups who also are poor and live in remote areas.

Country reports from the Mid-Decade Assessment of Education For All, conducted throughout Asia in 2007–08, highlight the following as disadvantaged groups, and it is clear that many of them are interdependent:

— Children from remote and rural communities
— Children from religious, linguistic and ethnic minorities as well as indigenous peoples
— Children from migrant families
— Persons/children with disabilities or with special need
— Street children, working children, in difficult circumstances (conflict or disaster areas)
— Orphans and abandoned children
— Children of very poor families
— Girls, especially from rural/ethnic communities.

Exclusion comprises a complex web of inter-linked dimensions of poverty (linked to location and livelihood), gender, caste/ status-based exclusion, ethnicity/language and disability. Children without adequate care and protection are particularly vulnerable to educational exclusion, and such children are not reached by general pro-poor policies. In South Asia, too, there is a compounding effect due to the prevalence of conflict and natural disasters (and HIV/AIDS).

The case of Dalits provides an example of the complexity of factors which prevent access to education for some children and is illustrated here. In this particular case there may be factors common with other disadvantaged children, but the example also illustrates that it is the compounding factors of both gender and caste which create the barriers and that particular types of discrimination, in this case the treatment by higher castes, will need to be addressed in a particular way.

Unequal Access

Factors resulting in unequal access are:

— *Poverty and vulnerable livelihoods:* Poor children are less likely to enrol in school, to complete the primary phase or achieve satisfactory learning outcomes. Poverty is inextricably linked with livelihood and location. Many of the poorest families live in rural areas, dependent on traditional agricultural occupations. Meanwhile, owing to rapid rural–urban migration, an increasing number live in the ever-growing urban slums. In both rural and urban areas, poor children are the most likely to be required to work to support themselves or their families, which affects their ability to attend school regularly, especially at certain times or seasons. Natural events such as floods or cyclones tend to disproportionately affect the poorest, further disrupting educational access and continuity. In South Asia, Huebler's study shows that attendance at primary school increases consistently from the lowest income quaintly to the highest. At secondary level the picture is even more marked: in Nepal, for example, there are almost four students from the highest income quintile for every one from the lowest; while in Bangladesh—where the differences at primary level are small—at secondary level there are nearly five students from the highest income quintile for every one from the lowest.

  Poor children have lower levels of health and nutrition than their better-off peers, which puts them at a disadvantage in learning and means they are more likely to be absent from school. Because of the linkage between education and poverty, poor children are also far more likely to have parents with little or no formal education. This might mean that parents are less convinced of the benefits of education and are also less able to support and encourage children in their studies.

— *Remoteness:* Many of the poorest children live in geographically remote communities. Across Asia, such environments include high mountains, island archipelagos, forest interiors or desert regions. Such areas tend to be the last to see the benefits of economic development and the provision of services, including education and transportation. In many Asian countries, it is in the remoter regions that indigenous and tribal peoples, cultures and languages have survived and maintained their distinctiveness, thus there is often an overlap between remoteness and social issues related to these population groups.

— *Illegally settled groups:* In many countries in the region, groups of people have migrated from their home areas and settled illegally in other areas, for a variety of reasons including poverty, conflict and social exclusion. Often these settlements are in urban slum areas, but may be on the fringes of other areas, such as national parks where there is a more reliable food supply. In such circumstances, government services such as education are not always provided.

— *Gender:* Gender discrimination against girls and women exists in almost every society. Women experience deeper levels of poverty and lesser access to services, resources, legal rights, power and decision-making than men. In many societies there continues to be a lower valuing of education for girls, lower expectations of girls, and the practice of early marriage, even if banned in law. These factors have the effect of directly reducing girls' enrolment and persistence in school, as well as indirectly influencing their educational opportunities through undermining their confidence and self-esteem.

In poor families, gender norms affect the types of work undertaken by girls and boys, and thus their patterns of school enrolment, attendance and completion. Many rural girls work particularly long hours on domestic and subsistence tasks within the household. In urban areas, gendered patterns of child work and exploitation are more complex. For example, girls often predominate in more 'hidden' forms of work, including as domestic servants and sex workers, whilst boys are often more prominent in the informal economy and are more visible as street children. Persistence and attendance of girls in education can also be affected by gender discrimination in the learning process, lack of facilities to manage menstruation privately, socialite attitudes to puberty and menstruation and safety on the way to school and within it.

— *Caste, social or occupational status:* Caste-based discrimination is significant in a number of South Asian countries, though in some it may go officially unrecognised. Caste discrimination, entrenched over many generations, has led to a combination of economic poverty and profound social exclusion—creating excluded communities with very little experience of the potential benefits of education and low levels of confidence and self esteem, putting them at great educational disadvantage. Those who do enrol face exclusionary practices within the school, related to their untouchability and the Hindu notions of 'purity' and 'pollution'. Other similar forms of status-based discrimination exist across South Asia, for example discrimination against sex workers and their children, which has a similar impact on the education of children.

— *Language, ethnicity or race:* Some linguistic minorities, ethnic or racial groups are disadvantaged in comparison with others in their societies who are considered the 'mainstream' or 'majority' language or culture. In South Asia this is particularly the case for ethnic minority, indigenous and tribal groups, whose cultures and languages are generally underrepresented, or not reflected, in mainstream institutions, politics or the media. Such groups are disadvantaged in education due to general factors of poverty and geographical remoteness and to a lack of congruence between the language and culture of the home and that of the formal education system.

— *Disability:* Children with disability now constitute the group of children most likely never to have attended school. They include children with general cognitive/intellectual disability, specific learning difficulties, physical/motor disabilities, sensory impairments, speech impairments or emotional difficulties. Many such children are hidden away at home, or institutionalised. Disabled children suffer from discrimination, the belief that they cannot learn, a lack of understanding (or even fear) of disability and a lack of knowledge of how to support disabled children to learn and develop, linked in turn to a lack of support for poor or isolated families.

— *Inadequate care and protection:* Because of economic stress or family breakdown, many children live without the presence of parents or other adult careers. For others these adults are physically present but unable to give children adequate care, attention and protection, or may even subject the children to active abuse. Other children have 'moved out' from their families, for example running away because of problems or abuse, being sent out to work, or being married off at an early age. Still others live in institutions that do not provide adequate care and support, including some in prison or detention. Many such children do not access a full cycle of good quality education. Even if they do go to school, their life situations put them at risk of poor attendance, low self-esteem, poorly developed social and emotional skills and thus of educational underachievement.

— *Conflict:* Conflict exacerbates poverty, gender-based violence, family breakdown and social exclusion. Children affected by conflict are at high risk of an undermining of their rights to education. Education services are often disrupted, security concerns affect attendance, the trauma of conflict very negatively affects children's learning capacity (and also their teachers' ability to work effectively) and increased poverty as well as loss of adult family members increases demands for children's labour. Children, especially teenage boys, are also at risk of direct involvement in conflict, and can become internally displaced (IDPs) or refugees.

— *Sudden onset emergencies:* Natural disasters also disrupt education, and those already vulnerable will be more at risk of not re-entering the education process, as new roles and responsibilities are taken on with loss of parental livelihoods when family members are lost or injured. Again, such vulnerable children are at higher risk of becoming IDPs or refugees.

— *HIV/AIDS and other communicable diseases:* HIV/AIDS is another factor that has seriously undermined children's educational rights in many countries, disproportionately affecting the poorest. Some children are sufferers themselves, whilst many more are affected by the illness or death of family and community members. High prevalence of HIV/AIDS exacerbates poverty and gender inequality and increases the incidence of child work, particularly for girls in caring roles. In some Asian countries, there are concerns that other epidemics, notably avian influenza, might emerge as a further 'exacerbated' of poverty and inequality. Both HIV/AIDS and other communicable diseases, such as leprosy and tuberculosis, carry stigma which can often 'chase' a child away from school.

Unequal Opportunities and Outcomes

The above discussion focuses on factors within society that create differential demand for education and differential ability to take the advantage of educational opportunities. However, equally significant—as well as more in the direct control of the duty bearers—are the supply factors that create barriers for some children in achieving their rights to, in and through education.

Building A Rights-based SWAp

Policy, Planning and SWAp Design

This section identifies and elaborates on the key stages leading to the design of a sectorwide approach in education. The order of these sections is for guidance only—in practice the development of a SWAp will be a complex iterative procedure which should be seen as a process of continual improvement rather than a linear exercise leading to a fixed outcome.

Achieving a conducive national policy and institutional environment

There are many factors in the wider policy, social and institutional environment that can support progress in the education sector towards equity, inclusion and rights. It is important to avoid staying in the sector—or government—box, being overly mechanistic whilst ignoring the political realities. Factors to consider include:

— Strengthen political commitment, human rights and legal frameworks for rights, gender equality and social inclusion.

— Develop poverty reduction strategies (PRSPs) that are based on a rigorous analysis of the linkages between poverty, gender, social exclusion and rights.

— Strengthen legislation that supports educational rights, for example related to the 'right to exist', birth registration, nondiscrimination or the status of minority languages; and improve enforcement and monitoring.

— Support 'good governance', transparency initiatives and civil service reform, which include strengthening of equal opportunities mechanisms and government-wide structures that facilitate mainstreaming of 'cross cutting' issues.

— Promote a general culture of respect for children and for education. Support an active media and civil society that promotes debate, challenges exclusionary practice and makes people aware of their rights.

— Strengthen structures and capacity for monitoring of political and economic change in order to predict crises and thus take steps to cushion children and families most likely to be negatively affected.

— Shape decentralisation processes so that they effectively promote equity and participation. Determine the balance between effective mechanisms for local level participation and the addressing of local level priorities, with targeting mechanisms and 'checks and balances' to ensure that poorer districts and regions are adequately supported and to avoid 'elite capture'.

— Support other sectors, with encouragement of synergist crosssectoral working. For example, this could include working more closely with social sectors to support children in difficult circumstances; and, conversely, encouraging the development of schools as focal points for children's services.

— Support national (and local) initiatives for children, gender equality or social inclusion, for example in getting research findings shared, or arguing a case.

— Keep schools and teachers non-political. Encourage the development of schools as 'Zones of Peace' in contexts of conflict.

— Intensify the emphasis on basic education and literacy in order to have an increased impact within poverty reduction initiatives across the sectors, for example agricultural extension, health worker training, media development.

Overarching policy directions that inform the SWAp

Sometimes, SWAps can founder through being created in a policy vacuum. Detailed sector plans or frameworks need to be informed by clear overall long-term policy directions and aspirations. To achieve equity and inclusion, it is particularly helpful to have clarity of intended broad directions in relation to the following areas:

— What constitutes 'free' (and compulsory) education? What costs are borne, and by whom; which educational levels should be free and compulsory; what provisions are in place to mitigate indirect costs for some children; what mechanisms are in place to claim these provisions; how free and compulsory education will be enforced.

— The overall goals and content of education, including an expanded definition of what is understood by educational 'quality' and a coherent vision for schools, using terms that are well understood in the context.

— What constitutes the 'sector'? Does it include pre-primary/ECE, non-formal and higher education? In terms of mainstreaming children and assisting transition, it should be inclusive of these levels, particularly as ECD and non-formal education are good strategies for bringing excluded children into the mainstream. Higher education would need to ensure that marginalised groups have access and can feed back into the development of the education sector (for example as teachers).

— The roles and responsibilities of different actors and stockholders at different levels in the education sector. These include school managers and management committees, teachers, community members, parents, different administrative officers and also other bodies involved in education such as NGOs or the private sector. These roles, responsibilities and relationships need to be clarified in relation to any wider governance changes, for example any ongoing processes of decentralisation or public service reform.

— Definition of comprehensive minimum quality standards being aimed for or—better still—a set of levels of standards to be progressively achieved. Some countries have found it useful to define a set of levels, so that resources and efforts can be focused first on those schools that have not yet achieved the fundamental level.

— Desired pupil: teacher ratios for different stages/age groups and geographical locations—with stated minima and maxima.

— The need for special measures within an inclusive education approach that includes both the formal and non-formal education systems. For example provision of extra teachers in classrooms where children have special needs, measures to reintegrate child soldiers, to reach street children or child domestic servants who currently cannot be reached by the formal system, or to ensure girls' access. Some of these measures need to be aimed at changing attitudes of teachers and other duty bearers. For example, in South Asia special measures are needed to overcome the discrimination experienced by Dalits.

— Equivalence of formal and non-formal education. Non-formal education systems provide an opportunity for those children for whom the formal education system is not appropriate to complete at least a basic education. However, such education must be seen to be valuable by the children and their families, and not be a second class system. It is in fact a strategy to reach education for all. For this reason, there needs to be equivalence with the formal education system, for example a certificate that is equivalent to a primary leaving certificate. Any qualification should therefore enable children to enter mainstream education at an appropriate point if they wish to do so, and also be equally acceptable to potential employers.

— Non-formal education needs to be part of the overall sector framework. This will facilitate children's transfer from non-formal to formal education, where appropriate, equivalence of qualifications, and allocation of resources. Non-formal education will probably always be needed to serve those not served by a traditional formal education.

— The roles and status of community and national languages in education. This needs to include clarity on their use at different stages, processes for language acquisition and literacy learning, languages for literacy and implications for teacher training/ professional development and deployment.

— The roles of, and interactions between, government and nongovernment educational provision, including the role of the state in quality assurance and ensuring universal access to quality provision.

Consultation and participation in SWAp design

A first requirement for a SWAp that·helps to achieve equity, inclusion and rights is that its design takes account of the stated priorities of the potential beneficiaries, especially those who are currently disadvantaged and excluded. This implies that they are able to participate meaningfully in its design. Thus stockholders need to be positioned as actors in their own development. Factors to consider include:

— When and for what purposes is consultation a need? This needs to be planned into the SWAp cycle. Processes such as particular reforms may require consultation with those implementing and affected by the reform such as teachers, school management committees, district officials.

— Who is included in consultation and design exercises? Stockholders consultation exercises need to actively include those whose voices are least likely to be heard and those who are currently denied their full educational rights. Children, both those in and out of school, can be actively engaged in meaningful dialogue about their education. Parents also need to be consulted.

— Who does the consultation? The undertaking of consultation should involve a range of stockholders at different levels, including those with strong backgrounds in community facilitation. The consultation teams should include members of the groups to be consulted and equally include men and women.

— Avoiding 'participation fatigue'. Repeated consultations can place unnecessary burdens on poor people, especially where the benefits of participating do not seem clear. It might prove possible to make use of recent exercises undertaken for other related purposes, for example by an NGO or for a PRSP or education policy reform. In this case, it is important to ensure that the education-related issues are explored in sufficient detail and that linkages to SWAp design are made explicit.

— Building in ongoing opportunities for participation. The full range of stockholders, and particularly more disadvantaged children and parents, should have regular opportunities for ongoing participation in educational management and monitoring at the local level.

Gender and social disparity analysis

If the system is to support the realisation of rights, then the SWAp design needs to be based on a thorough understanding and analysis of the range and patterns of disparities that exist in the context, the extent of different kinds of disparity, the dynamics and interactions and the underlying causes. It is also important to identify the groups who are particularly vulnerable in case of an emergency so that the response can be better targeted. Activities to consider include:

— Carry out thorough, multidimensional quantitative analysis of educational disparity, by gender, caste (or other social group), poverty level, disability and other relevant variables. Categories need to be agreed that are useful for identifying key relevant dimensions of educational disparity (not necessarily strictly medical, anthropological or linguistic), as well as being politically acceptable.

— Explore the causes and interrelationships of disparities. This could include SWAp-specific consultation exercises, existing research publications, specially commissioned studies and evidence from existing or previous policy initiatives or projects. One particularly important source of information should be studies undertaken by excluded groups themselves.

— Undertake both of the above at different levels. Individual schools and communities need to be able to undertake their own local analysis for responding to specific needs and priorities, and it is at this level that there can be active seeking out of the 'hidden' and 'hard to reach' children. Districts (or other intermediate levels) also need to have an overview of the main disparities that are operating locally, and how these fit into the national picture. At national level, it is important to have a picture of overall challenges and priorities, in order to priorities both specific geographic regions or population groups and particular policy areas.

— Analyse the political, cultural and historical context, in order to identify the forces that are influencing positive change in the direction of equity, inclusion and rights and, conversely, the forces and factors that might be obstacles.

— Carry out ongoing analysis linked to monitoring of progress and policy review.

The SWAp strategic framework/plan

A fundamental element of a SWAp is that there is a robust, comprehensive, coasted, strategy framework to guide the activities of the sub-sector or sector over a time-bound period. The framework needs to be flexible and implemental in the context. If the framework is to support a rights-based and inclusive system, then the following are important considerations:

— The set of strategies devised is sufficiently comprehensive to address the barriers to access and quality that have been identified during SWAp design, including attention to the aspects of a 'rights realising' system. There is balanced attention to rights to and in education, recognising their interdependence. Strategies are coherent and consistent through the use of unifying concepts and approaches.

— Gender and equity are mainstream across all general components and strategies, including those related to access, quality, management, teacher education, financing and institutional development.

— There is appropriate balance between general mainstream strategies for all schools or individuals and targeted programmes for specific schools, groups or individuals. For example, within the general strategy of provision of access to school for all children, there may be specific provision of transport/boarding facilities for girls who would otherwise not enrol for social or cultural reasons.

— Emergency preparedness and responsiveness, as appropriate to the context, is built into the strategic framework. The needs of children from vulnerable groups need to be specially considered, and suitable differentiated responses prepared.

— Non-governmental and private education provision is included within the strategic framework, as a strategy for reaching all children. Standards need to be set by government to apply to all providers, both government and nongovernmental.

— The framework sets the education sector (or relevant sub-sector) within the wider context. It is clear how the education system and specific activities within the SWAp will link or interact with other sectors that impact on education (for example health, gender/women, social development, water and sanitation).

— Scope for carrying out pilots and other small-scale strategies on equity is built into the SWAp; those which are successful can be scaled up and incorporated into the mainstream programme.

SWAp goals, objectives and targets

Education SWAps need to be based around a set of clear goals and objectives for a time bound period, to help ensure coherence and a common focus and direction. Shorter-term targets can also be helpful to ensure prioritisation of certain actions. Some of the characteristics of a SWAp that supports equity, inclusion and rights are given here:

— Objectives and targets are set with a view to an ultimate goal of 100 per cent access and completion of at least nine years of quality education. Objectives and targets are set with regard to the progressive realisation of basic education rights in the shortest possible time.

— Where there are disparities (e. g. By gender, income group, caste or ethnicity), disaggregated enrolment, completion and achievement milestone targets are set to focus attention on progressive narrowing of these gaps. In other words, success should not be judged only on increasing overall enrolment and completion, but also on improved equity and the reduction of disparity.

— Objectives are set in relation to 'access, quality and management', recognising the gender and equity dimensions of all three of these areas. While it is very common, and important, for SWAps to set goals in relation to improving gender equity in access, it is also important to consider disparities other than (and interacting with) gender, as well as to aim for equity in both quality and access.

— Targets are set for equitable learning outcomes, for equity in quality of provision (in terms of teachers, facilities, resources, etc.) and for all schools to reach identified minimum standards for quality and inclusion.

— Objectives and targets are sufficiently ambitious whilst remaining realistically achievable in the economic and political context. It is important to be ambitious and strategies should be developed to mobilise additional resources where a lack of these constitutes the major constraint. At the same time, real capacity and institutional constraints should be acknowledged and it is important that unrealistic goals do not lead to negative side-effects such as over-reporting of enrolment, the covering up of problems, or the use of practices that undermine the rights of individual children.

References

Crisp, Jeff, Christopher Talbot and Daiana B. Cipollone, eds., *Learning for a Future: Refugee education in developing countries*, United Nations Refugee Agency, Geneva, 2001.

Dahlberg, Gunilla, Peter Moss and Alan Pence, *Beyond Quality in Early Childhood Education and Care,* Routledge/Falmer, London and New York, 1999.

Fountain, Susan, *It's Only Right! A practical guide to learning about the Convention on the Rights of the Child*, United Nations Children's Fund, New York, 1993.

Kattan, Raja Bentaouet, and Nicholas Burnett, *User Fees in Primary Education*, World Bank, Washington, D.C., 2004.

Kerr, David, *Citizenship Education in Primary Schools*, Institute for Citizenship Studies, London, 1999.

6

Literacy and Human Rights

Literacy should be understood within a rights-based approach and among principles of inclusion for human development. The rationale for recognizing literacy as a right is the set of benefits it confers on individuals, families, communities and nations. Literacy is a right. It is implicit in the right to education. It is recognized as a right, explicitly for both children and adults, in certain international conventions. It is included in key international declarations :

- 1948: Universal Declaration of Human Rights
- 1966: International Covenant on Civil and Political Rights
- 1966: International Covenant on Economic, Social and Cultural Rights
- 1960: Convention Against Discrimination Education (CDE)
- 1975: Persepolis Declaration - 'literacy is not an end in itself. It is a fundamental human right'.
- 1979: Convention on the Elimination of all Forms of Discrimination Against Women (CEDAW)
- 1989: Convention on the Rights of the Child (CRC) explicitly recognizes literacy not just education
- 1993: Vienna Declaration and Programme of Action emphasizes the use of human rights -informed education as a means of combating illiteracy.

- 1997: Hamburg Declaration – 'literacy, broadly conceived as the basic knowledge and skills needed by all in a rapidly changing world, is a fundamental human right' (Resolution 11, UNESCO)
- 1990: The World Declaration on Education for All (Jomtien, Thailand)
- 2003: UNESCO round-table report Literacy as Freedom – literacy must be understood within a rights- based approach and among principles of inclusion for human development
- 2005: UNESCO B@bel Initiative

Literacy has been recognized not only as a right in itself but also as a mechanism for the pursuit of other human rights, just as human rights education is a tool for combating illiteracy.

Literacy, besides being a fundamental human right, is a foundation not only for achieving Education for All but, more broadly, for reaching the overarching goal of reducing human poverty. And yet, 140 million adults in sub-Saharan Africa lack the basic learning tools to make informed decisions and participate fully in the development of their societies.

In addition to being a right in itself, literacy allows the pursuit of other human rights. it confers a wide set of benefits and strengthens the capabilities of individuals, families and communities to access health, educational, economic, political and cultural opportunities. Yet, on average, less than sixty percent of the total adult population in sub-Saharan Africa can read and write with understanding – one of the lowest adult literacy rates in the world. The rates are below forty percent (the supposed threshold for rapid economic growth to take place) in Benin, Burkina Faso, Chad, Mali, the Niger, Senegal and Sierra Leone.

Importance of Literacy

Literacy plays a central role in preventing social exclusion and promoting equity and social justice. Poor literacy skills result in a lack of participation in education, employment, community life or citizenship. Literacy is key to inclusion, empowerment and improving the quality of life. Where illiterate people do not have access to literacy provision, this adds to their exclusion and serves to reproduce social inequalities.

When countries and donors priorities their investment in education, financially and politically, illiterate youth and adults are largely excluded. Within this huge group of illiterate people, many more women than men lack literacy skills. As literacy provision is often seen as the basic education for adults, major groups who should be targeted by literacy programmes do not receive sufficient attention. These include out-of-school children, youth and adolescents who, if not taken in charge early enough, will soon add to the number of illiterate adults. As many programmes target adults from age 15+, adolescents and youth (15-24) might find themselves in class with older learners whose needs are different. Given the age profile of population in many developing countries, it is imperative to provide relevant alternative learning opportunities to young people.

Among excluded population, certain groups in particular have been marginalised: minorities, indigenous population, migrants, refugees, nomads, prisoners, and others. Such social exclusion may be due to disability, to ascribed characteristics such as ethnicity, caste or religion (in addition to gender and age), or to 'acquired' characteristics such as poverty, income level, migration, displacement or incarceration. Socioeconomic status and 'class' are often determinants of access to quality learning opportunities.

It is difficult to consider one dimension of inequality in isolation as there are significant interactions between, for instance, gender and poverty in relation to literacy attainment. Promoting inclusive literacy, therefore, is not just about how to target literacy or schooling interventions effectively for specific groups but also about the impact that literacy can have on transforming traditional gender, socioeconomic, cultural and political inequalities within and between communities. Moreover, it is pertinent to link literacy programmes with development strategies that address poverty in integrated ways.

Literacy rates amongst indigenous population remain relatively low in many countries, as compared to the rest of the population. In Bolivia and Guatemala, for instance, over half the population is composed of indigenous groups and they also account for the largest number of illiterates. The main reasons are that (a) there are very few adequate educational programmes in the languages of these indigenous population and (b) the content of education pays insufficient attention to their cultural backgrounds. They often have to perform in the mainstream culture and in a language they may not have mastered.

Nomadic communities face similar problems regarding exclusion from mainstream education. Sedentary values are linked to notions of progress and shape ideas about how education should be provided. Becoming literate is often associated with adopting the dominant sedentary lifestyle and, to some extent, values that promote literate above oral practices. For this reason, mobile adult literacy provision - intended to respond to the nomadic lifestyle - is seen as excluding nomads from what they see as higher status education in formal settings. With growing numbers of children becoming literate through mainstream schools and in response to increasing interaction with 'dominant' cultural values and communicative practices, indigenous and nomadic cultures are changing. Approaches to literacy and broader learning which respect the nomadic lifestyle need much greater attention.

The literacy and basic learning needs of young people are critical for the future. Some particular groups of children and youth have been excluded from regular schooling due to the pressures of poverty or living in war-torn areas. The large numbers of children of school age who are not in school - currently 75 million "need alternative and often less formal learning opportunities.

In many countries, there are large numbers of illiterate or semiliterate adolescents and youth who are at the critical stage of entering productive life. However, they do not have the necessary skills to do so successfully, and most of the countries concerned do not have any well articulated policy to deal with this segment of the population. School dropouts, child soldiers, working children, street children and others who continue to be excluded from mainstream education, require literacy programmes tailored to their needs and circumstances. Literacy programmes for youth, most often defined as the 15-24 age group, should build on the specific needs, energy and enthusiasm of that age group. A focus on shaping their own lives and that of their communities offers a channel for their aspirations and ideals. Understanding youth subcultures is a starting point for addressing feelings of alienation from the values of mainstream society and thus a springboard for designing relevant learning. The process of learning literacy and the content of materials, when both are designed specifically for that age group, can stimulate young people to adopt learning habits which they can sustain throughout life. Within this group, the characteristics of adolescents, both girls and boys, need targeted approaches where literacy and numeracy skills are combined with confidence-building and skills for appropriate work.

Estimates indicate that about 70 per cent of poor population live in rural areas which have fewer schools and less well-developed opportunities for non-formal learning. Other factors such poverty, remoteness and cultural differences may compound relative disadvantage. As a means accessing new and wider sources of information, literacy enables rural people to manage their own development and take more autonomous decisions. The inclusion of skills enabling rural people to diversify their livelihoods - such as basic literacy and numeracy, agricultural skills, for off-farm activities as well as for micro-business management - contributes to reducing vulnerability and poverty. In many rural communities, other subjects such as human rights, nonviolent resolution of conflicts, HIV and AIDS prevention and treatment and other health topics are valued. Whatever the configuration of content may be, basic education should equip rural learners to continue learning, apply critical thinking and cope with the changes they will encounter in life. In rural areas, local artisans, storytellers, and others are human resources who can contribute to meeting learning needs based on the local culture and economy.

Globally, people with disabilities make up the world's largest and most disadvantaged minority and often live on the margins of society. An estimated 20 per cent of the world's poorest people are those with disabilities: over 90 per cent of children with disabilities in developing countries do not attend school, and the literacy rate for adults with disabilities is as low as 3 per cent, in some countries dropping to 1 per cent for women with disabilities. In many parts of the world, people with disabilities suffer from negative attitudes from their families and communities, and the education system may completely overlook them. Beyond the crucial questions of access, literacy programmes need to structure learning in ways that enable people with disabilities to make relevant use of literacy, with a firm commitment to avoid stigma and discrimination in learning materials.

Migrants often find themselves facing the challenges of a new language and possibly a new script which they must learn in order to live and work in their new environment. Skilled and experienced workers are unable to function at their previous socioeconomic level without the opportunity to acquire new literacy competencies. Migrants also encounter new literacy practices, for example in moving from a rural to urban environment.

The emphasis so far has been placed on enhancing access and it will be a major challenge for many countries in future years to use literacy as a means of tackling the sources of social equalities. Only a few programmes have explored new learning, teaching and curriculum approaches that respond to and build on the practices, languages and cultures of marginalised groups. Some examples may be found in Latin America, particularly in relation to indigenous communities. These examples suggest the potential to promote literacy as a process of engaging critically with existing inequalities, whether around disability, poverty, gender, ethnic group or language, following in the Freirean tradition of literacy for social transformation.

Sensitivity to cultural diversity means that a critical examination of the relevance and appropriateness of the curriculum is equally as important as addressing more structural obstacles to access such as, for instance, the emphasis on literacy by radio for remote groups.

Literacy Programmes

There are many ways to learn literacy as part of schooling, in non-formal programmes for youth and adults, or informally without any structured instruction. Literacy learning may stand on its own, be part of a package of basic competencies or have a place in programmes which teach other knowledge or skills.

Where the formal education system provides good quality basic education, it ensures effective literacy learning in schools. It reduces dropout rates and helps in retaining literacy and other skills. Literacy gets increasing attention as a particularly important area of the school curriculum because it lays the foundation of success in other subjects too. Children's home and community situations influence the education they receive at school. Schoolage children perform better if their parents have an education and if books and other reading materials are available at home or in the community.

For those who were not able to complete basic education successfully or to retain skills obtained in school, non-formal learning opportunities offer literacy programmes adapted to their specific needs. Non-formal programmes take a variety of shapes, of which some examples follow.

Equivalency or 'second chance' programmes provide young adults and out-of-school children access to an alternative route for gaining the same qualifications provided in the formal sector. Many Asian countries such as India, Indonesia, the Philippines and Thailand, for example, have considerable experience in designing and implementing equivalency programmes, and these are widespread in many regions. They are often more flexible and can better respond to the specific needs of the learners in terms of timing, and the pedagogical approaches used but also as far as content and learning material are concerned. To allow learners in non-formal programmes to join formal schooling again, efforts are made to link both systems and allow easy transition. In Madagascar, a Joint Malagasy Government-United Nations System Programme for the Promotion of Basic Education for All Malagasy Children offers as one of its components the 'school of the second chance' where the primary school cycle is covered in 10 months instead of 5 years. In Morocco, equivalency or second chance schooling, which caters for the out-of-school population and school dropouts aged 9 to 16, is one of the two main education programmes of the Department of Literacy and Non-Formal Education of the Ministry of Education.

Sometimes known as family literacy, an intergenerational approach to literacy learning has shown positive results as adults and children learn together, as programmes in Guatemala, Pakistan, Turkey, Uganda, and the USA have shown.

This approach takes account of the different learning styles and needs of both adult and child. At the same time, activities designed for parents and children together stimulate learning and the child receives valuable support. Family literacy also enable parents to engage much more with their children's experience at school and makes the links between school and community stronger.

In remote areas, neither formal nor non-formal literacy programmes might be available. In this context, distance education through television, video, radio and the Internet plays an important role. Information and Communication Technologies (ICTs) in general can be an interesting alternative to traditional modes of learning as they often provide for more individualised learning opportunities. ICTs are rarely the sole means of literacy learning, but they give support to learners and facilitates in a number of ways: stimulating awareness and raising motivation, facilitating learner-generated materials, providing input for facilitates, and gathering feedback on learner experiences. The explosive growth of access to mobile phones has enabled illiterate adults to use text messages to enhance their livelihoods: for example, fishermen in Bangladesh have compared prices through texting to possible market purchasers. A successful distance learning programme in Mongolia addressed the needs of nomadic herder families for stronger basic competencies and new skills to adjust to new economic realities. Using radio, print materials, district learning centres, 'core' learning families and itinerant facilitates, the programme made a difference to families nationwide.

In addition to formal learning in school or non-formal learning outside the formal education system, many young people and adults may learn literacy by informal means. This may involve learning to read certain texts that are necessary for work, learning through texting by mobile phone or using a computer for particular purposes. Informal learning by using literacy in practice is the way everyone improves their skills.

Literacy and gender

Two-thirds of the youth and adults without literacy skills are female. In some countries, this proportion reaches 80 per cent. However, the relationship between literacy and gender is more complex than these figures suggest. In Europe, North America, the Caribbean and some middle-income countries, educators are concerned about boys' relative lack of achievement in literacy. There is thus a striking difference between the discourse about literacy and gender in different regions of the world, which illustrates the importance of context in relation to the gendering of literacy practices and education generally.

In most countries of Africa, Asia and the Pacific, policy focuses on women's and girls' marginalisation from education due to the huge gender gap in adult literacy rates. This is also true in the countries of Latin America with indigenous majorities. Both structural barriers (inappropriate timing, lack of child care, lack of mobility, male teachers, etc.) and social factors (male opposition to women's education, women's low status in society, etc.) affect the participation of women in literacy programmes. Structural barriers are easier to tackle in the planning of programmes than social and cultural barriers which need a change in attitudes.

In Europe and North America where the trend disadvantages boys, gender inequalities are analysed in relation to the literacy curriculum which seems to be more 'girl friendly'. Assessments of literacy skills emphasise writing and reading which are girls' preferred activities in the classroom. In the Caribbean, the disadvantage that boys suffer reflects the socioeconomic status and circumstances of their families.

Research reveals a correlation between women's literacy and the positive development of the family and the community in terms of their economic situation, education and health. There is evidence that literate women, even those with relatively low levels of literacy, are more likely to send their daughters to school than those without any literacy at all.

Previously, literacy programmes tended to target women as a homogeneous group. Now there is more understanding of the differing needs of women according to age, marital status, location and economic situation. Many literacy programmes specifically target women in their roles as wives and mothers and adopt a functional literacy approach with lessons on health, child care, savings and loan clubs and income generation. In particular, poor women and women and girls in conflict situations need special attention.

Importantly, what attracts many women to attend a literacy class is the symbolic value of literacy and the self-confidence that learning generates. They wish to learn to read and write as a value in itself and learning about improved health and nutrition practices - aspects put forward by many providers - is secondary. The potential that literacy offers for increased status in their living and work situations holds greater value for many women.

An evaluation of approaches to literacy and gender reveals a deeper challenge. Most emphasis has so far been placed on how to change structures, curriculum and teaching approaches to ensure greater participation of the marginalised group, whether girls or boys, women or men. Many women welcome women-only classes as a safe space to discuss their lives and to learn new skills in a supportive environment. It is also more acceptable in many communities for women to learn literacy in places where men are not present. However, in order to challenge traditional gendered assumptions and change attitudes towards women, men also need to be included in the educational process. Promising examples come from REFLECT programmes which use a participatory approach to help men and women to discuss and address gender inequalities such as the gender division of labour and unequal workloads in their homes and communities. When gender equality is addressed holistically and specific programmes target both women and men, literacy programmes have an impact on transforming traditional gender inequalities.

Literacy for Poverty Education

Poverty is a complex cycle of deprivation, with a high level of vulnerability to changes in social, economic, ecological and demographic circumstances. It is not a homogeneous phenomenon, with a single solution. Whatever measure of poverty is used - for example US$1 or 2 a day to live on - the gap between rich and poor continues to grow. Moreover, a map of areas of high illiteracy in the world corresponds quite closely with a map of high levels of poverty, and literacy competence is an essential learning outcome contributing to economic development. In this perspective, it is not literacy on its own that makes a difference, but rather what it enables people to do in order to benefit from new freedoms and address poverty "accessing information, using services they have a right to and reducing vulnerability to disease or ecological change. Literacy is one of the features "but a universal one - that is linked with poverty reduction, economic growth and wealth creation.

Literacy, the Millennium Development Goals and Poverty Reduction Strategies

An analysis of the development frameworks informing both education and wider development policy can give an insight into how literacy is defined within international and national poverty reduction strategies. The Poverty Reduction Strategy Paper's (PRSP) conceptual framework for education is informed by two theories: human capital and an integrated approach to development. These two theories carry different assumptions about education: the former assumes that more education will improve capacity to raise income (i.e. more education = less poverty), whereas the latter approach, less prominent in PRSPs, promotes education both in its own right and for achieving economic, social and infrastructure targets in other sectors. Development policy frameworks have shaped and influenced approaches to literacy "particularly outside the formal school sector. In particular, the adoption of the Millennium Development Goals at the UN General Assembly in 2000 reinforced the prioritisation of funding for primary education. The lack of reference to adult literacy or non-formal education in the goals meant that the connections between literacy and poverty reduction were not directly addressed. However, literacy clearly has an important role to play in achieving all eight MDGs - for instance, the intergenerational effect of literate adults being more likely to send children to school, or learning about prevention of HIV and AIDS through literacy.

Education is a major element of Poverty Reduction Strategy Papers; however, a review of 18 PRSPs revealed that though most countries referred to the MDGs related to education, there was limited reference to the EFA goals that were not focused on formal education. Though many countries presented correlations between low levels of poverty and illiteracy rates and discussed illiteracy 'as a cause of poverty', some PRSPs did not contain any suggested actions to tackle literacy problems. This was partly due to the lack of any developed theoretical framework around learning and teaching to take the PRSP process beyond the recommendation that the poor should learn relevant skills.

Literacy in Conflict-affected Areas

A major obstacle to achieving literacy for all is the high proportion of countries that are experiencing or have recently emerged from conflict. Most conflicts today occur in poorer countries which often have the lowest literacy rates. Protracted violence and instability may mean that entire groups miss out on the chance to develop literacy skills.

Conflicts and their aftermath directly affect the provision of education. School buildings are destroyed, teachers are killed or flee and under qualified teachers are brought in but are often unpaid and untrained. Not surprisingly, families are unwilling to send their children to school when security is poor. Opportunities for non-formal education and youth and adult learning may similarly be curtailed.

The importance of access to literacy instruction for conflict-affected population, particularly women and marginalised youth, cannot be overemphasised. Building literacy is critical to protection, health and well-being during and after conflict, as well as to social and economic reintegration and development. Literacy programmes, especially when linked to life and livelihood skills, empowerment and peace-building initiatives, have the potential to improve human security, promote reconciliation and prevent future conflict.

Programmes in Sierra Leone, Afghanistan, Iraq and Kosovo show that integrated literacy, conflict resolution and peace-building programmes can play an important role in contributing to the reconstruction of post-conflict societies. Even more than under normal circumstances, it is crucial to use participatory approaches and elaborate literacy programmes in full dialogue with the affected communities.

A number of challenges to achieving literacy for all among conflict-affected population remain. Conflict imposes risks, responsibilities and burdens on adults and youth that may prevent them from accessing learning opportunities. Further, confl ict can intensify processes of marginalisation, increasing the vulnerability of certain groups or individuals whether because of economic status, age, gender, ethnicity, nationality, religion, disability, geographic location or some combination thereof.

Missed years of schooling during confl ict make it difficult for many young people to complete even a basic education, especially for those beyond the age limit for school entry, or build a solid base for further learning. It is critically important to offer learning opportunities tailored to the urgent needs of such groups. Despite growing emphasis on working with adolescents and youth, their educational needs typically exceed the number and scope of programmes available to address them.

Situations of displacement may present additional challenges as learners are often forced to adapt to a new language of instruction, whether in refugee or IDP camps or upon returning home. Where youth and adult learning opportunities exist in camps, literacy gains are not always sustained by appropriate follow-up strategies.

These possibilities and challenges highlight the need for additional investment in research, capacity development and programming, if literacy for all is to be achieved among confl ict affected population. Situations of reconstruction may open 'windows of opportunity'. As stated in the Global Monitoring Report 2006, "The necessary reconstruction of education after conflicts and other emergencies represents considerable potential for renewal and improvement. Policy change, for example, can be relatively easy, as old structures may have been swept away."

Where new opportunities open up during reconstruction a sustained commitment is necessary to make them meaningful and bring promising programmes to scale.

Making Policy for literacy

Designing literacy policies and strategies has to start with a process of reflection on the meaning and scope of literacy - a consistent definition is necessary as a yardstick for monitoring. Sound policies and planning need sound data - reliable and timely data on literacy levels of population groups, on patterns of literacy and illiteracy, and on the types, quality and outcomes of literacy programmes. Where this information is not available at national level, efficient planning and implementation are rendered difficult. Benchmarks provide a reference point for setting standards in implementing literacy policies.

In making policy for literacy, national development strategies, the Millennium Development Goals (MDGs), Poverty Reduction Strategies and other frameworks form the larger context, while education sector plans, gender policies and policies on linguistic minorities will shape literacy programming.

Policies in themselves are not enough - they must lead to feasible strategies for implementation and include sound projections of what the strategies entail in terms of human and financial resources. Making these resources available is a critical step towards action.

Feasible strategies will take account of which institutions deliver literacy - both governmental and nongovernmental - and how formal and non-formal education are linked. Partnerships at national and community level will be a feature of effectively reaching diverse population groups; as well as government departments and units, these partnerships will include both international agencies and community associations.

Strategies that are realistic will address the essential aspects of literacy in order to deliver literacy successfully on the ground. These include curriculum design, facilitates training, fostering an environment which encourages the use of literacy, both reading and writing, as well as assessing how local communities can manage and sustain relevant literacy efforts. No strategy is complete without appropriate and adequate provision for monitoring and evaluation, in order to measure progress made.

Many national governments have integrated youth and adult literacy into their education plans and poverty reduction strategies. These policies express a growing commitment to literacy and its links with other aspects of development. During the first half of the UN Literacy Decade, countries in all regions strengthened literacy policies, for example:

Brazil: Coinciding with the start of the Literacy Decade, the government gave fresh impetus to youth and adult literacy by establishing a new national secretariat. The Secretariat of Continuing Education, Literacy and Diversity focuses on population groups which had historically been denied access. There was a budget increase in 2005 of 25 per cent - part of a new concern for the quality of literacy programmes which also led to longer programmes and new monitoring and evaluation tools. States and municipalities in particular have raised levels of investment. Currently, there are steps to offer continuing basic education at primary and secondary levels to those who participated in the government's 2003-2008 basic literacy programme Brazil Alfabetizado.

Burkina Faso: With the goal of increasing the literacy rate from 28 to 40 per cent by 2010, literacy policy focuses on offering opportunities to young people and adults who did not benefit from primary schooling or who dropped out. Permanent literacy training centres and centres for non-formal basic education are the practical expression of this policy. Graduates from these centres grew by 24 per cent between 2003 and 2007. As part of the agreement with the EFA Fast Track Initiative, the government included funding for adult literacy as part of its strategy to promote EFA holistically at local level.

China: Having achieved major increases in the adult literacy rate over the last 15 years with over 90 million new literates, literacy policy in China now focuses on groups that experience particular disadvantage: poor areas, rural population, women and ethnic minorities, especially those with a population of less than 100,000.

India: The National Literacy Mission focuses on functional literacy and stresses female literacy. It has a target of achieving an 85 per cent literacy rate (90 per cent for males and 80 per cent for females) by 2011. Having stressed literacy needs among youth and younger adults, particularly girls and women, a major policy shift is to add the 35+ age group population to the target group for adult literacy programmes, and to focus on low literacy areas, particularly in the northern part of the country (i.e. Bihar, Jharkhand, Rajasthan and Uttar Pradesh), tribal areas and some states in north-eastern India.

Morocco: The National Initiative for Human Development, launched in May 2005, provides the policy framework for the National Literacy and Non-Formal Education Strategy, and this means that literacy action is increasingly integrated into local development projects aiming at the promotion of income-generating activities and health awareness, specifically for women.

Niger: The 10-year Education Development Plan (2003-2013) aims to double the overall literacy rate from 19 per cent (2000) to 38 per cent, with a focus on partnership with civil society, community participation, and improving the quality of literacy provision.

Literacy Policy

Governments set education policy - it is part of their responsibility to fulfil the right to education for the citizens of the country. A coherent policy and plan for the whole education sector is the best way to organise learning opportunities for all ages, within a lifelong learning perspective. Literacy for young people and adults who had no chance to learn it as children must be part of that. In recent years, and particularly since the Dakar World Education Forum in 2000, other stockholders have come to the policymaking table, either for the first time or in a more deliberate way - civil society, the private sector and bilateral/multilateral partners.

In literacy, the participation of civil society is particularly crucial since CSOs run so many programmes on the ground. They bring experience and knowledge to the table and can lobby for policies that respond to grassroots realities. The private sector, with its concern for a well-educated work force, brings a clear focus and some resources to the policy debate, for example on workplace literacy. External partners, in particular bilateral and multilateral agencies, have played a critical role in shaping efforts to achieve the EFA goals, but have shied away from engaging with youth and adult literacy. Whereas planning for EFA is the obvious forum to plan for meeting literacy needs, in practice this has rarely happened, or has not given enough focus to this aspect of education. It is time for collaborative policy and planning arenas to address literacy seriously, particularly at national level.

Benchmarks for literacy

A benchmark is a norm or standard which represents practices in literacy which will lead to effective learning and use. There are two reasons why benchmarks are useful in literacy. First, adult literacy provision is a neglected area in education and quality control is frequently absent or haphazard - thus benchmarks provide a valuable reference point. Second, literacy learning takes different forms in different contexts, with content and approach being dependent on particular circumstances and population groups "thus it is difficult to establish which programmes are effective and therefore worth investing in. Benchmarks provide an external marker for assessing how close a programme is to known quality standards.

When it addressed the theme of literacy in its 2006 edition, the EFA Global Monitoring Report commissioned work from Auctioned to propose a set of benchmarks. These benchmarks, however, are not universal and do not command unquestioning support from literacy professionals, and application of the benchmarks will vary according to context. Refinement and wider use of the benchmarks will require further testing and research.

Putting policy into Practice

Literacy calls for collaboration across institutional boundaries. Literacy is not only the concern of the Ministry of Education. Others such as the Ministry of Social Affairs, the Ministry of Labour, the Ministry of Women's Affairs, the Ministry of Agriculture, etc., often offer literacy programmes too or link other subjects within their concern to literacy because of its role as a tool for learning of all kinds. Civil society, the private sector and bilateral/multilateral partners also play a prominent role in implementing literacy and influencing policy.

Young people and adults have a variety of reasons for learning literacy and they use it for different purposes. Therefore, it is only natural that a range of ministries and agencies provide literacy for different groups. Special initiatives have integrated literacy into learning for farmers and fishermen in Morocco, border guards in Thailand, army recruits in Saudi Arabia and Mongolia, job seekers in the United Kingdom, village craftsmen and women in Bhutan, and rural development groups in Ethiopia. In some countries, particularly in South Asia and Sub-Saharan Africa, civil society organisations and NGOs are the main providers of literacy on the ground.

Coordination among these organisations and with government departments varies greatly from one context to another, but is crucial in reaching all groups with learning needs and in achieving sustainable results. Strengthening coordination is therefore a vital concern - the best scenario is where there is mutual support. In this respect, three important issues require attention if the quality and scope of literacy are to improve:

Coordination: the government is best placed to coordinate action, not by insisting on the same approach by everyone, but by enabling literacy providers to learn from each other and to complement each other's efforts. This needs to take place across the government ministries concerned, as well as with civil society, the private sector and other providers.

Quality assurance: governments have the responsibility for setting standards and monitoring their application, receiving feedback from the multiple actors involved.

Funding: there may be no central budget for literacy, so it is important for the government to allocate sufficient funds for literacy through all the ministries concerned. Similarly, external funding partners must be ready to see funds for literacy channelled through a range of organisations and interventions.

Often the best way to achieve coordination and to target funding is to concentrate attention at the local level, decentralising certain aspects of literacy work.

Promoting quality literacy

Literacy needs are highly diverse and no single approach or literacy method will meet them. At the macro level, three major components fundamental for improving the quality of literacy efforts emerged from the UNESCO Regional Conferences in Support of Global Literacy and from the studies undertaken for the mid-Decade review of UNLD: strong policies, evidence of what works emerging from sound research, and developing capacity. At the programme level, planning must take into account the many dimensions specific to working with youth and adults.

Setting the Macro-level Framework

Clear policies will provide a framework within which all actors can make literacy learning effective and relevant to learners in diverse contexts. Such a framework will avoid standardised, centralised or top-down approach, but rather be responsive to local circumstances.

Sound policies are based on solid evidence of what works best and of what does not work well. There are lessons to learn both from success and failure - the key is to make sure that learning from experience does actually take place. Currently, there is not enough research to supply sound evidence for policy formulation. While governments, civil society organisations and others document particular programmes, systematic research is harder to come by. Research requirements in adult literacy will necessarily vary between countries. There are many areas of youth and adult literacy which could benefit from more vigorous and extensive research, including:

- Factors at the national level: to optimise policy, implementation strategies, budgeting and coordination; to respond to linguistic diversity and changing literacy environments, including digital literacy and ICTs;

— Factors at the programme level: to understand what contributes to quality "including content, pedagogical approaches, group dynamics, facilitates, materials, language of instruction and other aspects;
— Learning purposes: to maximise the relevance, usefulness and impact of literacy programmes;
— Analysis of costs and benefits: to inform investment and resource needs, to improve programme quality and to demonstrate impact;
— Analysis of the costs of illiteracy to the society and the economy;
— Asynergy between children's education and adult literacy: to understand intergenerational benefits and reading acquisition, and the impacts of expanded primary education on adult literacy programmes and on the literate environment.

Further evidence comes from documenting and sharing good practices. However, a literacy programme which works in one context will not necessarily work in another. Rather, the exchange of experience sheds new light and stimulates new approaches. On the one hand, practices from very different situations can challenge existing patterns and stimulate change. On the other hand, experience from similar contexts can bring highly relevant perspectives, and this is why regional sharing can work well. The 2007-2008 UNESCO Regional Conferences in Support of Global Literacy provided a useful opportunity for this, and numerous examples of good practice from all regions of the world are available online at: portal. Unesco. Org/ Education.

The UNESCO International Literacy Prizes reward outstanding and innovative efforts in the field of literacy and non-formal education throughout the world. The three prizes are: the International Reading Association Prize, the King Sejong Prize (Korea), and the Confucius Prize (China). Since the beginning of the UNLD, these prestigious prizes have rewarded literacy projects and programmes - undertaken by governments and NGOs - in Bangladesh, Brazil, China, Cuba, India, Mauritius, Morocco, Mozambique, Nigeria, Pakistan, Senegal, Spain, South Africa, Sudan, Tanzania, Turkey, and the USA.

Capacity development is a sine quanon of quality literacy. Many literacy programmes work because of the motivation and enthusiasm of the people involved often from the local community with a commitment to its education and development. The skills that literacy personnel bring to their work are frequently derived from their experience in the formal school system, whether as teachers, trainers or managers. However, youth and adult literacy requires specific approaches, and the management of these programmes is different from running schools. In today's world, the scale of the literacy need and the complexity of programmes necessitate the development of greater capacity at country level - it is essential to move away from amateur and volunteer methods to a fully professional approach to literacy. Developing capacity must take place at both the institutional and programme levels.

Designing Good Literacy Programmes

A good literacy programme is one that is accessible, relevant, useful and leads to learning outcomes that participants can put to use in their daily lives and for further learning. Experience has shown that literacy for youth and adults must recognise their existing knowledge and experience and build on it. Good programmes will avoid treating youth and adults like children "they bring considerable life experience into the learning environment and frequently "demand that learning should be relevant, with the possibility of applying new knowledge and skills directly in their lives. These characteristics mean that the local context of literacy is critical "language, culture, social relationships, economic activity, religion, history, and future hopes and aspirations. They also mean that local ownership and management of literacy programmes are the best way forward.

Another important factor is the duration of programmes, in terms of the number of contact hours. There are models which claim that literacy can be attained with a rather limited number of "contact hours, which reduces costs. However, an Auditioned study concluded that most good quality adult literacy programmes involve about two contact hours twice or three times a week, for about two years or more - an estimate of the whole process amounting to about 600 contact hours over nearly three years.

The first half of the Literacy Decade has witnessed a good deal of innovation in pedagogic approaches to adult literacy, and some consolidation of approaches that were developed in the 1990s. There are now multiple pedagogical approaches used in adult literacy programmes and campaigns. All have their merits as well as their challenges. No single method can be considered the most appropriate to be adopted by everyone. Below are examples of existing methods:

— *Initial literacy:* including conventional primer-based approaches, family literacy such as 'Reading with Children' of Save the Children US, for example in Pakistan, Bangladesh and Afghanistan.
— *Community Literacy and Social Literacy approaches:* working with specific groups and their development needs, for example in India and Nepal.
— *Reflect:* focusing on local learning circles, community mobilisation and generation of local materials, in at least 55 countries.
— Methods based on the Labiate 'each one teach one' method, for example in Bangladesh.
— The Cuban Yo sí puedo method combining radio/TV and systematised instruction in some Latin American countries and other regions.
— *Critical Literacy and Legal Literacy:* combining literacy with other skills for social participation, in Scotland, India, Nepal, Nigeria and Sierra Leone.
— *Intercultural and multilingual literacy:* combining literacy and language learning with cultural exploration, for example in Bolivia, Ecuador, Mexico, Paraguay, Peru, Philippines, Senegal and South Africa.

Some approaches adopt a campaign mode, while others involve national programmes, or community-based initiatives. There are approaches that include the use of new information technologies, and specialist methods developed for working with people with disabilities, learning difficulties and dyslexia. Family literacy and intergenerational learning programmes have met with success, for example, in Pakistan, Turkey and the USA.

Assessing Effective Learning

'Formative assessment' has emerged as a useful way of both assessing learning and improving the process. This approach extends also to assessing how much and how well adults learn. Adults bring their life experience into the learning environment, and effective teaching/ learning approaches build on this knowledge. An interactive and facilitated approach has demonstrated its value in many contexts. While it is important in particular contexts to assess, and possibly certify, outcomes at the end of learning cycle, it is equally important to make sure that adults take responsibility for their own progress and that they have real input into what kind of learning processes best fit their needs.

Community Participation

Communities participate in literacy not merely as learners, but also in management roles. They may select facilitation, write materials, determine content or organise the programme. In Asia, Community Learning Centres (CLCs) have provided a focus for community participation in 22 countries. As a local educational institution outside the formal education system, they offer an opportunity for people to learn literacy together with other skills and may become a focus for development activities. Usually, local people set up and manage these centres, ensuring strong ownership of what happens in them. In terms of literacy programmes, CLCs give a better chance of aligning literacy more strongly with local development priorities, thus increasing its relevance and value.

In 17 countries of Asia and the Pacific, Literacy Resource Centres (LRCs) for Girls and Women develop innovative literacy and NFE teaching learning materials and strategies and provide information and training opportunities on literacy and NFE to NGOs, government organisations and field workers. The Centres are integrated into local organisations, with support from Japan's Asia/Pacific Cultural Centre for UNESCO (ACCU).

Developing Capacity for Literacy

As many international meetings such as the 2007-2008 UNESCO Regional Conferences in Support of Global Literacy have stated, there are three areas where a systematic approach to capacity development would make a difference.

Institutional Capacity

Sustainable work in literacy depends in part on the vision, resources and capacity of the institutions which coordinate it. For literacy, this can be a complex matter, since often more than one government department is involved, together with a range of nongovernmental and community-based organisations. There is a need for capacity in government to ensure overall planning, management and quality control, while at a programme level, it is organisations of civil society or other providers that require the full range of capacities to carry out literacy work. In order to sustain institutional capacity, it is essential to develop staff with the depth of experience to pass on high-level management and planning skills, mentoring and training others.

The national level is where the focus must be - with support for integrating literacy into development and education strategies. In implementing literacy programmes, the emphasis must be on capacity development in all aspects of literacy - from content development, material production and facilitates training, to management, monitoring, evaluation, research and planning. In these efforts, productive cooperation between civil society and governments will add value, based on regular and open communication and mutual support.

Capacity within Programmes

This includes a range of other skills and levels:

— *Managers:* planning the programme within a district or province, mobilising resources, keeping track of programme data, monitoring the quality of facilitation and learning, and compiling reports.

— *Supervisors:* giving support and encouragement to literacy facilitation, providing feedback and monitoring programme implementation, fostering community ownership, linking with other development activities, collecting data on progress on the ground.

— *Facilitation:* a linchpin for effective literacy learning, well-trained facilitators are crucial for the success of any programme.

— *Writers:* able to produce materials for learning, for entertainment, for instruction in useful skills and techniques, as well as documenting local life, culture and history.

— *Publishers and distributors of materials:* local publishing using appropriate technologies, and distribution using local outlets and networks.

Networking and community relations, accounting, data collection and analysis, and report-writing also form part of the skill-set needed for effective work on the ground.

Training and Motivating Facilitators

The success of literacy programmes largely depends on the facilitators and their efficiency depends on the training and regular supervision they are given. However, literacy facilitators are one of the least supported groups of educators worldwide. They receive little if any regular remuneration, lack job security, and receive few training opportunities and little ongoing professional support. This is a poor basis for major improvements in adult literacy.

Literacy facilitators are a diverse group. The great majority, especially in developing countries, come from the communities in which the literacy programme is situated. They often have no formal qualifications and no previous experience of teaching. Many of them are unpaid. A second group are qualified primary schoolteachers who teach adults after hours but do not get specific training for teaching adults. Literacy facilitators need professional training and status. Voluntarism makes a valuable contribution, but is likely to be unsustainable. A slow trend towards professionalisation can be observed, especially in developed countries with long-term professional training and entry qualifications for literacy facilitators.

Motivated, respected, supported and supervised teachers and facilitators are crucial to the success of literacy programmes.

Capacity for research and evaluation

Research capacities vary considerably between country and region. This is most clearly evident when comparing the high investment and capacities in literacy research in North America and Europe, where there are research centres and academic journals, with the resources of many developing countries. On a global scale, there is a need for improved research capacity for investigating all aspects of adult literacy. Progress in this area requires a major shift in approach, from the allocation of small-scale funds within adult literacy programmes for 'monitoring and evaluation', to large-scale investment in programmes of literacy research and processes of institutional development. In most cases, this will require sustained collaboration between literacy providers, universities, and other specialist research institutions, such as government statistics departments.

Literate Environments

The literate environment is a concept now being used to evoke the larger context in which people learn and use literacy. This includes what people write and what they read; it refers to who produces, publishes and distributes text and materials and how and why they do it; addresses the institutions that promote literacy as well as the purposes, languages, scripts, modes and methods of literacy. In other words, the concept is a way of understanding and describing what it means to be literate and what the wider connections of literacy may be. The literate environment is an expendable idea - one which offers ways to think about all the different aspects of promoting literacy in an integrated way.

The notion of a rich and dynamic literate environment was one of the three thrusts proposed by the 2006 EFA Global Monitoring Report as part of the strategy needed to address the literacy challenge systematically. Situated within the larger concept of a 'literate society', action to enrich the literate environment was deemed to include support for libraries, local language newspapers, book publishing and other related actions. This reflects the concern that people should not only acquire literacy competencies, but have the means and the opportunity to use them meaningfully and sustain them.

Up to the present, literacy policies generally have not focused on the literate environment, and there is more work to do to understand how policies might take the broader view that would address the literate environment in an integrated way. As a starting point, policy-makers would need answers to at least the following questions for a given context, although this is not an exhaustive list:

- What do people read? For what purposes - learning, information, entertainment, communication with others? Who reads?
- What does literacy give access to?
- Employment and jobs? A better job? New media and communication tools? Capacity to claim rights and services?
- What do people write? Who writes?
- How is it published or disseminated? In print or electronically? Who controls the channels of publication and distribution?
- How do people acquire literacy? In what institutions? Who teaches literacy and why?
- In what languages and scripts do people acquire literacy? What different purposes does literacy in different languages serve? How is literacy acquired in different languages? What are the gender patterns of literacy use in different languages?

The notion of a literate environment also has the flexibility to be applied at any level: individual, household, community/village/town/city, and for a country as a whole. In specific contexts, the promotion of a literate environment depends on an understanding of how different population groups define for themselves the purposes and uses of literacy.

The questions above relate to a variety of spheres of life - education, work, communication, media, and more - and, in policy terms, each is the responsibility of different government departments. It is therefore a complex undertaking to promote a richer and more dynamic literate environment - working with these multiple dimensions and fostering the cooperation necessary to do so is a key challenge in promoting literacy in today's world.

Something to read

'What can we read?' This is one of the regular cries of adolescents, youth and adults who pass through literacy programmes, frequently echoed by those who organise the programmes. The existence - or not - of materials that people want to read is a key parameter in enriching a literate environment.

Sometimes there is nothing culturally suitable for learners, or books are too expensive. In languages without a long written tradition, it may simply be that reading materials do not exist. Clearly, reading and writing improve through use, so opportunities to read and to produce materials are critical to sustained literacy for individuals and communities. Making reading material available is a key strategy in developing a rich literate environment - enabling learners to produce their own materials and become writers themselves helps ensure that the literate environment dynamic, motivating people both to write and to read.

For newly literate youth and adults, material should be relevant and familiar, with new concepts and language being introduced subsequently. Hence the local production of material by communities themselves is an important step, especially for 'initial learning' of 'absolutely' illiterate learners. Workshops to train local writers in different types of literature have shown themselves to be a valuable strategy. 'Learner Generated Materials' (LGM) can now be rapidly edited and reproduced using computer-based software, and translated into local languages or bilingual formats. These can include transcription of local testimonies, songs, folklore, epics and histories, for instance. Examples include the use of learner testimonies in Egypt, the production of CD-based materials in Nepal to enable local adaptation for linguistic and cultural variation, and REFLECT where participated material production is integral to the method.

Producing materials flexibly requires new capacities at local level and needs therefore to be part of plans for programme training, funding, management and delivery. This requires a shift away from centralised and nationally 'authorised' materials and curriculum toward more diverse and responsive approaches.

Many literacy instruction methods now advocate the use of authentic, 'real life' literacy materials "those that people need or want to read in their daily lives. These 'real' uses of literacy "and materials increasingly involve the use of computers and other forms of digital technology, for example mobile phones.

United Nations Literacy Decade

UNESCO leads the United Nations Literacy Decade (UNLD) under the slogan of "Literacy as Freedom". Launched at UN Headquarters in 2003, the Decade aims to increase literacy levels and to empower all people everywhere. In declaring this Decade, the international community recognised that the promotion of literacy is in the interest of all, as part of efforts towards peace, respect and exchange in a globalizing world.

At the request of the UN General Assembly, UNESCO is coordinating the Decade and its international activities. UNESCO launched the Literacy Initiative for Empowerment (LIFE) in 2005 as a framework for achieving the Decade's goals.

The UN Literacy Decade expresses the collective will of the international community to promote a literate environment for all, girls and boys, women and men in both developing and developed countries. The Decade was established for three reasons:

On a global scale, one in five adults cannot read nor write. According to the latest estimates, 776 million people are illiterate and two-thirds of these are women.

Literacy is a human right. Basic education, within which literacy is the key learning tool, was recognised as a human right over 50 years ago, in the Universal Declaration of Human Rights. This right continues to be violated for a large proportion of humanity.

Literacy efforts up to now have proved inadequate, at national and international levels. The Decade is an opportunity to make a sustained collective effort which will go beyond one-shot programmes or campaigns.

In response to these factors, efforts undertaken during the Decade are to target the poorest and most marginal social groups (including women) and to accompany initiatives to reduce poverty. According to the draft proposal and plan for the UNLD, "Literacy policies and programmes today require going beyond the limited view of literacy that has dominated in the past. Literacy for all requires a renewed vision of literacy…." In order to survive in today's globalized world, it has become necessary for everyone to learn new forms of literacy and to develop the ability to locate, evaluate and effectively use information in a variety of ways.

Resolution 56/116 adopted by the General Assembly entitled United Nations Literacy Decade: education for all evokes that literacy is crucial to the acquisition, by every child, youth and adult, of essential life skills that enable them to address the challenges they can face in life, and represents an essential step in basic education, which is an indispensable means for effective participation in the societies and economies of the twenty-first century. It also affirms that the realization of the right to education, especially for girls, contributes to the eradication of poverty.

The Education for All goal of increasing literacy rates by 50% by 2015 provides the overall target for the Decade, and the Millennium Development Goals set the Decade in the context of poverty reduction.

United Nations Literacy Decade - International Plan of Action

As part of its lead coordination role in the Decade, UNESCO prepared the International Plan of Action for the Literacy Decade. The International Plan of Action outlines the strategy and expected outcomes for the Decade. It proposes six key areas of action to implement literacy for all:

- Policy change to provide a framework for local participation in literacy;
- Development of flexible programmes;
- Capacity building for literacy workers;
- Research;
- Community participation; and
- Monitoring and evaluation to measure progress in the respective regions.

The Plan was submitted to the UN General Assembly at its 57th session in 2002.

UNESCO's Literacy Initiative for Empowerment (LIFE)

UNESCO's Literacy Initiative for Empowerment (LIFE) is a global strategic framework for the implementation of United Nations Literacy Decade (2003–2012), in order to meet the Education for All (EFA) goals, with particular focus on adult literacy and out-of-school children. It was created when it became apparent that existing literacy efforts would not be sufficient to achieve a 50 per cent improvement in levels of adult literacy by 2015. LIFE targets the 35 countries that have a literacy rate of less than 50 percent or a population of more than 10 million people who cannot read nor write. Eighty-five percent of the world's non-literate population resides in these countries, and two-thirds are women and girls. The UNESCO Institute for Lifelong Learning (UIL) is coordinating LIFE.

UNLD Mid-Decade Review

Halfway through the United Nations Literacy Decade (UNLD) 2003-2012, UNESCO has conducted a review of progress. The review has been a key opportunity to take stock and set a clear direction for the promotion of literacy between 2007 and 2012 in all key areas of the UNLD Plan of Action.

Taking place during 2007 and 2008, the review has used the 2006 Education for All Global Monitoring Report as a benchmark. It also used the momentum generated from the Regional Conferences to promote stronger policies and greater investment in literacy. The review aimed to identify concrete actions for the second half of the Decade. UNESCO has set up a UNLD Experts' Group which advised on the further development of the UN Literacy Decade as well as on other literacy related matters. The results of the mid-decade review have been submitted to the UN General Assembly in October 2008.

References

Alan K. Bowman and Greg Woolf, eds., *Literacy and Power in the Ancient World*, (Cambridge) 1994.

Knobel, M. (1999). *Everyday literacies: Students, discourse, and social practice.* New York: Lang; Gee, J. P. (1996). *Social linguistics and literacies: Ideologies in Discourses.* Philadelphia: Falmer.

Stuart Selber (2004). *Multiliteracies for a digital age.* Carbondale: Southern Illinois University Press.

Torres, R.M. *One decade of 'Education for All': The challenge ahead.* Buenos Aires: IIPE-UNESCO, 2000.

7

Convention against Discrimination in Education

The *Convention against Discrimination in Education*, adopted by the General Conference of UNESCO at its eleventh session (Paris,14 December 1960) aims not only the elimination of discrimination in Education, but also the adoption of measures aimed at promoting equality of opportunity and treatment in this field. It is therefore based upon two distinct fundamental principles which are embodied in both UNESCO's Constitution and the Universal Declaration of Human Rights, Articles 2 and 26 of which proscribe any form of discrimination and are aimed at promoting the right to education for all. However, the scope of the commitments entered into by States varies according to whether discrimination or equality of opportunity is involved. Under Article 3, the States undertake to take immediate measures with a view to eliminating and preventing any discrimination within the meaning of the Convention, preventing differences of treatment and forbidding preferences and restrictions in various fields. On the other hand, in many countries, the action to be taken in order to ensure equality of educational opportunity requires a complex effort which is not confined to education, together with a large budgetary outlay which must be spread over a period of time. The Convention therefore stipulates that States must formulate, develop and apply a national policy, which, by methods appropriate to the circumstances and to national usage, will tend to promote equality of opportunity and of treatment in the matter of education. The Convention came into force on 22 May 1962.

The Protocol instituting a Conciliation and Good Offices Commission to be responsible for seeking the settlement of any disputes, which may arise between States Parties to the Convention against Discrimination in Education was adopted as an instrument complementary to the Convention against Discrimination in Education. It establishes a Commission to settle possible disputes arising in the event of a State Party to the Protocol not giving effect to a provision or provisions of the aforementioned convention. The Commission consists of eleven members elected by the General Conference for terms of six years. The Protocol came into force on 24 October 1968.

Fulltext of the Convention

The General Conference of the United Nations Educational, Scientific and Cultural Organization, meeting in Paris from 14 November to 15 December 1960, at its eleventh session;

Recalling that the Universal Declaration of Human Rights asserts the principle of non-discrimination and proclaims that every person has the right to education,

Considering that discrimination in education is a violation of rights enunciated in that Declaration,

Considering that, under the terms of its Constitution, the United Nations Educational, Scientific and Cultural Organization has the purpose of instituting collaboration among the nations with a view to furthering for all universal respect for human rights and equality of educational opportunity,

Recognizing that, consequently, the United Nations Educational, Scientific and Cultural Organization, while respecting the diversity of national educational systems, has the duty not only to proscribe any form of discrimination in education but also to promote equality of opportunity and treatment for all in education,

Having before it proposals concerning the different aspects of discrimination in education, constituting item 17.1.4 of the agenda of the session,

Having decided at its tenth session that this question should be made the subject of an international convention as well as of recommendations to Member States,

Adopts this Convention on the fourteenth day of December 1960.

Article 1

1. For the purposes of this Convention, the term 'discrimination' includes any distinction, exclusion, limitation or preference which, being based on race, colour, sex, language, religion, political or other opinion, national or social origin, economic condition or birth, has the purpose or effect of nullifying or impairing equality of treatment in education and in particular:
   (a) Of depriving any person or group of persons of access to education of any type or at any level;
   (b) Of limiting any person or group of persons to education of an inferior standard;
   (c) Subject to the provisions of Article 2 of this Convention, of establishing or maintaining separate educational systems or institutions for persons or groups of persons; or
   (d) Of inflicting on any person or group of persons conditions which are in-compatible with the dignity of man.
2. For the purposes of this Convention, the term 'education' refers to all types and levels of education, and includes access to education, the standard and quality of education, and the conditions under which it is given.

Article 2

When permitted in a State, the following situations shall not be deemed to constitute discrimination, within the meaning of Article I of this Convention:

(a) The establishment or maintenance of separate educational systems or institutions for pupils of the two sexes, if these systems or institutions offer equivalent access to education, provide a teaching staff with qualifications of the same standard as well as school premises and equipment of the same quality, and afford the opportunity to take the same or equivalent courses of study;

(b) The establishment or maintenance, for religious or linguistic reasons, of separate educational systems or institutions offering an education which is in keeping with the wishes of the pupil's parents or legal guardians, if participation in such systems or attendance at such institutions is optional and if the education provided conforms to such standards as may be laid down or approved by the competent authorities, in particular for education of the same level;

(c) The establishment or maintenance of private educational institutions, if the object of the institutions is not to secure the exclusion of any group but to provide educational facilities in addition to those provided by the public authorities, if the institutions are conducted in accordance with that object, and if the education provided conforms with such standards as may be laid down or approved by the competent authorities, in particular for education of the same level.

Article 3

In order to eliminate and prevent discrimination within the meaning of this Convention, the States Parties thereto undertake:

(a) To abrogate any statutory provisions and any administrative instructions and to discontinue any administrative practices which involve discrimination in education;

(b) To ensure, by legislation where necessary, that there is no discrimination in the admission of pupils to educational institutions;

(c) Not to allow any differences of treatment by the public authorities between nationals, except on the basis of merit or need, in the matter of school fees and the grant of scholarships or other forms of assistance to pupils and necessary permits and facilities for the pursuit of studies in foreign countries;

(d) Not to allow, in any form of assistance granted by the public authorities to educational institutions, any restrictions or preference based solely on the ground that pupils belong to a particular group;

(e) To give foreign nationals resident within their territory the same access to education as that given to their own nationals.

Article 4

The States Parties to this Convention undertake furthermore to formulate, develop and apply a national policy which, by methods appropriate to the circumstances and to national usage, will tend to promote equality of opportunity and of treatment in the matter of education and in particular:

(a) To make primary education free and compulsory; make secondary education in its different forms generally available and accessible to all; make higher education equally accessible to all on the basis of individual capacity; assure compliance by all with the obligation to attend school prescribed by law;

(b) To ensure that the standards of education are equivalent in all public educational institutions of the same level, and that the conditions relating to the quality of the education provided are also equivalent;

(c) To encourage and intensify by appropriate methods the education of persons who have not received any primary education or who have not completed the entire primary education course and the continuation of their education on the basis of individual capacity;

(d) To provide training for the teaching profession without discrimination.

Article 5

1. The States Parties to this Convention agree that:

   (a) Education shall be directed to the full development of the human personality and to the strengthening of respect for human rights and fundamental freedoms; it shall promote understanding, tolerance and friendship among all nations, racial or religious groups, and shall further the activities of the United Nations for the maintenance of peace;

   (b) It is essential to respect the liberty of parents and, where applicable, of legal-guardians firstly to choose for their children institutions other than those maintained by the public authorities but conforming to such minimum educational standards as may be laid down or approved by the competent authorities and, secondly, to ensure in a manner consistent with the procedures followed in the State for the application of its legislation, the religious and moral education of the children in conformity with their own convictions; and no person or group of persons should be compelled to receive religious instruction inconsistent with his or their convictions;

   (c) It is essential to recognize the right of members of national minorities to carry on their own educational activities, including the maintenance of schools and, depending on the educational policy of each State, the use or the teaching of their own language, provided however:

(i) That this right is not exercised in a manner which prevents the members of these minorities from understanding the culture and language of the community as a whole and from participating in its activities, or which prejudices national sovereignty;

(ii) That the standard of education is not lower than the general standard laid down or approved by the competent authorities; and

(iii) That attendance at such schools is optional.

2. The States Parties to this Convention undertake to take all necessary measures to ensure the application of the principles enunciated in paragraph 1 of this Article.

Article 6

In the application of this Convention, the States Parties to it undertake to pay the greatest attention to any recommendations hereafter adopted by the General Conference of the United Nations Educational, Scientific and Cultural Organization defining the measures to be taken against the different forms of discrimination in education and for the purpose of ensuring equality of opportunity and treatment in education.

Article 7

The States Parties to this Convention shall in their periodic reports submitted to the General Conference of the United Nations Educational, Scientific and Cultural Organization on dates and in a manner to be determined by it, give information on the legislative and administrative provisions which they have adopted and other action which they have taken for the application of this Convention, including that taken for the formulation and the development of the national policy defined in Article 4 as well as the results achieved and the obstacles encountered in the application of that policy.

Article 8

Any dispute which may arise between any two or more States Parties to this Convention concerning the interpretation or application of this Convention, which is not settled by negociation shall at the request of the parties to the dispute be referred, failing other means of settling the dispute, to the International Court of Justice for decision.

Article 9

Reservations to this Convention shall not be permitted.

Article 10

This Convention shall not have the effect of diminishing the rights which individuals or groups may enjoy by virtue of agreements concluded between two or more States, where such rights are not contrary to the letter or spirit of this Convention.

Article 11

This Convention is drawn up in English, French, Russian and Spanish, the four texts being equally authoritative.

Article 12

1. This Convention shall be subject to ratification or acceptance by States Members of the United Nations Educational, Scientific and Cultural Organization in accordance with their respective constitutional procedures.
2. The instruments of ratification or acceptance shall be deposited with the Director-General of the United Nations Educational, Scientific and Cultural Organization.

Article 13

1. This Convention shall be open to accession by all States not Members of the United Nations Educational, Scientific and Cultural Organization which are invited to do so by the Executive Board of the Organization.
2. Accession shall be effected by the deposit of an instrument of accession with the Director-General of the United Nations Educational, Scientific and Cultural Organization.

Article 14

This Convention shall enter into force three months after the date of the deposit of the third instrument of ratification, acceptance or accession, but only with respect to those States which have deposited their respective instruments on or before that date. It shall enter into force with respect to any other State three months after the deposit of its instrument of ratification, acceptance or accession.

Article 15

The States Parties to this Convention recognize that the Convention is applicable not only to their metropolitan territory but also to all non-self-governing, trust, colonial and other territories for the international relations of which they are responsible; they undertake to consult, if necessary, the governments or other competent authorities of these territories on or before ratification, acceptance or accession with a view to securing the application of the Convention to those territories, and to notify the Director-General of the United Nations Educational, Scientific and Cultural Organization of the territories to which it is accordingly applied, the notification to take effect three months after the date of its receipt.

Article 16

1. Each State Party to this Convention may denounce the Convention on its own behalf or on behalf of any territory for whose international relations it is responsible.
2. The denunciation shall be notified by an instrument in writing, deposited with the Director-General of the United Nations Educational, Scientific and Cultural Organization.
3. The denunciation shall take effect twelve months after the receipt of the instrument of denunciation.

Article 17

The Director-General of the United Nations Educational, Scientific and Cultural Organization shall inform the States Members of the Organization, the States not members of the Organization which are referred to in Article 13, as well as the United Nations, of the deposit of all the instruments of ratification, acceptance and accession provided for in Articles 12 and 13, and of the notifications and denunciations provided for in Articles 15 and 16 respectively.

Article 18

1. This Convention may be revised by the General Conference of the United Nations Educational, Scientific and Cultural Organization. Any such revision shall, however, bind only the States which shall become Parties to the revising convention.

2. If the General Conference should adopt a new convention revising this Convention in whole or in part, then, unless the new convention otherwise provides, this Convention shall cease to be open to ratification, acceptance or accession as from the date on which the new revising convention enters into force.

Article 19

In conformity with Article 102 of the Charter of the United Nations, this Convention shall be registered with the Secretariat of the United Nations at the request of the Director-General of the United Nations Educational, Scientific and Cultural Organization.

Done in Paris, this fifteenth day of December 1960, in two authentic copies bearing the signatures of the President of the eleventh session of the General Conference and of the Director-General of the United Nations Educational, Scientific and Cultural Organization, which shall be deposited in the archives of the United Nations Educational, Scientific and Cultural Organization, and certified true copies of which shall be delivered to all the States referred to in Articles 12 and 13 as well as to the United Nations.

The foregoing is the authentic text of the Convention duly adopted by the General Conference of the United Nations Educational, Scientific and Cultural Organization during its eleventh session, which was held in Paris and declared closed the fifteenth day of December 1960.

IN FAITH WHEREOF we have appended our signatures this fifteenth day of December 1960.

The President of the General Conference *The Director-General*

Aim and Scope of the Convention

In our globalized world, education and the fight against discrimination remains a major issue. Thus discriminatory practices still exist today despite the fact that discrimination has no justification in international law.

Faced with this challenge, not only is education required to play an important role in the fight against discrimination, but access to all levels of education must be ensured systematically and without discrimination. This is one of the major issues involved in the right to education.

The right to education forms an integral part of the mandate of UNESCO, whose mission is to ensure "full and equal opportunities for education for all". UNESCO's Constitution establishes the fundamental principle of equality of opportunity for all in education. By the terms of Article I.2(b) of its Constitution, the Organization shall "advance the ideal of equality of educational opportunity without regard to race, sex or any distinctions, economic or social".

The Convention against Discrimination in Education gives expression to the fundamental principles of non-discrimination and equality of opportunity for all, as enshrined in the UNESCO Constitution. UNESCO has addressed the question of the right to education by affirming, through the Convention, its determination to apply the prescriptions and principles of the Universal Declaration of Human Rights (1948). The Convention prohibits any discrimination in the field of education "based on race, colour, sex, language, religion, political or other opinion, national or social origin, economic condition or birth".

The Convention against Discrimination in Education, as UNESCO's first international treaty instrument to have binding force in international law, draws its inspiration from two distinct and fundamental principles found in both the UNESCO Constitution (1945) and the Universal Declaration of Human Rights (1948), Articles 2 and 26 of which proscribe any form of discrimination and seek to promote the right to education for all. The aim, therefore, is, on the one hand, to prohibit any discrimination in education and, on the other hand, to promote equality of opportunity and treatment for all persons in this field.

The Convention, the result of a lengthy process involving a great deal of work and numerous studies carried out some years beforehand, was adopted by the General Conference of UNESCO on 14 December 1960. It should be noted that a Recommendation against Discrimination in Education was also adopted by the General Conference on the same date. While identical to the Convention in content, the Recommendation enables States that are not in a position to ratify the Convention to contribute to the fight against discrimination in education.

These two instruments are entirely consistent with UNESCO's constitutional mandate.

Like the major texts adopted by UNESCO concerning the right to education, the Convention is of major interest from several standpoints. Firstly, it reaffirms the principles of non-discrimination and equality of opportunity in education as set forth in the founding texts and gives them a specific content without which they would be mere "principles" and therefore difficult to apply. Secondly, it makes it easier to mobilize the commitment of States in the field of the right to education by updating the principles and the means of exercising that right.

The Convention, as an essential part of the body of international law, has developed the content, and taken into account all the aspects of the right to education - a fundamental human right at the heart of UNESCO's mission. In order to ful-fil that mission, the Organization has had to draw up a number of standard-setting instruments. It is through such normative action, in tandem with follow-up mechanisms, that the many facets of the right to education – "extending from initial or basic education to lifelong learning ..." can find practical expression.

The Convention, which entered into force on 22 May 1962, has been ratified by 91 Member States (as of December 2004). It seeks not only to eliminate discrimination in education but also to adopt positive measures to promote equality of opportunity and treatment in that field.

The Obligations of the States Parties to the Convention against Discrimination in Education

Implementation of the provisions of the Convention imposes a number of obligations upon the States Parties.

The Convention has binding force and the States Parties to it must incorporate its provisions in their national constitutions or domestic law. Consequently, they must give effect to those provisions in their national legal systems and in their education policies. In particular, the States Parties are obliged to take a set of measures to guarantee minimum educational standards having regard to the rights of parents or legal guardians with respect to their children's religious and moral education and the choice of educational institutions, in accordance with the provisions of Article 5.1(b).

The obligations of the States Parties to the Convention deriving from the provisions of Articles 3 and 4 of the Convention are particularly significant. These articles contain the provisions relating to the commitments made by the States Parties to the Convention. These principles having been set, the States that have ratified the Convention (with no reservation possible) must, under their obligation to implement the Convention, take all the domestic legislative and regulatory measures necessary to abrogate any texts that are contrary to the Convention and to adopt those that will bring their legislation into line with it.

Accordingly, Article 3 provides that:

"In order to eliminate and prevent discrimination within the meaning of this Convention, the States Parties thereto undertake:

(a) To abrogate any statutory provisions and any administrative instructions and to discontinue any administrative practices which involve discrimination in education;

(b) To ensure, by legislation where necessary, that there is no discrimination in the admission of pupils to educational institutions;

(c) Not to allow any differences of treatment by the public authorities between nationals, except on the basis of merit or need, in the matter of school fees and the grant of scholarships or other forms of assistance to pupils and necessary permits and facilities for the pursuit of studies in foreign countries;

(d) Not to allow, in any form of assistance granted by the public authorities to educational institutions, any restrictions or preference based solely on the ground that pupils belong to a particular group;

(e) To give foreign nationals resident within their territory the same access to education as that given to their own nationals."

Similarly, under the provisions of Article 4:

"The States Parties to this Convention undertake furthermore to formulate, develop and apply a national policy which, by methods appropriate to the circumstances and to national usage, will tend to promote equality of opportunity and of treatment in the matter of education and in particular:

(a) To make primary education free and compulsory; make secondary education in its different forms generally available and accessible to all; make higher education equally accessible to all on the basis of individual capacity; assure compliance by all with the obligation to attend school prescribed by law;

(b) To ensure that the standards of education are equivalent in all public educational institutions of the same level, and that the conditions relating to the quality of the education provided are also equivalent;

(c) To encourage and intensify by appropriate methods the education of persons who have not received any primary education or who have not completed the entire primary education course and the continuation of their education on the basis of individual capacity;

(d) To provide training for the teaching profession without discrimination."

The States Parties to the Convention are obliged to employ means to proscribe discrimination in education based on the grounds specified, in particular regarding acts specified in paragraphs (a), (b), (c) and (d) of Article 4, and to indicate, in accordance with the provisions of Article 2(a), measures taken to ensure gender parity in education; 2(b) measures relating to parental choice and the establishment or maintenance, for religious or linguistic purposes, of separate education systems or establishments; and 2(c) the regulatory framework for private educational institutions in order to ensure equality of educational opportunities and treatment.

The Convention also protects the right of national minorities to carry out their own educational activities. In accordance with Article 5.1(c) of the Convention, the States Parties are obliged to take all the necessary measures to guarantee a minimum level of teaching in establishments administered by minorities, while recognizing their right to use and teach their own language in certain conditions.

By taking positive measures to implement the Convention, Member States would contribute to the process of undertaking activities at the national level aimed at creating conditions favourable to equality of opportunity with regard to educational access and would reinforce the right to education.

The fundamental principle of equality of opportunity in the field of education is refl ected in the other instruments elaborated by UNESCO in that field, which develop the many different dimensions of the right to education.

Thus, the *Convention on Technical and Vocational Education* (1989) reiterates the principles contained in the Convention against Discrimination in Education; the *Hamburg Declaration on Adult Learning* (1997) establishes that "The state remains the essential vehicle for ensuring the right to education for all, particularly for the most vulnerable groups of society, such as minorities and indigenous peoples, and for providing an overall policy framework"(§ 8); the *World Declaration on Higher Education for the Twenty-First Century: Vision and Action* (1998) provides that "… no discrimination can be accepted in granting access to higher education on grounds of race, gender, language or religion, or economic, cultural or social distinctions, or physical disabilities" (Article 3 §a); and the *Declaration on Race and Racial Prejudice* (1978) states that: "Any distinction, exclusion, restriction or preference based on race, colour, ethnic or national origin or religious intolerance motivated by racist considerations, which destroys or compromises the sovereign equality of States and the right of peoples to self-determination, or which limits in an arbitrary or discriminatory manner the right of every human being and group to full development is incompatible with the requirements of an international order which is just and guarantees respect for human rights."

International Recognition of the Convention

The particular significance of the Convention is demonstrated by the frequency with which it is mentioned in other instruments concerning the right to education adopted by the United Nations and by its recognition under modern international law, not to mention the case law of many members of the international community.

The basic principle of equality of opportunity is refl ected in the International Convention on the Rights of the Child adopted on 20 November 1989 by United Nations, Article 28, paragraph 1 of which provides that "States Parties recognize the right of the child to education and with a view to achieving this right progressively and on the basis of equal opportunity ...". Furthermore, Article 30 of the Convention provides that "In those States in which ethnic, religious or linguistic minorities or persons of indigenous origin exist, a child belonging to such a minority or who is indigenous shall not be denied the right, in community with other members of his or her group, to enjoy his or her own culture, to profess and practise his or her own religion, or to use his or her own language."

Outside the field of education properly speaking, equality of opportunity and treatment is one of the basic objectives of the International Labour Organization, and this principle is enshrined in two of its most important conventions, namely Convention No. 100 concerning Equal Remuneration adopted in 1951 and Convention No. 111 concerning Discrimination in Respect of Employment and Occupation adopted in 1958. These convention codify the basic principle of "the elimination of discrimination in respect of employment and occupation" which must be observed absolutely and in all circumstances.

Resolutions adopted by the Commission on Human Rights refer systematically to the Convention and the principles it illustrates. Accordingly, resolutions 2002/23, 2003/19, 2004/25 and 2005/21 on the right to education mention all the grounds of discrimination prohibited by the Convention and urge all States "to give full effect to the right to education and to guarantee that this right is recognized and exercised without discrimination of any kind".

In addition, it is to be noted that the importance of the Convention has also been recognized in General Comment No. 13, on the Right to Education formulated by the United Nations Committee on Economic, Social and Cultural Rights (CESCR) concerning Article 13 of the International Covenant on Economic, Social and Cultural Rights. The provisions concerning non-discrimination and equality of treatment are set out in the section on special topics of broad application. Paragraph 31 thus provides that the "Committee interprets Articles 2(2) and 3 in the light of the UNESCO Convention against Discrimination in Education". In subsequent paragraphs, the Committee draws attention to specific considerations that make specific reference to and restate provisions set out in the 1960 Convention. The Committee confirms that the principle of non-discrimination extends to all persons of school age residing in the territory of a State Party, including non-nationals, and irrespective of their legal status.

The 1960 Convention has become all the more relevant in the context of the Declaration adopted on 8 September 2001 at the World Conference against Racism, Racial Discrimination, Xenophobia and Related Intolerance (Durban, South Africa), in regard to "action-oriented policies and action plans, including affirmative action to ensure non-discrimination, in particular as regards access to ... education".

8

The World Declaration on Education for All and the Framework for Action to Meet Basic Learning Needs

The World Declaration on Education for All and the Framework for Action to Meet Basic Learning Needs are products of a wide and systematic process of consultation conducted from October 1989 through January 1990 under the auspices of the Inter-Agency Commission established to organize the World Conference. In March 1990 in Jomtien, Thailand, some 1,500 participants met in order to address the critical importance of providing basic education for all. It was recognized that, following a slowing down of school enrolment in several regions throughout the 1980s, mobilization of new partnerships and support for basic education were urgently needed. A declaration and framework for action was agreed upon which encouraged action at global, regional and national levels. Each government was asked to set its goals and objectives on the basis of the Jomtien Declaration and Framework for Action. It was agreed that the crucial part of education is not mere school attendance but learning. In this connection, it was recognized that school enrolment would frequently give a false impression of the efficiency of a particular education system where learning achievement is often dismally low. The quality of education was thus presented as ultimately more important than mere access to schooling.

The World Declaration on Education for All underlined the importance of 'meeting basic learning needs' for all and set out an expanded vision and a renewed commitment. This expanded vision would encompass:

- universalizing access and promoting equity;
- focusing on learning;
- broadening the means and scope of basic education;
- strengthening partnerships.

The Framework for Action encouraged countries to set their own targets for the 1990s around the following six dimensions:

1. expansion of early childhood care and development;
2. universal access to and completion of primary education by the year 2000;
3. improvement of learning achievement;
4. reduction of the adult illiteracy rate;
5. expansion of basic education and training in essential skills required by young people and adults;
6. increased acquisition by individuals and families of the knowledge, skills and values
7. required for better living and for sustainable development through all educational channels.

At the central level, the Education for All (EFA) Forum was officially constituted on the initiative of the five conveners—the United Nations Development Programme, the United Nations Educational, Scientific and Cultural Organization, the United Nations Population Fund, the United Nations Children's Fund and the World Bank—with the following objectives:

- to monitor progress by countries and organizations towards education for all;
- to ensure that basic education remains on the world's development agenda (advocacy and information);
- to promote dialogue and co-operation among Education for All partners.

UNESCO, whose mandate gives the highest priority to education, offered to host the EFA Forum Secretariat, which was consequently established in Paris at UNESCO Headquarters in order to execute the programme approved by the EFA Forum Steering Committee. This Steering Committee has a very broad representation of all major partners at international level involved in different ways in supporting and developing education for all world-wide. The members include, in addition to the above mentioned conveners, UNDESA, the World Health Organization as well as other international governmental bodies, all major bilateral donors, a broad representation of leading non-governmental organizations and regional representation.

The fulltext of the "World Declaration on Education For All is given below.

Preamble

More than 40 years ago, the nations of the world, speaking through the Universal Declaration of Human Rights, asserted that "everyone has a right to education".

". Despite notable efforts by countries around the globe to ensure the right to education for all, the following realities persist:

More than 100 million children, including at least 60 million girls, have no access to primary schooling;

More than 960 million adults, two-thirds of whom are women, are illiterate, and functional illiteracy is a significant problem in all countries, industrialized and developing;

More than one-third of the world's adults have no access to the printed knowledge, new skills and technologies that could improve the quality of their lives and help them shape, and adapt to, social and cultural change; and

More than 100 million children and countless adults fail to complete basic education programmes; millions more satisfy the attendance requirements but do not acquire essential knowledge and skills;

At the same time, the world faces daunting problems: notably mounting debt burdens, the threat of economic stagnation and decline, rapid population growth, widening economic disparities among and within nations, war, occupation, civil strife, violent crime, the preventable deaths of millions of children and widespread environmental degradation. These problems constrain efforts to meet basic learning needs, while the lack of basic education among a significant proportion of the population prevents societies from addressing such problems with strength and purpose.

These problems have led to major setbacks in basic education in the 1980s in many of the least developed countries. In some other countries, economic growth has been available to finance education expansion, but even so, many millions remain in poverty and unschooled or illiterate. In certain industrialized countries too, cutbacks in government expenditure over the 1980s have led to the deterioration of education

Yet the world is also at the threshold of a new century, with all its promise and possibilities. Today, there is genuine progress toward peaceful detente and greater cooperation among nations. Today, the essential rights and capacities of women are being realized. Today, there are many useful scientific and cultural developments. Today, the sheer quantity of information available in the world - much of it relevant to survival and basic well-being - is exponentially greater than that available only a few years ago, and the rate of its growth is accelerating. This includes information about obtaining more life-enhancing knowledge - or learning how to learn. A synergistic effect occurs when important information is coupled with another modern advance - our new capacity to communicate. These new forces, when combined with the cumulative experience of reform, innovation, research and the remarkable educational progress of many countries, make the goal of basic education for all - for the first time in history - an attainable goal.

Therefore, we participants in the World Conference on Education for All, assembled in Jomtien, Thailand, from 5 to 9 March, 1990:

— Recalling that education is a fundamental right for all people, women and men, of all ages, throughout our world;

— Understanding that education can help ensure a safer, healthier, more prosperous and environmentally sound world, while simultaneously contributing to social, economic, and cultural progress, tolerance, and international cooperation;

— Knowing that education is an indispensable key to, though not a sufficient condition for, personal and social improvement;

— Recognizing that traditional knowledge and indigenous cultural heritage have a value and validity in their own right and a capacity to both define and promote development;

— Acknowledging that, overall, the current provision of education is seriously deficient and that it must be made more relevant and qualitatively improved, and made universally available;

— Recognizing that sound basic education is fundamental to the strengthening of higher levels of education and of scientific and technological literacy and capacity and thus to self-reliant development; and

— Recognizing the necessity to give to present and coming generations an expanded vision of, and a renewed commitment to, basic education to address the scale and complexity of the challenge; proclaim the following

Education For All: The Purpose

Article I - Meeting Basic Learning Needs

1. Every person - child, youth and adult - shall be able to benefit from educational opportunities designed to meet their basic learning needs. These needs comprise both essential learning tools (such as literacy, oral expression, numeracy, and problem solving) and the basic learning content (such as knowledge, skills, values, and attitudes) required by human beings to be able to survive, to develop their full capacities, to live and work in dignity, to participate fully in development, to improve the quality of their lives, to make informed decisions, and to continue learning. The scope of basic learning needs and how they should be met varies with individual countries and cultures, and inevitably, changes with the passage of time.
2. The satisfaction of these needs empowers individuals in any society and confers upon them a responsibility to respect and build upon their collective cultural, linguistic and spiritual heritage, to promote the education of others, to further the cause of social justice, to achieve environmental protection, to be tolerant towards social, political and religious systems which differ from their own, ensuring that commonly accepted humanistic values and human rights are upheld, and to work for international peace and solidarity in an interdependent world.
3. Another and no less fundamental aim of educational development is the transmission and enrichment of common cultural and moral values. It is in these values that the individual and society find their identity and worth.
4. Basic education is more than an end in itself. It is the foundation for lifelong learning and human development on which countries may build, systematically, further levels and types of education and training.:

Education For All: An Expanded Vision And A Renewed Commitment

Article II - Shaping The Vision

To serve the basic learning needs of all requires more than a recommitment to basic education as it now exists. What is needed is an "expanded vision" that surpasses present resource levels, institutional structures, curricula, and conventional delivery systems while building on the best in current practices. New possibilities exist today which result from the convergence of the increase in information and the unprecedented capacity to communicate. We must seize them with creativity and a determination for increased effectiveness. As elaborated in Articles III-VII, the expanded vision encompasses:

- Universalizing access and promoting equity;
- Focussing on learning;
- Broadening the means and scope of basic education;
- Enhancing the environment for learning;
- Strengthening partnerships.

The realization of an enormous potential for human progress and empowerment is contingent upon whether people can be enabled to acquire the education and the start needed to tap into the ever-expanding pool of relevant knowledge and the new means for sharing this knowledge.

Article III- Universalizing Access And Promoting Equity

1. Basic education should be provided to all children, youth and adults. To this end, basic education services of quality should be expanded and consistent measures must be taken to reduce disparities.
2. For basic education to be equitable, all children, youth and adults must be given the opportunity to achieve and maintain an acceptable level of learning.
3. The most urgent priority is to ensure access to, and improve the quality of, education for girls and women, and to remove every obstacle that hampers their active participation. All gender stereotyping in education should be eliminated.
4. An active commitment must be made to removing educational disparities. Underserved groups: the poor; street and working children;

rural and remote populations; nomads and migrant workers; indigenous peoples; ethnic, racial, and linguistic minorities; refugees; those displaced by war; and people under occupation, should not suffer any discrimination in access to learning opportunities.

5. The learning needs of the disabled demand special attention. Steps need to be taken to provide equal access to education to every category of disabled persons as an integral part of the education system.

Article IV - Focussing On Learning

Whether or not expanded educational opportunities will translate into meaningful development - for an individual or for society - depends ultimately on whether people actually learn as a result of those opportunities, i.e., whether they incorporate useful knowledge, reasoning ability, skills, and values. The focus of basic education must, therefore, be on actual learning acquisition and outcome, rather than exclusively upon enrolment, continued participation in organized programmes and completion of certification requirements. Active and participatory approaches are particularly valuable in assuring learning acquisition and allowing learners to reach their fullest potential. It is, therefore, necessary to define acceptable levels of learning acquisition for educational programmes and to improve and apply systems of assessing learning achievement.

Article V - Broadening The Means And Scope Of Basic Education

The diversity, complexity, and changing nature of basic learning needs of children, youth and adults necessitates broadening and constantly redefining the scope of basic education to include the following components:

— Learning begins at birth. This calls for early childhood care and initial education. These can be provided through arrangements involving families, communities, or institutional programmes, as appropriate.

— The main delivery system for the basic education of children outside the family is primary schooling. Primary education must be universal, ensure that the basic learning needs of all children are satisfied, and take into account the culture, needs, and opportunities of the community. Supplementary alternative programmes can help meet the basic learning needs of children with limited or no access to formal schooling, provided that they share the same standards of learning applied to schools, and are adequately supported.

— The basic learning needs of youth and adults are diverse and should be met through a variety of delivery systems. Literacy programmes are indispensable because literacy is a necessary skill in itself and the foundation of other life skills. Literacy in the mother-tongue strengthens cultural identity and heritage. Other needs can be served by: skills training, apprenticeships, and formal and non-formal education programmes in health, nutrition, population, agricultural techniques, the environment, science, technology, family life, including fertility awareness, and other societal issues.

— All available instruments and channels of information, communications, and social action could be used to help convey essential knowledge and inform and educate people on social issues. In addition to the traditional means, libraries, television, radio and other media can be mobilized to realize their potential towards meeting basic education needs of all.

These components should constitute an integrated system - complementary, mutually reinforcing, and of comparable standards, and they should contribute to creating and developing possibilities for lifelong learning.

Article VI - Enhancing The Environment For Learning

Learning does not take place in isolation. Societies, therefore, must ensure that all learners receive the nutrition, health care, and general physical and emotional support they need in order to participate actively in and benefit from their education. Knowledge and skills that will enhance the learning environment of children should be integrated into community learning programmes for adults. The education of children and their parents or other caretakers is mutually supportive and this interaction should be used to create, for all, a learning environment of vibrancy and warmth.

Article VII - Strengthening Partnerships

National, regional, and local educational authorities have a unique obligation to provide basic education for all, but they cannot be expected to supply every human, financial or organizational requirement for this task. New and revitalized partnerships at all levels will be necessary: partnerships among all sub-sectors and forms of education, recognizing the special role of teachers and that of administrators and other educational personnel; partnerships between education and other government departments, including planning, finance, labour, communications, and other social sectors; partnerships between government and non-governmental organizations, the private sector, local communities, religious groups, and families. The recognition of the vital role of both families and teachers is particularly important. In this context, the terms and conditions of service of teachers and their status, which constitute a determining factor in the implementation of education for all, must be urgently improved in all countries in line with the joint ILO/ UNESCO Recommendation Concerning the Status of Teachers (1966). Genuine partnerships contribute to the planning, implementing, managing and evaluating of basic education programmes. When we speak of "an expanded vision and a renewed commitment", partnerships are at the heart of it.

Education For All: The Requirements

Article VIII- Developing A Supportive Policy Context

1. Supportive policies in the social, cultural, and economic sectors are required in order to realize the full provision and utitlization of basic education for individual and societal improvement. The provision of basic education for all depends on political commitment and political will backed by appropriate fiscal measures and reinforced by educational policy reforms and institutional strengthening. Suitable economic, trade, labour, employment and health policies will enhance learners' incentives and contributions to societal development.
2. Societies should also insure a strong intellectual and scientific environment for basic education. This implies improving higher education and developing scientific research. Close contact with contemporary technological and scientific knowledge should be possible at every level of education.

Article IX - Mobilizing Resources

1. If the basic learning needs of all are to be met through a much broader scope of action than in the past, it will be essential to mobilize existing and new financial and human resources, public, private and voluntary. All of society has a contribution to make, recognizing that time, energy and funding directed to basic education are perhaps the most profound investment in people and in the future of a country which can be made.

2. Enlarged public-sector support means drawing on the resources of all the government agencies responsible for human development, through increased absolute and proportional allocations to basic education services with the clear recognition of competing claims on national resources of which education is an important one, but not the only one. Serious attention to improving the efficiency of existing educational resources and programmes will not only produce more, it can also be expected to attract new resources. The urgent task of meeting basic learning needs may require a reallocation between sectors, as, for example, a transfer from military to educational expenditure. Above all, special protection for basic education will be required in countries undergoing structural adjustment and facing severe external debt burdens. Today, more than ever, education must be seen as a fundamental dimension of any social, cultural, and economic design.

Article X - Strengthening International Solidarity

1. Meeting basic learning needs constitutes a common and universal human responsibility. It requires international solidarity and equitable and fair economic relations in order to redress existing economic disparities. All nations have valuable knowledge and experiences to share for designing effective educational policies and programmes.
2. Substantial and long-term increases in resources for basic education will be needed. The world community, including intergovernmental agencies and institutions, has an urgent responsibility to alleviate the constraints that prevent some countries from achieving the goal of education for all. It will mean the adoption of measures that augment the national budgets of the poorest countries or serve to relieve heavy debt burdens. Creditors and debtors must seek innovative and equitable formulae to resolve these burdens, since the capacity of many developing countries to respond effectively to education and other basic needs will be greatly helped by finding solutions to the debt problem.
3. Basic learning needs of adults and children must be addressed wherever they exist. Least developed and low-income countries have special needs which require priority in international support for basic education in the 1990s.
4. All nations must also work together to resolve conflicts and strife, to end military occupations, and to settle displaced populations, or to

facilitate their return to their countries of origin, and ensure that their basic learning needs are met. Only a stable and peaceful environment can create the conditions in which every human being, child and adult alike, may benefit from the goals of this Declaration.

We, the participants in the World Conference on Education for All, reaffirm the right of all people to education. This is the foundation of our determination, singly and together, to ensure education for all.

We commit ourselves to act cooperatively through our own spheres of responsibility, taking all necessary steps to achieve the goals of education for all. Together we call on governments, concerned organizations and individuals to join in this urgent undertaking.

The basic learning needs of all can and must be met. There can be no more meaningful way to begin the International Literacy Year, to move forward the goals of the United Nations Decade of Disabled Persons (1983-92), the World Decade for Cultural Development (1988-97), the Fourth United Nations Development Decade (1991-2000), of the Convention on the Elimination of Discrimination against Women and the Forward Looking Strategies for the Advancement of Women, and of the Convention on the Rights of the Child. There has never been a more propitious time to commit ourselves to providing basic learning opportunities for all the people of the world.

We adopt, therefore, this World Declaration on Education for All: Meeting Basic Learning Needs and agree on the Framework for Action to Meet Basic Learning Needs, to achieve the goals set forth in this Declaration.

Framework For Action: Meeting Basic Learning Needs—Guidelines for implementing the World Declaration on Education for All

This Framework for Action to Meet Basic Learning Needs derives from the World Declaration on Education for All, adopted by the World Conference on Education for All, which brought together representatives of governments, international and bilateral development agencies, and non-governmental organizations. Based on the best collective knowledge and the commitment of these partners, the Framework is intended as a reference and guide for national governments, international organizations, bilateral aid agencies, non-governmental organizations (NGOs), and all those committed to the goal of Education for All in formulating their own plans of action for implementing the World Declaration. It describes three broad levels of concerted action:

- direct action within individual countries,
- co-operation among groups of countries sharing certain characteristics and concerns, and
- multilateral and bilateral co-operation in the world community.

Individual countries and groups of countries, as well as international, regional and national organizations, may use the Framework to develop their own specific plans of action and programmes in line with their particular objectives, mandates and constituencies. This indeed has been the case in the ten-year experience of the UNESCO Major Project on Education for Latin America and the Caribbean. Further examples of such related initiatives are the UNESCO Plan of Action for the Eradication of Illiteracy by the Year 2000, adopted by the UNESCO General Conference at its 25th session (1989); the ISESCO Special Programme (1990); the current review by the World Bank of its policy for primary education; and USAID's programme for Advancing Basic Education and Literacy. Insofar as such plans of action, policies and programmes are consistent with this Framework, efforts throughout the world to meet basic learning needs will converge and facilitate co-operation.

While countries have many common concerns in meeting the basic learning needs of their populations, these concerns do, of course, vary in nature and intensity from country to country depending on the actual status of basic education as well as the cultural and socio-economic context. Globally by the year 2000, if enrolment rates remain at current levels, there will be more than 160 million children without access to primary schooling simply because of population growth. In much of sub-Saharan Africa and in many low income countries elsewhere, the provision of universal primary education for rapidly growing numbers of children remains a long-term challenge. Despite progress in promoting adult literacy, most of these same countries still have high illiteracy rates, while the numbers of functionally illiterate adults continue to grow and constitute a major social problem in much of Asia and the Arab States, as well as in Europe and North America. Many people are denied equal access on grounds of race, gender, language, disability, ethnic origin, or political convictions. In addition, high drop-out rates and poor learning achievement are commonly recognized problems throughout the world. These very general characterizations illustrate the need for decisive action on a large scale, with clear goals and targets.

Goals and Targets

The ultimate goal affirmed by the World Declaration on Education for All is to meet the basic learning needs of all children, youth, and adults. The long-term effort to attain that goal can be maintained more effectively if intermediate goals are established and progress toward these goals is measured. Appropriate authorities at the national and subnational levels may establish such intermediate goals, taking into account the objectives of the Declaration as well as overall national development goals and priorities.

- Intermediate goals can usefully be formulated as specific targets within national and subnational plans for educational development. Such targets usually
- specify expected attainments and outcomes in reference to terminal performance specifications within an appropriate time-frame,
- specify priority categories (e.g. the poor, the disabled), and
- are formulated in terms such that progress toward them can be observed and measured. These targets represent a "floor" (but not a "ceiling") for the continued development of education programmes and services.

Time-bound targets convey a sense of urgency and serve as a reference against which indices of implementation and accomplishment can be compared. As societal conditions change, plans and targets can be reviewed and updated. Where basic education efforts must be focussed to meet the needs of specific social groups or population categories, linking targets to such priority categories of learners can help to maintain the attention of planners, practitioners and evaluators on meeting the needs of these learners. Observable and measurable targets assist in the objective evaluation of progress.

Targets need not be based solely on current trends and resources. Initial targets can reflect a realistic appraisal of the possibilities presented by the Declaration to mobilize additional human, organizational, and financial capacities within a cooperative commitment to human development. Countries with low literacy and school enrolment rates, and very limited national resources, will need to make hard choices in establishing national targets within a realistic timeframe.

Countries may wish to set their own targets for the 1990s in terms of the following proposed dimensions:

- Expansion of early childhood care and developmental activities, including family and community interventions, especially for poor, disadvantaged and disabled children;
- Universal access to, and completion of, primary education (or whatever higher level of education is considered as "basic") by the year 2000;
- Improvement in learning achievement such that an agreed percentage of an appropriate age cohort (e. g. 80% of 14 year-olds) attains or surpasses a defined level of necessary learning achievement;
- Reduction of the adult illiteracy rate (the appropriate age group to be determined in each country) to, say, one-half its 1990 level by the year 2000, with sufficient emphasis on female literacy to significantly reduce the current disparity between male and female illiteracy rates;
- Expansion of provisions of basic education and training in other essential skills required by youth and adults, with programme effectiveness assessed in terms of behavioural changes and impacts on health, employment and productivity;
- Increased acquisition by individuals and families of the knowledge, skills and values required for better living and sound and sustainable development, made available through all education channels including the mass media, other forms of modern and traditional communication, and social action, with effectiveness assessed in terms of behavioural change.

Levels of performance in the above should be established, when possible. These should be consistent with the focus of basic education both on universalization of access and on learning acquisition, as joint and inseparable concerns. In all cases, the performance targets should include equity by gender. However, setting levels of performance and of the proportions of participants who are expected to reach these levels in specific basic education programmes must be an autonomous task of individual countries.

Principles of Action

The first step consists in identifying, preferably through an active participatory process involving groups and the community, the traditional learning systems which exist in the society, and the actual demand for basic education services, whether expressed in terms of formal schooling or non-formal education programmes. Addressing the basic learning needs of all means: early childhood care and development opportunities; relevant, quality primary schooling or equivalent out-of-school education for children; and literacy, basic knowledge and life skills training for youth and adults. It also means capitalizing on the use of traditional and modern information media and technologies to educate the public on matters of social concern and to support basic education activities. These complementary components of basic education need to be designed to ensure equitable access, sustained participation, and effective learning achievement. Meeting basic learning needs also involves action to enhance the family and community environments for learning and to correlate basic education and the larger socio-economic context. The complementarity and synergistic effects of related human resources investments in population, health and nutrition should be recognized.

Because basic learning needs are complex and diverse, meeting them requires multisectoral strategies and action which are integral to overall development efforts. Many partners must join with the education authorities, teachers, and other educational personnel in developing basic education if it is to be seen, once again, as the responsibility of the entire society. This implies the active involvement of a wide range of partners

Because basic learning needs are complex and diverse, meeting them requires

- families, teachers, communities, private enterprises (including those involved in information and communication), government and non-governmental organizations, institutions, etc.
- in planning, managing and evaluating the many forms of basic education.

Current practices and institutional arrangements for delivering basic education, and the existing mechanisms for co-operation in this regard, should be carefully evaluated before new institutions or mechanisms are created. Rehabilitating dilapidated schools and improving the training and working conditions of teachers and literacy workers, building on existing learning schemes, are likely to bring greater and more immediate returns on investment than attempts to start afresh.

Great potential lies in possible joint actions with non-governmental organizations on all levels. These autonomous bodies, while advocating independent and critical public views, might play roles in monitoring, research, training and material production for the sake of non-formal and life-long educational processes.

The primary purpose of bilateral and multilateral co-operation should appear in a true spirit of partnership - it should not be to transplant familiar models, but to help develop the endogenous capacities of national authorities and their in-country partners to meet basic learning needs effectively. Action and resources should be used to strengthen essential features of basic education services, focussing on managerial and analytical capacities, which can stimulate further developments. International co-operation and funding can be particularly valuable in supporting major reforms or sectoral adjustments, and in helping to develop and test innovative approaches to teaching and management, where new approaches need to be tried and/or extraordinary levels of expenditure are involved and where knowledge of relevant experiences elsewhere can often be useful.

International co-operation should give priority to the countries currently least able to meet the basic learning needs of their populations. It should also help countries redress their internal disparities in educational opportunity. Because two-thirds of illiterate adults and out-of-school children are female, wherever such inequities exist, a most urgent priority is to improve access to education for girls and women, and to remove every obstacle that hampers their active participation.

Priority Action at National Level

Progress in meeting the basic learning needs of all will depend ultimately on the actions taken within individual countries. While regional and international co-operation and financial assistance can support and facilitate such actions, government authorities, communities and their several in-country partners are the key agents for improvement, and national governments have the main responsibility for coordinating the effective use of internal and external resources. Given the diversity of countries' situations, capacities and development plans and goals, this Framework can only suggest certain areas that merit priority attention. Each country will determine for itself what specific actions beyond current efforts may be necessary in each of the following areas.

Assessing Needs and Planning Action

To achieve the targets set for itself, each country is encouraged to develop or update comprehensive and long-term plans of action (from local to national levels) to meet the learning needs it has defined as "basic". Within the context of existing education-sector and general development plans and strategies, a plan of action for basic education for all will necessarily be multisectoral, to guide activities in the sectors involved (e. g. education, information, communications/ media, labour, agriculture, health). Models of strategic planning, by definition, vary. However, most of them involve constant adjustments among objectives, resources, actions, and constraints. At the national level, objectives are normally couched in broad terms and central government resources are also determined, while actions are taken at the local level. Thus, local plans in the same national setting will naturally differ not only in scope but in content. National and subnational frameworks and local plans should allow for varying conditions and circumstances. These might, therefore, specify:

- studies for the evaluation of existing systems (analysis of problems, failures and successes):
- the basic learning needs to be met, including cognitive skills, values, attitudes, as well as subject knowledge;
- the languages to be used in education
- means to promote the demand for, and broadscale participation in, basic education;
- modalities to mobilize family and local community support;
- targets and specific objectives;
- the required capital and recurrent resources, duly costed, as well as possible measures for cost effectiveness;
- indicators and procedures to be used to monitor progress in reaching the targets;
- priorities for using resources and for developing services and programmes over time;
- the priority groups that require special measures;
- the kinds of expertise required to implement the plan;
- institutional and administrative arrangements needed;

- modalities for ensuring information sharing among formal and other basic education programmes; and
- an implementation strategy and timetable.

Developing a Supportive Policy Environment

A multisectoral plan of action implies adjustments to sectoral policies so that sectors interact in a mutually supportive and beneficial manner in line with the country's overall development goals. Action to meet basic learning needs should be an integral part of a country's national and subnational development strategies, which should reflect the priority given to human development. Legislative and other measures may be needed to promote and facilitate co-operation among the various partners involved. Advocacy and public information about basic education are important in creating a supportive policy environment at national, subnational and local levels.

Four specific steps that merit attention are:

- initiation of national and subnational level activities to create a broad, public recommitment to the goal of education for all;
- reduction of inefficiency in the public sector and exploitative practices in the private sector;
- provision of improved training for public administrators and of incentives to retain qualified women and men in public service; and
- provision of measures to encourage wider participation in the design and implementation of basic education programmes.

Designing Policies to Improve Basic Education

The preconditions for educational quality, equity and efficiency, are set in the early childhood years, making attention to early childhood care and development essential to the achievement of basic education goals. Basic education must correspond to actual needs, interests, and problems of the participants in the learning process. The relevance of curricula could be enhanced by linking literacy and numeracy skills and scientific concepts with learners' concerns and earlier experiences, for example, nutrition, health, and work. While many needs vary considerably within and among countries, and therefore much of a curriculum should be sensitive to local conditions, there are also many universal needs and shared concerns which should be addressed in education curricula and in educational messages. Issues such as protecting the environment, achieving a balance between population and resources, slowing the spread of AIDS, and preventing drug abuse are everyone's issues.

Specific strategies addressed to improve the conditions of schooling may focus on: learners and the learning process, personnel (teachers, administrators, others), curriculum and learning assessment, materials and physical facilities. Such strategies should be conducted in an integrated manner; their design, management, and evaluation should take into account the acquisition of knowledge and problem-solving skills as well as the social, cultural, and ethical dimensions of human development.

Depending on the outcomes desired, teachers have to be trained accordingly, whilst benefiting from in-service programmes as well as other incentives of opportunity which put a premium on the achievement of these outcomes; curriculum and assessment must reflect a variety of criteria while materials - and conceivably buildings and facilities as well - must be adapted along the same lines.

In some countries, the strategy may include ways to improve conditions for teaching and learning such that absenteeism is reduced and learning time increased. In order to meet the educational needs of groups not covered by formal schooling, appropriate strategies are needed for non-formal education. These include but go far beyond the aspects described above, but may also give special attention to the need for coordination with other forms of education, to the support of all interested partners, to sustained financial resources and to full community participation.

An example for such an approach applied to literacy can be found in UNESCO's Plan of Action for the Eradication of Illiteracy by the Year 2000. Other strategies still may rely on the media to meet the broader education needs of the entire community. Such strategies need to be linked to formal education, non-formal education or a combination of both. The use of the communications media holds a tremendous potential to educate the public and to share important information among those who need to know.

Expanding access to basic education of satisfactory quality is an effective way to improve equity. Ensuring that girls and women stay involved in basic education activities until they have attained at least the agreed necessary level of learning, can be encouraged through special measures designed, wherever possible, in consultation with them. Similar approaches are necessary to expand learning opportunities for various disadvantaged groups.

Efficiency in basic education does not mean providing education at the lowest cost, but rather the most effective use of all resources (human, organizational, and financial) to produce the desired levels of access and of necessary learning achievement. The foregoing considerations of relevance, quality, and equity are not alternatives to efficiency but represent the specific conditions within which efficiency should be attained. For some programmes, efficiency will require more, not fewer, resources. However, if existing resources can be used by more learners or if the same learning targets can be reached at a lower cost per learner, then the capacity of basic education to meet the targets of access and achievement for presently underserved groups can be increased.

Improving Managerial, Analytical and Technological Capacities

Many kinds of expertise and skills will be needed to carry out these initiatives. Managerial and supervisory personnel, as well as planners, school architects, teacher educators, curriculum developers, researchers, analysts, etc., are important for any strategy to improve basic education, but many countries do not provide specialized training to prepare them for their responsibilities; this is especially true in literacy and other out-of-school basic education activities. A broadening of outlook toward basic education will be a crucial prerequisite to the effective co-ordination of efforts among these many participants, and strengthening and developing capacities for planning and management at regional and local levels with a greater sharing of responsibilities will be necessary in many countries. Pre- and in-service training programmes for key personnel should be initiated, or strengthened where they do exist. Such training can be particularly useful in introducing administrative reforms and innovative management and supervisory techniques.

The technical services and mechanisms to collect, process and analyze data pertaining to basic education can be improved in all countries. This is an urgent task in many countries that have little reliable information and/or research on the basic learning needs of their people and on existing basic education activities. A country's information and knowledge base is vital in preparing and implementing a plan of action. One major implication of the focus on learning acquisition is that systems have to be developed and improved to assess the performance of individual learners and delivery mechanisms. Process and outcome assessment data should serve as the core of a management information system for basic education.

The quality and delivery of basic education can be enhanced through the judicious use of instructional technologies. Where such technologies are not now widely used, their introduction will require the selection and/or development of suitable technologies, acquisition of the necessary equipment and operating systems, and the recruitment or training of teachers and other educational personnel to work with them. The definition of a suitable technology varies by societal characteristics and will change rapidly over time as new technologies (educational radio and television, computers, and various audio-visual instructional devices) become less expensive and more adaptable to a range of environments. The use of modern technology can also improve the management of basic education. Each country may reexamine periodically its present and potential technological capacity in relation to its basic educational needs and resources.

Mobilizing Information and Communication Channels

New possibilities are emerging which already show a powerful impact on meeting basic learning needs, and it is clear that the educational potential of these new possibilities has barely been tapped. These new possibilities exist largely as a result of two converging forces, both recent by-products of the general development process. First, the quantity of information available in the world - much of it relevant to survival and basic well-being - is exponentially greater than that available only a few years ago, and the rate of its growth is accelerating. A synergistic effect occurs when important information is coupled with a second modern advance - the new capacity to communicate among the people of the world. The opportunity exists to harness this force and use it positively, consciously, and with design, in order to contribute to meeting defined learning needs.

Building Partnerships and Mobilizing Resources

In designing the plan of action and creating a supportive policy environment for promoting basic education, maximum use of opportunities should be considered to expand existing collaborations and to bring together new partners: e.g., family and community organizations, non-governmental and other voluntary associations, teachers' unions, other professional groups, employers, the media, political parties, co-operatives, universities, research institutions, religious bodies, as well as education authorities and other government departments and services (labour, agriculture, health, information, commerce, industry, defence, etc.). The human and organizational resources these domestic partners represent need to be effectively mobilized to play their parts in implementing the plan of action. Partnerships at the community level and at the intermediate and national levels should be encouraged; they can help harmonize activities, utilize resources more effectively, and mobilize additional financial and human resources where necessary.

Governments and their partners can analyze the current allocation and use of financial and other resources for education and training in different sectors to determine if additional support for basic education can be obtained by

- improving efficiency,
- mobilizing additional sources of funding within and outside the government budget, and
- allocating funds within existing education and training budgets, taking into account efficiency and equity concerns. Countries where the total fiscal support for education is low need to explore the possibility of reallocating some public funds used for other purposes to basic education.

Assessing the resources actually or potentially available for basic education and comparing them to the budget estimates underlying the plan of action, can help identify possible inadequacies of resources that may affect the scheduling of planned activities over time or may require choices to be made. Countries that require external assistance to meet the basic learning needs of their people can use the resource assessment and plan of action as a basis for discussions with their international partners and for coordinating external funding.

The individual learners themselves constitute a vital human resource that needs to be mobilized. The demand for, and participation in, learning opportunities cannot simply be assumed, but must be actively encouraged. Potential learners need to see that the benefits of basic education activities exceed the costs the participants must bear, such as earnings foregone and reduced time available for community and household activities and for leisure. Women and girls especially may be deterred from taking full advantage of basic education opportunities because of reasons specific to individual cultures. Such barriers to participation may be overcome through the use of incentives and by programmes adapted to the local context and seen by the learners, their families and communities to be "productive activities". Also, learners tend to benefit more from education when they are partners in the instructional process, rather than treated simply as "inputs" or "beneficiaries". Attention to the issues of demand and participation will help assure that the learners' personal capacities are mobilized for education.

Family resources, including time and mutual support, are vital for the success of basic education activities. Families can be offered incentives and assistance to ensure that their resources are invested to enable all family members to benefit as fully and equitably as possible from basic education opportunities.

The preeminent role of teachers as well as of other educational personnel in providing quality basic education needs to be recognized and developed to optimize their contribution. This must entail measures to respect teachers' trade union rights and professional freedoms, and to improve their working conditions and status, notably in respect to their recruitment, initial and in-service training, remuneration and career development possibilities, as well as to allow teachers to fulfill their aspirations, social obligations, and ethical responsibilities.

In partnerships with school and community workers, libraries need to become a vital link in providing educational resources for all learners - pre-school through adulthood - in school and non-school settings. There is therefore a need to recognize libraries as invaluable information resources.

Community associations, co-operatives, religious bodies, and other non-governmental organizations also play important roles in supporting and in providing basic education. Their experience, expertise, energy and direct relationships with various constituencies are valuable resources for identifying and meeting basic learning needs. Their active involvement in partnerships for basic education should be promoted through policies and mechanisms that strengthen their capacities and recognize their autonomy.

Priority Action at Regional Level

Basic learning needs must be met through collaborative action within each country, but there are many forms of co-operation between countries with similar conditions and concerns that could, and do, assist in this endeavour. Regions have already developed plans, such as the Jakarta Plan of Action on Human Resources, adopted by ESCAP in 1988. By exchanging information and experience, pooling expertise, sharing facilities, and undertaking joint activities, several countries, working together, can increase their resource base and lower costs to their mutual benefit. Such arrangements are often set up among neighboring countries (sub-regional), among all countries in a major geo-cultural region, or among countries sharing a common language or having cultural and commercial relations. Regional and international organizations often play an important role in facilitating such co-operation between countries. In the following discussion, all such arrangements are included in the term "regional". In general, existing regional partnerships will need to be strengthened and provided with the resources necessary for their effective functioning in helping countries meet the basic learning needs of their populations.

Exchanging Information, Experience and Expertise

Various regional mechanisms, both intergovernmental and nongovernmental, promote co-operation in education and training, health, agricultural development, research and information, communications, and in other fields relevant to meeting basic learning needs. Such mechanisms can be further developed in response to the evolving needs of their constituents. Among several possible examples are the four regional programmes established through UNESCO in the 1980s to support national efforts to achieve universal primary education and eliminate adult illiteracy:

- Major Project in the Field of Education in Latin America and the Caribbean;
- Regional Programme for the Eradication of Illiteracy in Africa;
- Asia-Pacific Programme of Education for All (APPEAL);
- Regional Programme for the Universalization and Renewal of Primary Education and the Eradication of Illiteracy in the Arab States by the Year 2000 (ARABUPEAL).

In addition to the technical and policy consultations organized in connection with these programmes, other existing mechanisms can be used for consulting on policy issues in basic education. The conferences of ministers of education organized by UNESCO and by several regional organizations, the regular sessions of the regional commissions of the United Nations, and certain trans-regional conferences organized by the Commonwealth Secretariat, CONFEMEN (standing conference of ministers of education of francophone countries), the Organization of Economic Co-operation and Development (OECD), and the Islamic Educational, Scientific and Cultural

Organization (ISESCO), could be used for this purpose as needs arise. In addition, numerous conferences and meetings organized by non-governmental bodies provide opportunities for professionals to share information and views on technical and policy issues. The conveners of these various conferences and meetings may consider ways of extending participation, where appropriate, to include representatives of other constituencies engaged in meeting basic learning needs.

Full advantage should be taken of opportunities to share media messages or programmes that can be exchanged among countries or collaboratively developed, especially where language and cultural similarities extend beyond political boundaries.

Undertaking Joint Activities

There are many possible joint activities among countries in support of national efforts to implement action plans for basic education. Joint activities should be designed to exploit economies of scale and the comparative advantages of participating countries. Six areas where this form of regional collaboration seems particularly appropriate are:

- training of key personnel, such as planners, managers, teacher educators, researchers, etc.;
- efforts to improve information collection and analysis;
- research;
- production of educational materials;
- use of communication media to meet basic learning needs; and
- management and use of distance education services.

Here, too, there are several existing mechanisms that could be utilized to foster such activities, including UNESCO's International Institute of Educational Planning and its networks of trainees and research as well as IBE's information network and the Unesco Institute for Education, the five networks for educational innovation operating under UNESCO's auspices, the research and review advisory groups (RRAGs) associated with the International Development Research Centre, the Commonwealth of Learning, the Asian Cultural Center for UNESCO, the participatory network established by the International Council for Adult Education, and the International Association for the Evaluation of Educational Achievement, which links major national research institutions in some 35 countries. Certain multilateral and bilateral development agencies that have accumulated valuable experience in one or more of these areas might be interested in participating in joint activities. The five United Nations regional commissions could provide further support to such regional collaboration, especially by mobilizing policymakers to take appropriate action.

Priority Action at World Level

The world community has a well-established record of co-operation in education and development. However, international funding for education stagnated during the early 1980s; at the same time, many countries have been handicapped by growing debt burdens and economic relationships that channel their financial and human resources to wealthier countries. Because concern about the issues in basic education is shared by industrialized and developing countries alike, international co-operation can provide valuable support for national efforts and regional actions to implement the expanded vision of basic Education for All. Time, energy, and funding directed to basic education are perhaps the most profound investment in people and in the future of a country which can be made; there is a clear need and strong moral and economic argument for international solidarity to provide technical co-operation and financial assistance to countries that lack the resources to meet the basic learning needs of their populations.

Cooperation within the International Context

Meeting basic learning needs constitutes a common and universal human responsibility. The prospects for meeting basic learning needs around the world are determined in part by the dynamics of international relations and trade. With the current relaxation of tensions and the decreasing number of armed conflicts, there are now real possibilities to reduce the tremendous waste of military spending and shift those resources into socially useful areas, including basic education. The urgent task of meeting basic learning needs may require such a reallocation between sectors, and the world community and individual governments need to plan this conversion of resources for peaceful uses with courage and vision, and in a thoughtful and careful manner. Similarly, international measures to reduce or eliminate current imbalances in trade relations and to reduce debt burdens must be taken to enable many low-income countries to rebuild their own economies, releasing and retaining human and financial resources needed for development and for providing basic education to their populations. Structural adjustment policies should protect appropriate funding levels for education.

Enhancing National Capacities

International support should be provided, on request, to countries seeking to develop the national capacities needed for planning and managing basic education programmes and services. Ultimate responsibility rests within each nation to design and manage its own programmes to meet the learning needs of all its population. International support could include training and institutional development in data collection, analysis and research, technological innovation, and educational methodologies. Management information systems and other modern management methods could also be introduced, with an emphasis on low and middle level managers. These capabilities will be even more in demand to support quality improvements in primary education and to introduce innovative out-of-school programmes. In addition to direct support to countries and institutions, international assistance can also be usefully channelled to support the activities of international, regional and other inter-country structures that organize joint research, training and information exchanges. The latter should be based on, and supported by, existing institutions and programmes, if need be improved and strengthened, rather than on the establishment of new structures. Support will be especially valuable for technical cooperation among developing countries, among whom both circumstances and resources available to respond to circumstances are often similar.

Providing Sustained Long-term Support for National and Regional Actions

Meeting the basic learning needs of all people in all countries is obviously a long-term undertaking. This Framework provides guidelines for preparing national and subnational plans of action for the development of basic education through a long-term commitment of governments and their national partners to work together to reach the targets and achieve the objectives they set for themselves. International agencies and institutions, many of which are sponsors, co-sponsors, and associate sponsors of the World Conference on Education for All, should actively seek to plan together and sustain their long-term support for the kinds of national and regional actions outlined in the preceding sections. In particular, the core sponsors of the Education for All initiative (UNDP, UNESCO, UNICEF, World Bank) affirm their commitments to supporting the priority areas for international action presented below and to making appropriate arrangements for meeting the objectives of Education for All, each acting within its mandate, special responsibilities, and decisions of its governing bodies. Given that UNESCO is the UN agency with a particular responsibility for education, it will give priority to implementing the Framework for Action and to facilitating provision of services needed for reinforced international co-ordination and co-operation.

Increased international funding is needed to help the less developed countries implement their own autonomous plans of action in line with the expanded vision of basic Education for All. Genuine partnerships characterized by co-operation and joint long-term commitments will accomplish more and provide the basis for a substantial increase in overall funding for this important sub-sector of education. Upon governments' request, multilateral and bilateral agencies should focus on supporting priority actions, particularly at the country level, in areas such as the following:

The design or updating of national and subnational multisectoral plans of action, which will need to be elaborated very early in the 1990s. Both financial and technical assistance are needed by many developing countries, particularly in collecting and analyzing data, as well as in organizing domestic consultations.

National efforts and related inter-country co-operation to attain a satisfactory level of quality and relevance in primary education. Experiences involving the participation of families, local communities, and non-governmental organizations in increasing the relevance and improving the quality of education could profitably be shared among countries.

The provision of universal primary education in the economically poorer countries. International funding agencies should consider negotiating arrangements to provide long-term support, on a case-by-case basis, to help countries move toward universal primary education according to their timetable. The external agencies should examine current assistance practices in order to find ways of effectively assisting basic education programmes which do not require capital- and technology-intensive assistance, but often need longer-term budgetary support. In this context, greater attention should be given to criteria for development co-operation in education to include more than mere economic considerations.

Programmes designed to meet the basic learning needs of disadvantaged groups, out-of-school youth, and adults with little or no access to basic learning opportunities. All partners can share their experience and expertise in designing and implementing innovative measures and activities, and focus their funding for basic education on specific categories and groups to improve significantly the learning opportunities and conditions available for them.

Education programmes for women and girls. These programmes should be designed to eliminate the social and cultural barriers which have discouraged or even excluded women and girls from benefits of regular education programmes, as well as to promote equal opportunities in all aspects of their lives.

Education programmes for refugees. The programmes run by such organizations as the United Nations High Commission for Refugees (UNHCR) and the United Nations Relief and Works Agency for Palestine (UNRWA) need more substantial and reliable long-term financial support for this recognized international responsibility. Where countries of refuge need international financial and technical assistance to cope with the basic needs of refugees, including their learning needs, the international community can help to share this burden through increased cooperation. The world community will also endeavour to ensure that people under occupation or displaced by war and other calamities continue to have access to basic education programmes that preserve their cultural identity.

Basic education programmes of all kinds in countries with high rates of illiteracy (as in sub-Saharan Africa) and with large illiterate populations (as in South Asia). Substantial assistance will be needed to reduce significantly the world's large number of illiterate adults.Capacity building for research and planning and the experimentation of small-scale innovations. The success of Education for All actions will ultimately be determined by the capacity of each country to design and implement programs that reflect national conditions. A strengthened knowledge base nourished by research findings and the lessons of experiments and innovations as well as the availablity of competent educational planners will be essential in this respect.

The coordination of external funding for education is an area of shared responsibility at country level, in which host governments need to take the lead to ensure the efficient use of resources in accordance with their priorities. Development funding agencies should explore innovative and more flexible modalities of co-operation in consultation with the governments and institutions with which they work and co-operate in regional initiatives, such as the Task Force of Donors to African Education. Other forums need to be developed in which funding agencies and developing countries can collaborate in the design of inter-country projects and discuss general issues relating to financial assistance.

Consultations on Policy Issues

Existing channels of communication and forums for consultation among the many partners involved in meeting basic learning needs should be fully utilized in the 1990s to maintain and extend the international consensus underlying this Framework for Action. Some channels and forums, such as the biannual International Conference on Education, operate globally, while others focus on particular regions or groups of countries or categories of partners. Insofar as possible, organizers should seek to coordinate these consultations and share results.

Moreover, in order to maintain and expand the Education for All initiative, the international community will need to make appropriate arrangements, which will ensure co-operation among the interested agencies using the existing mechanisms insofar as possible:

- to continue advocacy of basic Education for All, building on the momentum generated by the World Conference;
- to facilitate sharing information on the progress made in achieving basic education targets set by countries for themselves and on the resources and organizational requirements for successful initiatives;
- to encourage new partners to join this global endeavor; and
- to ensure that all partners are fully aware of the importance of maintaining strong support for basic education.

Indicative Phasing of Implementation for the 1990s

Each country, in determining its own intermediate goals and targets and in designing its plan of action for achieving them, will, in the process, establish a timetable to harmonize and schedule specific activities. Similarly, regional and international action will need to be scheduled to help countries meet their targets on time.

Governments and organizations set specific targets and complete or update their plans of action to meet basic learning needs; take measures to create a supportive policy environment; devise policies to improve the relevance, quality, equity and efficiency of basic education services and programmes; design the means to adapt information and communication media to meet basic learning needs and mobilize resources and establish operational partnerships. International partners assist countries, through direct support and through regional co-operation, to complete this preparatory stage. (1990-1991)

Development agencies establish policies and plans for the 1990s, in line with their commitments to sustained, long-term support for national and regional actions and increase their financial and technical assistance to basic education accordingly. All partners strengthen and use relevant existing mechanisms for consultation and co-operation and establish procedures for monitoring progress at regional and international levels. (1990-1993)

First stage of implementation of plans of action: national coordinating bodies monitor implementation and propose appropriate adjustments to plans. Regional and international supporting actions are carried out. (1990-1995)

Governments and organizations undertake mid-term evaluation of the implementation of their respective plans and adjust them as needed. Governments, organizations and development agencies undertake comprehensive policy reviews at regional and global levels. (1995-1996)

Second stage of implementation of plans of action and of supporting action at regional and international levels. Development agencies adjust their plans as necessary and increase their assistance to basic education accordingly. (1996-2000)

Governments, organizations and development agencies evaluate achievements and undertake comprehensive policy review at regional and global levels. (2000-2001)

There will never be a better time to renew commitment to the inevitable and long-term effort to meet the basic learning needs of all children, youth and adults. This effort will require a much greater and wiser investment of resources in basic education and training than ever before, but benefits will begin accruing immediately and will extend well into the future - where the global challenges of today will be met, in good measure, by the world community's commitment and perseverance in attaining its goal of education for all.

9

The Dakar Framework for Action—Education for All: Meeting our Collective Commitments

The Dakar Framework for Action—Education for All: Meeting our Collective Commitments, adopted by the World Education Forum (Dakar, Senegal, 28 April 2000), is based on the most extensive evaluation ever undertaken, the Education for All (EFA) 2000 Assessment, presented at the World Education Forum (Dakar, April 2000). By adopting this Framework for Action, 1100 participants from 164 countries, coming from any horizon – teachers, ministers, decision makers, academics, political figures or leaders of international organizations – subscribed to a collective commitment. They reaffirmed that basic education is a fundamental human right and that it is the key to personal, social and sustainable development. The Dakar Framework for Action reaffirms that every person – child, youth and adult – shall be able to benefit from an education designed to meet their basic learning needs in the best and fullest sense of the term.

Sharing a common vision of basic education, the *Dakar Framework for Action* expresses the commitment of the entire international community in favour of basic education for all in order to accelerate the progress towards EFA goals. In conformity with this collective commitment, it sets out six goals in order to achieve Basic Education for All by 2015. It presents an affirmed practical approach, envisaging three principal levels of joint action: (i) a direct action inside the various countries, (ii) a cooperation between groups of countries sharing certain common characteristics and concerns, (iii) a bilateral and multilateral cooperation within the international community. The *Dakar Framework for Action* invites all the States to develop national action plans or to reinforce those which already exist, in order to give a form and a concrete reality to the goals and strategies. These plans will also set out clear strategies for overcoming the special problems facing those currently excluded from educational opportunities, with a clear commitment to girl's education and gender equity. *The Framework for Action* is intended to be used as instrument of reference and guide to governments, international organizations, multilateral and bilateral funding agencies, non-governmental organizations, and those which work in favour of education for all by helping them formulate their own action plans to fulfil their collective commitment.

The implementation of the Dakar Framework for Action and the formulation of the Action Plans at the national level call for inter-agency cooperation. As the lead agency in this international movement, UNESCO has the responsibility to co-ordinate the actions undertaken to follow up the collective commitments resulting from the *Dakar Framework for Action* so as to broaden the field of cooperation at international level.

While doing so, the four official partners of UNESCO, the World Bank, UNFPA, UNDP, UNICEF, but also other *multilateral agencies*, such as ILO, FAO, WHO must be involved in this follow-up.

The *Dakar Framework for Action* strengthens accountable international and regional mechanisms to give clear expression to the commitments made by the World Education Forum and to ensure that the *Dakar Framework for Action* is on the agenda of every international and regional organization, every national legislature and every local decision-making forum (Paragraph 13).

The Full text

1. Meeting in Dakar, Senegal, in April 2000, we, the participants in the World Education Forum, commit ourselves to the achievement of education for all (EFA) goals and targets for every citizen and for every society.
2. The Dakar Framework is a collective commitment to action. Governments have an obligation to ensure that EFA goals and targets are reached and sustained. This is a responsibility that will be met most

effectively through broad-based partnerships within countries, supported by cooperation with regional and international agencies and institutions.

3. We re-affirm the vision of the World Declaration on Education for All (Jomtien 1990), supported by the Universal Declaration of Human Rights and the Convention on the Rights of the Child, that all children, young people and adults have the human right to benefit from an education that will meet their basic learning needs in the best and fullest sense of the term, an education that includes learning to know, to do, to live together and to be. It is an education geared to tapping each individual's talents and potential and developing learners' personalities, so that they can improve their lives and transform their societies.

4. We welcome the commitments made by the international community to basic education throughout the 1990s, notably at the World Summit for Children (1990), the Conference on Environment and Development (1992), the World Conference on Human Rights (1993), the World Conference on Special Needs Education: Access and Quality (1994), the International Conference on Population and Development (1994), the World Summit for Social Development (1995), the Fourth World Conference on Women (1995), the mid-term Meeting of the International Consultative Forum on Education for All (1996), the Fifth International Conference on Adult Education (1997), and the International Conference on Child Labour (1997). The challenge now is to deliver on these commitments.

5. The EFA 2000 Assessment demonstrates that there has been significant progress in many countries. But it is unacceptable in the year 2000 that more than 113 million children have no access to primary education, 880 million adults are illiterate, gender discrimination continues to permeate education systems, and the quality of learning and the acquisition of human values and skills fall far short of the aspirations and needs of individuals and societies. Youth and adults are denied access to the skills and knowledge necessary for gainful employment and full participation in their societies. Without accelerated progress towards education for all, national and internationally agreed targets for poverty reduction will be missed, and inequalities between countries and within societies will widen.

6. Education is a fundamental human right. It is the key to sustainable development and peace and stability within and among countries, and thus an indispensable means for effective participation in the societies and economies of the twenty-first century, which are affected by rapid globalization. Achieving EFA goals should be postponed no longer. The basic learning needs of all can and must be met as a matter of urgency.

7. We hereby collectively commit ourselves to the attainment of the following goals:
   (i) expanding and improving comprehensive early childhood care and education, especially for the most vulnerable and disadvantaged children;
   (ii) ensuring that by 2015 all children, particularly girls, children in difficult circumstances and those belonging to ethnic minorities, have access to and complete free and compulsory primary education of good quality;
   (iii) ensuring that the learning needs of all young people and adults are met through equitable access to appropriate learning and life-skills programmes;
   (iv) achieving a 50 per cent improvement in levels of adult literacy by 2015, especially for women, and equitable access to basic and continuing education for all adults;
   (v) eliminating gender disparities in primary and secondary education by 2005, and achieving gender equality in education by 2015, with a focus on ensuring girls' full and equal access to and achievement in basic education of good quality;
   (vi) improving all aspects of the quality of education and ensuring excellence of all so that recognized and measurable learning outcomes are achieved by all, especially in literacy, numeracy and essential life skills.

8. To achieve these goals, we the governments, organizations, agencies, groups and associations represented at the World Education Forum pledge ourselves to:
   (i) mobilize strong national and international political commitment for education for all, develop national action plans and enhance significantly investment in basic education;

(ii) promote EFA policies within a sustainable and well-integrated sector framework clearly linked to poverty elimination and development strategies;

(iii) ensure the engagement and participation of civil society in the formulation, implementation and monitoring of strategies for educational development;

(iv) develop responsive, participatory and accountable systems of educational governance and management;

(v) meet the needs of education systems affected by conflict, national calamities and instability and conduct educational programmes in ways that promote mutual understanding, peace and tolerance, and that help to prevent violence and conflict;

(vi) implement integrated strategies for gender equality in education which recognize the need for changes in attitudes, values and practices;

(vii) implement as a matter of urgency education programmes and actions to combat the HIV/AIDS pandemic;

(viii) create safe, healthy, inclusive and equitably resourced educational environments conducive to excellence in learning with clearly defined levels of achievement for all;

(ix) enhance the status, morale and professionalism of teachers;

(x) harness new information and communication technologies to help achieve EFA goals;

(xi) systematically monitor progress towards EFA goals and strategies at the national, regional and international levels;

(xii) build on existing mechanisms to accelerate progress towards education for all.

9. Drawing on the evidence accumulated during the national and regional EFA assessments, and building on existing national sector strategies, all States will be requested to develop or strengthen existing national plans of action by 2002 at the latest. These plans should be integrated into a wider poverty reduction and development framework, and should be developed through more transparent and democratic processes, involving stakeholders, especially peoples' representatives, community leaders, parents, learners, non-governmental organizations (NGOs) and

civil society. The plans will address problems associated with the chronic under-financing of basic education by establishing budget priorities that reflect a commitment to achieving EFA goals and targets at the earliest possible date, and no later than 2015. They will also set out clear strategies for overcoming the special problems facing those currently excluded from educational opportunities, with a clear commitment to girls' education and gender equity. The plans will give substance and form to the goals and strategies set out in this Framework, and to the commitments made during a succession of international conferences in the 1990s. Regional activities to support national strategies will be based on strengthened regional and subregional organizations, networks and initiatives.

10. Political will and stronger national leadership are needed for the effective and successful implementation of national plans in each of the countries concerned. However, political will must be underpinned by resources. The international community acknowledges that many countries currently lack the resources to achieve education for all within an acceptable time-frame. New financial resources, preferably in the form of grants and concessional assistance, must therefore be mobilized by bilateral and multilateral funding agencies, including the World Bank and regional development banks, and the private sector. We affirm that no countries seriously committed to education for all will be thwarted in their achievement of this goal by a lack of resources.

11. The international community will deliver on this collective commitment by launching with immediate effect a global initiative aimed at developing the strategies and mobilizing the resources needed to provide effective support to national efforts. Options to be considered under this initiative will include:

    (i) increasing external finance for education, in particular basic education;

    (ii) ensuring greater predictability in the flow of external assistance;

    (iii) facilitating more effective donor coordination;

    (iv) strengthening sector-wide approaches;

    (v) providing earlier, more extensive and broader debt relief and/or debt cancellation for poverty reduction, with a strong commitment to basic education;

(vi) undertaking more effective and regular monitoring of progress towards EFA goals and targets, including periodic assessments.

12. There is already evidence from many countries of what can be achieved through strong national strategies supported by effective development cooperation. Progress under these strategies could – and must – be accelerated through increased international support. At the same time, countries with less developed strategies – including countries in transition, countries affected by conflict, and post-crisis countries – must be given the support they need to achieve more rapid progress towards education for all.

13. We will strengthen accountable international and regional mechanisms to give clear expression to these commitments and to ensure that the Dakar Framework for Action is on the agenda of every international and regional organization, every national legislature and every local decision-making forum.

14. The EFA 2000 Assessment highlights that the challenge of education for all is greatest in sub-Saharan Africa, in South Asia, and in the least developed countries. Accordingly, while no country in need should be denied international assistance, priority should be given to these regions and countries. Countries in conflict or undergoing reconstruction should also be given special attention in building up their education systems to meet the needs of all learners.

15. Implementation of the preceding goals and strategies will require national, regional and international mechanisms to be galvanized immediately. To be most effective these mechanisms will be participatory and, wherever possible, build on what already exists. They will include representatives of all stakeholders and partners and they will operate in transparent and accountable ways. They will respond comprehensively to the word and spirit of the Jomtien Declaration and this Dakar Framework for Action. The functions of these mechanisms will include, to varying degrees, advocacy, resource mobilization, monitoring, and EFA knowledge generation and sharing.

16. The heart of EFA activity lies at the country level. National EFA Forums will be strengthened or established to support the achievement of EFA. All relevant ministries and national civil society organizations will be systematically represented in these Forums. They should be transparent

and democratic and should constitute a framework for implementation at subnational levels. Countries will prepare comprehensive National EFA Plans by 2002 at the latest. For those countries with significant challenges, such as complex crises or natural disasters, special technical support will be provided by the international community. Each National EFA Plan will:

(i) be developed by government leadership in direct and systematic consultation with national civil society;

(ii) attract co-ordinated support of all development partners;

(iii) specify reforms addressing the six EFA goals;

(iv) establish a sustainable financial framework;

(v) be time-bound and action-oriented;

(vi) include mid-term performance indicators; and

(vii) achieve a synergy of all human development efforts, through its inclusion within the national development planning framework and process.

17. Where these processes and a credible plan are in place, partner members of the international community undertake to work in a consistent, co-ordinated and coherent manner. Each partner will contribute according to its comparative advantage in support of the National EFA Plans to ensure that resource gaps are filled.

18. Regional activities to support national efforts will be based on existing regional and subregional organizations, networks and initiatives, augmented where necessary. Regions and subregions will decide on a lead EFA network that will become the Regional or Subregional Forum with an explicit EFA mandate. Systematic involvement of, and co-ordination with, all relevant civil society and other regional and subregional organizations are essential. These Regional and Subregional EFA Forums will be linked organically with, and be accountable to, National EFA Forums. Their functions will be: co-ordination with all relevant networks; setting and monitoring regional/subregional targets; advocacy; policy dialogue; the promotion of partnerships and technical cooperation; the sharing of best practices and lessons learned; monitoring and reporting for accountability; and promoting resource mobilization. Regional and international support

will be available to strengthen Regional and Subregional Forums and relevant EFA capacities, especially within Africa and South Asia.

19. UNESCO will continue its mandated role in co-ordinating EFA partners and maintaining their collaborative momentum. In line with this, UNESCO's Director-General will convene annually a high-level, small and flexible group. It will serve as a lever for political commitment and technical and financial resource mobilization. Informed by a monitoring report from the UNESCO International Institute for Educational Planning (IIEP), the UNESCO International Bureau of Education (IBE), the UNESCO Institute for Education (UIE) and, in particular, the UNESCO Institute for Statistics, and inputs from Regional and Subregional EFA Forums, it will also be an opportunity to hold the global community to account for commitments made in Dakar. It will be composed of highest-level leaders from governments and civil society of developing and developed countries, and from development agencies.
20. UNESCO will serve as the Secretariat. It will refocus its education programme in order to place the outcomes and priorities of Dakar at the heart of its work. This will involve working groups on each of the six goals adopted at Dakar. This Secretariat will work closely with other organizations and may include staff seconded from them.
21. Achieving Education for All will require additional financial support by countries and increased development assistance and debt relief for education by bilateral and multilateral donors, estimated to cost in the order of $8 billion a year. It is therefore essential that new, concrete financial commitments be made by national governments and also by bilateral and multilateral donors including the World Bank and the regional development banks, by civil society and by foundations.

Expanded Commentary on the Dakar Framework for Action

This commentary provides details on each goal and strategy of the Framework for Action on the basis of the many suggestions provided before and during the World Education Forum, most notably from its twenty-four strategy sessions.

I.Introduction

1. The Dakar Framework for Action is a re-affirmation of the vision set

out in the World Declaration on Education for All in Jomtien a decade ago. It expresses the international community's collective commitment to pursue a broad-based strategy for ensuring that the basic learning needs of every child, youth and adult are met within a generation and sustained thereafter.

2. The World Education Forum in Dakar provided the opportunity to assess the achievements, lessons and failures of the past decade. The EFA 2000 Assessment represents an unparalleled effort to take stock of the state of basic education in the world. It includes national assessments of the progress achieved since Jomtien in 183 countries, the problems encountered and recommendations for future action. Synthesis reports summarize the main findings of these assessments by region. In addition, fourteen special thematic studies were undertaken, surveys were conducted on the quality of learning achievement in over thirty countries, and a comprehensive collection and synthesis of case-studies on the involvement of NGOs in education was prepared.

3. The Assessment is a rich store of information and analysis. Five regional EFA conferences (sub-Saharan Africa, Johannesburg; Asia and the Pacific, Bangkok; Arab States and North Africa, Cairo; the Americas and the Caribbean, Santo Domingo; and Europe and North America, Warsaw) and a conference of the nine high-population (E-9) countries (Recife) discussed and translated the outcomes of the Assessment into regional frameworks for action which are an integral part of this document and underpin the Dakar Framework for Action.

4. The vision of Jomtien remains pertinent and powerful. It provides a broad and comprehensive view of education and its critical role in empowering individuals and transforming societies. Its key points and principles include universal access to learning; a focus on equity; emphasis on learning outcomes; broadening the means and the scope of basic education; enhancing the environment for learning; and strengthening partnerships. Tragically, reality has fallen far short of this vision: millions of people are still denied their right to education and the opportunities it brings to live safer, healthier, more productive and more fulfilling lives. Such a failure has multiple causes: weak political will, insufficient financial resources and the inefficient use of those available, the burden of debt, inadequate attention to the learning needs

of the poor and the excluded, a lack of attention to the quality of learning and an absence of commitment to overcoming gender disparities. There can be no doubt that the barriers to achieving Education for All are formidable. Yet they can and must be overcome.

5. The Assessment shows that progress has been achieved, proving that Education for All is a realistic and achievable goal. But it needs to be frankly acknowledged that progress has been uneven and far too slow. At the start of a new millennium, the EFA 2000 Assessment shows the following:
   (i) Of the more than 800 million children under 6 years of age, fewer than a third benefit from any form of early childhood education.
   (ii) Some 113 million children, 60 per cent of whom are girls, have no access to primary schooling.
   (iii) At least 880 million adults are illiterate, of whom the majority are women.

6. These figures represent an affront to human dignity and a denial of the right to education. They stand as major barriers to eliminating poverty and attaining sustainable development, and are clearly unacceptable.

7. The Dakar Framework sets six major EFA goals and proposes twelve major strategies. It puts forward twelve major strategies informed by the experience of the past decade and the changing global context. These include the international development targets for education to which national governments and the international community are already committed.

8. Starting from early childhood and extending throughout life, the learners of the twenty-first century will require access to high quality educational opportunities that are responsive to their needs, equitable and gender-sensitive. These opportunities must neither exclude nor discriminate. Since the pace, style, language and circumstances of learning will never be uniform for all, there should be room for diverse formal or less formal approaches, as long as they ensure sound learning and confer equivalent status.

9. The right to education imposes an obligation upon states to ensure that all citizens have opportunities to meet their basic learning needs. Primary education should be free, compulsory and of good quality. The

education systems of tomorrow, however diversified they may be, will need to be transparent and accountable in how they are governed, managed and financed. The indispensable role of the state in education must be supplemented and supported by bold and comprehensive educational partnerships at all levels of society. Education for All implies the involvement and commitment of all to education.

II.Achievements and Challenges

Achievements and lessons

10. The EFA 2000 Assessment conducted at national, regional, and global levels shows that progress has been made over the past decade towards the vision reflected in the Jomtien Declaration.

11. Worldwide, primary school enrolments increased by some 82 million pupils since 1990, with 44 million more girls in school in 1998 than in 1990 – figures which more than any other symbolize the serious efforts of many countries to advance in the face of often severe economic constraints and continued rapid population growth. At the end of the 1990s, developing countries as a whole had achieved net enrolment rates in excess of 80 per cent. Repetition and dropout rates had declined. There has been some improvement, albeit limited, in gender equality in primary enrolment in many regions, with the critical exception of sub-Saharan Africa. Early childhood care and education have expanded modestly, mainly in urban areas. Virtually all countries in the world have ratified the United Nations Convention on the Rights of the Child and have thereby accepted an obligation to ensure the right of every child to a basic education. There has been a gradual growth in non-formal education and skills training. While levels of illiteracy remain unacceptably high, a measure of progress has been achieved. The overall adult literacy rate has risen to 85 per cent for men and to 74 per cent for women. Increased levels of education have enabled men and women to make more informed choices about family size. This is having an impact on demographic growth rates, a factor of great importance for both education and development.

12. These quantitative achievements tell nothing of the plight of the millions who are still excluded from education or of alienated youth and their painful struggle to find a place and retain their values in changing societies. Information is also sparse on the nature and quality

of teaching and learning and of educational outcomes at all levels in education systems.

13. There is a powerful correlation between low enrolment, poor retention and unsatisfactory learning outcomes and the incidence of poverty. Experience in the post-Jomtien decade, however, has demonstrated that significant progress can be made towards the goals of Education for All where there is a strong political commitment, backed by new partnerships with civil society and more strategic support from funding agencies. It is also clear that ensuring that girls and boys benefit equally from education requires nothing less than the integration of gender equality concerns into the design and implementation of sector policies and strategies. The importance of gathering and carefully analysing reliable gender-disaggregated data at national and subnational levels is evident.

14. The many factors that impinge on the demand for education are now better understood, as are the multiple causes that exclude children, young people and adults from learning opportunities. The range of actions required to increase the participation and retention of girls in school has received widespread attention. Knowledge about the effectiveness of teachers and other educators, the central role of appropri ate learning materials, the need for a context-specific mix of 'old' and 'new' technologies, the importance of local languages for initial literacy and the major influence of the community in the life of schools and other education pro grammes has increased. The value of early childhood care and education for later school success and the need for strong linkages between the different subsectors of education and among basic education, health, nutrition, safe water and the natural environment have received greater attention and are better understood.

Challenges and opportunities

15. The tangible but modest gains overall of the past decade still call for caution. Many countries continue to face the challenges of defining the meaning, purpose and content of basic education in the context of a fast-moving world and of assessing learning outcomes and achievement. Many of the qualitative and informal aspects of education have still not been clearly assessed. The huge diversity of contexts makes performance and achievements difficult to measure and

compare. Moreover, growing educational disparities within and between countries are a matter for serious concern.

16. Many governments and agencies have focused their efforts on the easy to reach and they have neglected those excluded from a basic education, whether for social, economic or geographic reasons. What is clear is that quality must not suffer as access expands and that improvements in quality should not benefit the economically well-off at the expense of the poor, as has happened, for example, in the expansion of early childhood care and education.

17. The education of girls remains a major challenge: despite the international attention that it has received, 60 per cent of all children without access to primary education are girls.

18. South Asia and sub-Saharan Africa, where progress has been most difficult to achieve, clearly present a much deeper challenge than world averages imply and will require particular attention if the goals of Education for All are to be reached in each and every country. In the Americas and the Caribbean, deep differences between regions and social groups based on income inequality continue to hamper progress towards Education for All and must receive due attention.

19. A key challenge is to ensure that the broad vision of Education for All as an inclusive concept is reflected in national government and funding agency policies. Education for All must encompass not only primary education, but also early childhood education, literacy and life-skills programmes. Using both formal and non-formal approaches, it must take account of the needs of the poor and the most disadvan-taged, including working children, remote rural dwellers and nomads, and ethnic and linguistic minorities, children, young people and adults affected by conflict, HIV/AIDS, hunger and poor health; and those with special learning needs. It is encouraging to see that many governments, funding agencies and civil society organizations are increasingly rallying to this more inclusive and comprehensive view of education.

20. Ensuring that Education for All is provided with adequate, equitable and sustainable resources is the foremost challenge. Many governments do not give education sufficient priority in their national budgets. Too many do not use resources for education effectively and efficiently, and often subsidize better-off groups at the expense of the poor. At the same

time, stabilization programmes often fail to protect education budgets. As a direct consequence, user charges continue to be a major deterrent to poor children attending school and to young people and adults in need of non-formal learning. In some countries, passing the cost burden on to poor parents has had a devastating impact on enrolment and retention. Education must neither exclude nor discriminate. Every government has the responsibility to provide free, quality basic education, so that no child will be denied access because of an inability to pay.

21. Governments need to explore more actively alternative and innovative ways of increasing the resources available to support Education for All and to develop clearly defined strategies for achieving EFA goals, for which they take real and sustained ownership. Debt relief to the poorest countries remains inadequate, with too little being provided to too few countries too late. Debt reduction programmes should offer governments an opportunity to give priority to education within overall poverty reduction frameworks.

22. While the proportion of international assistance allocated to basic education increased in the 1990s, there was an overall decline in total development assistance. The first trend should be supported and the second reversed. There is considerable scope for the international community to demonstrate, in a co-operative and accountable way, that it can be effective in supporting well-defined national sector strategies and in helping to release the significant additional resources that many funding agencies are willing to provide.

23. New ways of working that are emerging within the wider development context also represent opportunities for achieving EFA goals. Greater co-operation between national and international agencies at the country level, through structures and mechanisms such as Comprehensive Development Frameworks, Poverty Reduction Strategy Plans and United Nations Development Assistance Frameworks, offers the potential for resource-related partnerships for basic education.

24. Genuinely participatory development is more likely to occur where there is a stronger and more vocal recognition of education as a fundamental human right and where representative democracy has taken root. The growing importance of participatory poverty assessments and household surveys also highlights a positive trend in

the development of education programmes and systems that are genuinely responsive to well-defined needs and priorities.

25. While inadequate institutional capacity and weak political processes still prevent many governments from responding to the priorities of their citizens, the spread of democratic principles around the world, the growing contribution of civil society to democratic processes, the fight against corruption and the process of decentralization that is ongoing in many countries all have the potential to contribute greatly to building a solid foundation for the achievement of effective, equitable and sustainable Education for All.

26. Globalization is both an opportunity and a challenge. It is a process which must be shaped and managed so as to ensure equity and sustainability. Globalization is generating new wealth and resulting in the greater interconnectedness and interdependence of economies and societies. Driven by the revolution in information technologies and the increased mobility of capital, it has the potential to help reduce poverty and inequality throughout the world, and to harness the new technologies for basic education. Yet globalization carries with it the danger of creating a market place in knowledge that excludes the poor and the disadvantaged. Countries and households denied access to opportunities for basic education in an increasingly knowledge-based global economy face the prospect of deepening marginalization within an increasingly prosperous international economy.

27. The threat posed by HIV/AIDS to the achievement of EFA goals and to development more broadly, especially in sub-Saharan Africa, presents an enormous challenge. The terrifying impact of HIV/AIDS on educational demand, supply and quality requires explicit and immediate attention in national policy-making and planning. Programmes to control and reduce the spread of the virus must make maximum use of education's potential to transmit messages on prevention and to change attitudes and behaviours.

28. The significant growth of tensions, conflict and war, both within nations and between nations and peoples, is a cause of great concern. Education has a key role to play in preventing conflict in the future and building lasting peace and stability.

III. Goals

> Basic learning needs . . . comprise both essential learning tools . . . and the basic learning content . . . required by human beings to be able to survive, to develop their full capacities, to live and work in dignity, to participate fully in development, to improve the quality of their lives, to make informed decisions, and to continue learning. (World Declaration on Education for All, Article 1, Paragraph 1)

29. The goals and strategies set out below establish a Framework for Action that is designed to enable all individuals to realize their right to learn and to fulfil their responsibility to contribute to the development of their society. They are global in nature, drawn from the outcomes of the regional EFA conferences and the international development targets to which countries are already committed. Individual countries, through a process of consultation among all stakeholders in education and with the assistance of the wider international community and EFA follow-up mechanisms, should set their own goals, intermediate targets and timelines within existing or new national education plans.

1. Expanding and improving comprehensive early childhood care and education, especially for the most vulnerable and disadvantaged children

30. All young children must be nurtured in safe and caring environments that allow them to become healthy, alert and secure and be able to learn. The past decade has provided more evidence that good quality early childhood care and education, both in families and in more structured programmes, have a positive impact on the survival, growth, development and learning potential of children. Such programmes should be comprehensive, focusing on all of the child's needs and encompassing health, nutrition and hygiene as well as cognitive and psycho-social development. They should be provided in the child's mother tongue and help to identify and enrich the care and education of children with special needs. Partnerships between governments, NGOs, communities and families can help ensure the provision of good care and education for children, especially for those most disadvantaged, through activities centred on the child, focused on the family, based within the community and supported by national, multi-sectoral policies and adequate resources.

31. Governments, through relevant ministries, have the primary responsibility of formulating early childhood care and education policies within the context of national EFA plans, mobilizing political and popular support, and promoting flexible, adaptable programmes for young children that are appropriate to their age and not mere downward extensions of formal school systems. The education of parents and other caregivers in better child care, building on traditional practices, and the systematic use of early childhood indicators, are important elements in achieving this goal.

2 Ensuring that by 2015 all children, particularly girls, children in difficult circumstances and those belonging to ethnic minorities, have access to and complete free and compulsory primary education of good quality

32. All children must have the opportunity to fulfil their right to quality education in schools or alternative programmes at whatever level of education is considered 'basic'. All states must fulfil their obligation to offer free and compulsory primary education in accordance with the United Nations Convention on the Rights of the Child and other international commitments. The international agreement on the 2015 target date for achieving Universal Primary Education (UPE) in all countries will require commitment and political will from all levels of government. For the millions of children living in poverty, who suffer multiple disadvantages, there must be an unequivocal commitment that education be free of tuition and other fees, and that everything possible be done to reduce or eliminate costs such as those for learning materials, uniforms, school meals and transport. Wider social policies, interventions and incentives should be used to mitigate indirect opportunity costs of attending school. No one should be denied the opportunity to complete a good quality primary education because it is unaffordable. Child labour must not stand in the way of education. The inclusion of children with special needs, from disadvantaged ethnic minorities and migrant populations, from remote and isolated communities and from urban slums, and others excluded from education, must be an integral part of strategies to achieve UPE by 2015.

33. While commitment to attaining universal enrolment is essential, improving and sustaining the quality of basic education is equally important in ensuring effective learning outcomes. In order to attract

and retain children from marginalized and excluded groups, education systems should respond flexibly, providing relevant content in an accessible and appealing format. Education systems must be inclusive, actively seeking out children who are not enrolled, and responding flexibly to the circumstances and needs of all learners. The EFA 2000 Assessment suggests a wide range of ways in which schools can respond to the needs of their pupils, including affirmative action programmes for girls that seek to remove the obstacles to their enrolment, bilingual education for the children of ethnic minorities, and a range of imaginative and diverse approaches to address and actively engage children who are not enrolled in school.

3 Ensuring that the learning needs of all young people and adults are met through equitable access to appropriate learning and life skills programmes

34. All young people and adults must be given the opportunity to gain the knowledge and develop the values, attitudes and skills that will enable them to develop their capacities to work, to participate fully in their society, to take control of their own lives and to continue learning. No country can be expected to develop into a modern and open economy without a certain proportion of its work force having completed secondary education. In most countries this requires an expansion of the secondary system.

35. Young people, especially adolescent girls, face risks and threats that limit learning opportunities and challenge education systems. These include exploitative labour, the lack of employment, conflict and violence, drug abuse, school-age pregnancy and HIV/AIDS. Youth-friendly programmes must be made available to provide the information, skills, counselling and services needed to protect them from these risks.

36. All young people should be given the opportunity for ongoing education. For those who drop out of school or complete school without acquiring the literacy, numeracy and life skills they need, there must be a range of options for continuing their learning. Such opportunities should be both meaningful and relevant to their environment and needs, help them become active agents in shaping their future and develop useful work-related skills.

4 Achieving a 50 per cent improvement in levels of adult literacy by 2015, especially for women, and equitable access to basic and continuing education for all adults

37. All adults have a right to basic education, beginning with literacy, which allows them to engage actively in, and to transform, the world in which they live. There are still some 880 million people who cannot read or write in the world; two-thirds are women. The fragile levels of literacy acquired by many new literates compound the problem. Yet the education of adults remains isolated, often at the periphery of national education systems and budgets.
38. Adult and continuing education must be greatly expanded and diversified, and integrated into the mainstream of national education and poverty reduction strategies. The vital role literacy plays in lifelong learning, sustainable livelihoods, good health, active citizenship and the improved quality of life for individuals, communities and societies must be more widely recognized. Literacy and continuing education are essential for women's empowerment and gender equality. Closer linkages among formal, non-formal and informal approaches to learning must be fostered to respond to the diverse needs and circumstances of adults.
39. Sufficient resources, well-targeted literacy programmes, better trained teachers and the innovative use of technologies are essential in promoting these activities. The scaling up of practical, participatory learning methodologies developed by non-government organizations, which link literacy with empowerment and local development, is especially important. The success of adult education efforts in the next decade will be essentially demonstrated by substantial reduction in disparities between male/female and urban/ rural literacy rates.

5 Eliminating gender disparities in primary and secondary education by 2005, and achieving gender equality in education by 2015, with a focus on ensuring girls' full and equal access to and achievement in basic education of good quality

40. Gender-based discrimination remains one of the most intractable constraints to realizing the right to education. Without overcoming this obstacle, Education for All cannot be achieved. Girls are a majority among out-of-school children and youth, although in an increasing

number of countries boys are at a disadvantage. Even though the education of girls and women has a powerful trans-generational effect and is a key determinant of social development and women's empowerment, limited progress has been made in increasing girls' participation in basic education.

41. International agreement has already been reached to eliminate gender disparities in primary and secondary education by 2005. This requires that gender issues be mainstreamed throughout the education system, supported by adequate resources and strong political commitment. Merely ensuring access to education for girls is not enough; unsafe school environments and biases in teacher behaviour and training, teaching and learning processes, and curricula and textbooks often lead to lower completion and achievement rates for girls. By creating safe and gender-sensitive learning environments, it should be possible to remove a major hurdle to girls' participation in education. Increasing levels of women's literacy is another crucial factor in promoting girls' education. Comprehensive efforts therefore need to be made at all levels and in all areas to eliminate gender discrimination and to promote mutual respect between girls and boys, women and men. To make this possible, changes in attitudes, values and behaviour are required.

6 Improving every aspect of the quality of education, and ensuring their excellence so that recognized and measurable learning outcomes are achieved by all, especially in literacy, numeracy and essential life skills

42. Quality is at the heart of education, and what takes place in classrooms and other learning environments is fundamentally important to the future well-being of children, young people and adults. A quality education is one that satisfies basic learning needs, and enriches the lives of learners and their overall experience of living.

43. Evidence over the past decade has shown that efforts to expand enrolment must be accompanied by attempts to enhance educational quality if children are to be attracted to school, stay there and achieve meaningful learning outcomes. Scarce resources have frequently been used for expanding systems with insufficient attention to quality improvement in areas such as teacher training and materials development. Recent assessments of learning achievement in some countries have shown that a sizeable percentage of children is acquiring

only a fraction of the knowledge and skills they are expected to master. What students are meant to learn has often not been clearly defined, well-taught or accurately assessed.

44. Governments and all other EFA partners must work together to ensure basic education of quality for all, regardless of gender, wealth, location, language or ethnic origin. Successful education programmes require: (1) healthy, well-nourished and motivated students; (2) well-trained teachers and active learning techniques; (3) adequate facilities and learning materials; (4) a relevant curriculum that can be taught and learned in a local language and builds upon the knowledge and experience of the teachers and learners; (5) an environment that not only encourages learning but is welcoming, gender-sensitive, healthy and safe; (6) a clear definition and accurate assessment of learning outcomes, including knowledge, skills, attitudes and values; (7) participatory governance and management; and (8) respect for and engagement with local communities and cultures.

IV.Strategies

45. Education for All is a basic human right at the heart of development. It must be a national and international priority, and it requires a strong and sustained political commitment, enhanced financial allocations and the participation of all EFA partners in the processes of policy design, strategic planning and the implementation of programmes. Achieving the six goals outlined above necessitates a broad-based approach which extends well beyond the confines of formal education systems. Building on the lessons of the last decade, the implementation of the following strategies will be critical in achieving Education for All.

1 Mobilize strong national and international political commitment for Education for All, develop national action plans and enhance significantly investment in basic education

46. The Jomtien Framework for Action stated that progress in meeting the basic learning needs of all will depend ultimately on the actions taken within individual countries. This means first that governments must make firm political commitments and allocate sufficient resources to all components of basic education – an absolutely essential step to meeting the state's obligation to all of its citizens. In many countries

this will require increasing the share of national income and budgets allocated to education and, within that, to basic education, balanced by reduced allocations to sectors of lower development priority. Resources have to be used with much greater efficiency and integrity, and governments should set goals for more equitable spending across education sub-sectors. Corruption is a major drain on the effective use of resources for education and should be drastically curbed. Structures are needed to enable civil society to be part of transparent and accountable budgeting and financing systems. Achieving Education for All will also require more creative and sustained mobilization of resources from other parts of society, including different levels of government, the private sector and nongovernmental organizations.

47. Even with improved mobilization and allocation of domestic resources, and enhanced efficiency in their use, meeting all the education goals will require additional funding from international development agencies. Funding agencies should allocate a larger share of their resources to support primary and other forms of basic education. The regions and countries where challenges are greatest, which include much of sub-Saharan Africa and South Asia, least developed countries and countries emerging from conflict, deserve particular attention.

48. No countries seriously committed to Education for All will be thwarted in their achievement of this goal by lack of resources. Funding agencies are willing to allocate significant resources towards Education for All. The keys to releasing these resources are evidence of, or potential for, sustained political commitment; effective and transparent mechanisms for consultation with civil society organizations in developing, implementing and monitoring EFA plans; and a well-defined, consultative processes for sector planning and management.

49. This commitment requires that funding agencies coordinate their efforts to provide flexible development assistance within the framework of sectorwide reforms and support sector priorities within sound and coherent government-owned poverty reduction programmes. High priority should be given to providing earlier, deeper and broader debt relief and/or debt cancellation for poverty reduction, with a strong commitment to basic education. Debt relief should not be a substitute for aid.

50. Funding agencies will need to make longer-term and more predictable commitments, and to be more accountable and transparent. They must provide timely and accurate information on their disbursements, and ensure that there is regular reporting at regional and international levels.

2 Promote EFA policies within a sustainable and well-integrated sector framework clearly linked to poverty elimination and development strategies

51. Education, starting with the care and education of young children and continuing through lifelong learning, is central to individual empowerment, the elimination of poverty at household and community level, and broader social and economic development. At the same time, the reduction of poverty facilitates progress toward basic education goals. There are evident synergies between strategies for promoting education and those for reducing poverty that must be exploited both in programme planning and implementation.

52. A multi-sectoral approach to poverty elimination requires that education strategies complement those of the productive sectors as well as of health, population, social welfare, labour, the environment and finance, and be closely linked with civil society. Specific actions in this regard include: (1) integrating basic education strategies into broader national and international poverty alleviation measures such as United Nations Development Assistance Frameworks (UNDAFs), Comprehensive Development Frameworks and Poverty Reduction Strategy Papers; and (2) developing 'inclusive' education systems which explicitly identify, target and respond flexibly to the needs and circumstances of the poorest and the most marginalized.

3 Ensure the engagement and participation of civil society in the formulation, implementation and monitoring of strategies for educational development

53. Learners, teachers, parents, communities, non-governmental organizations and other bodies representing civil society must be granted new and expanded political and social scope, at all levels of society, in order to engage governments in dialogue, decision-making and innovation around the goals of basic education. Civil society has much experience and a crucial role to play in identifying barriers to EFA goals, and developing policies and strategies to remove them.

54. Such participation, especially at the local level through partnerships between schools and communities, should not only be limited to

endorsing decisions of, or financing programmes designed by, the state. Rather, at all levels of decision-making, governments must put in place regular mechanisms for dialogue that will enable citizens and civil society organizations to contribute to the planning, implementation, monitoring and evaluation of basic education. This is essential in order to foster the development of accountable, comprehensive and flexible educational management frameworks. In order to facilitate this process, capacity will often have to be developed in the civil society organizations.

4 Develop responsive, participatory and accountable systems of educational governance and management

55. The experience of the past decade has underscored the need for better governance of education systems in terms of efficiency, accountability, transparency and flexibility so that they can respond more effectively to the diverse and continuously changing needs of learners. Reform of educational management is urgently needed — to move from highly centralized, standardized and command-driven forms of management to more decentralized and participatory decision-making, implementation and monitoring at lower levels of accountability. These processes must be buttressed by a management information system that benefits from both new technologies and community participation to produce timely, relevant and accurate information.

56. Country EFA reports and regional action frameworks stemming from the EFA 2000 Assessment recommend the following: (1) establish better regulatory frameworks and administrative mechanisms for managing not only formal and non-formal primary education, but also early childhood, youth and adult education programmes; (2) more sharply delineate responsibilities among different levels of government; (3) ensure that decentralization does not lead to inequitable distribution of resources; (4) make more efficient use of existing human and financial resources; (5) improve capacities for managing diversity, disparity and change; (6) integrate programmes within education and strengthen their convergence with those of other sectors, especially health, labour and social welfare; and (7) provide training for school leaders and other education personnel.

5 Meet the needs of education systems affected by conflict, natural calamities and instability, and conduct educational programmes in ways that promote mutual understanding, peace and tolerance, and that help to prevent violence and conflict

57. Conflicts, instability and natural disasters take their toll on education and are a major barrier towards attaining Education for All. The capacity of governments and civil society should be enhanced to rapidly assess educational needs in contexts of crisis and post-conflict situations for children and adults, to restore learning opportunities in secure and friendly environments, and to reconstruct destroyed or damaged education systems.

58. Schools should be respected and protected as sanctuaries and zones of peace. Education programmes should be designed to promote the full development of the human personality and strengthen respect for human rights and fundamental freedoms as proclaimed in the Universal Declaration of Human Rights (Article 26). Such programmes should promote understanding, tolerance and friendship among all nations, and all ethnic and religious groups; and they should be sensitive to cultural and linguistic identities, and respectful of diversity and reinforce a culture of peace. Education should promote not only skills such as the prevention and peaceful resolution of conflict, but also social and ethical values.

6 Implement integrated strategies for gender equality in education that recognize the need for change in attitudes, values and practices

59. Achieving Education for All demands that high-level commitment and priority be given to gender equality. Schools, other learning environments and education systems usually mirror the larger society. Efforts in support of gender equality must include specific actions to address discrimination resulting from social attitudes and practices, economic status and culture.

60. Throughout the education system, there must be a commitment to the development of attitudes and behaviours that incorporate gender awareness and analysis. Education systems must also act explicitly to remove gender bias. This includes ensuring that policies and their implementation are supportive of girls' and boys' learning. Teaching and supervisory bodies must be fair and transparent, and rules and

regulations, including promotion and disciplinary action, must have equal impact on girls and boys, women and men. Attention must be given to boys' needs in cases where they are disadvantaged.

61. In the learning environment, the content, processes and context of education must be free of gender bias, and encourage and support equality and respect. This includes teachers' behaviours and attitudes, curriculum and textbooks, and student interactions. Efforts must be made to ensure personal security: girls are often especially vulnerable to abuse and harassment on the journey to and from school and at school.

7 Implement education programmes and actions to combat the HIV/AIDS pandemic as a matter of urgency

62. The HIV/AIDS pandemic is undermining progress towards Education for All in many parts of the world by seriously affecting educational demand, supply and quality. This situation requires the urgent attention of governments, civil society and the international community. Education systems must go through significant changes if they are to survive the impact of HIV/AIDS and counter its spread, especially in response to the impact on teacher supply and student demand. To achieve EFA goals will necessitate putting HIV/AIDS as the highest priority in the most affected countries, with strong, sustained political commitment; mainstreaming HIV/AIDS perspectives in all aspects of policy; redesigning teacher training and curricula; and significantly enhancing resources to these efforts.

63. The decade has shown that the pandemic has had, and will increasingly have, a devastating effect on education systems, teachers and learners, with a particularly adverse impact on girls. Stigma and poverty brought about by HIV/AIDS are creating new social castes of children excluded from education and adults with reduced livelihood opportunities. A rights-based response to HIV/AIDS mitigation and ongoing monitoring impact of the pandemic on EFA goals are essential. This response should include appropriate legislation and administrative actions to ensure the right of HIV/AIDS-affected people to receive education and to combat discrimination within the education sector.

64. Education institutions and structures should create a safe and supportive environment for children and young people in a world with HIV/AIDS,

and strengthen their protection from sexual abuse and other forms of exploitation. Flexible non-formal approaches should be adopted to reach children and adults infected and affected by HIV/AIDS, with particular attention to AIDS orphans. Curricula based on life-skills approaches should include all aspects of HIV/AIDS care and prevention. Parents and communities should also benefit from HIV/AIDS-related programmes. Teachers must be adequately trained, both in-service and pre-service, in providing HIV/AIDS education, and teachers affected by the pandemic should be supported at all levels.

8 Create safe, healthy, inclusive and equitably resourced educational environments conducive to excellence in learning, with clearly defined levels of achievement for all

65. The quality of learning is and must be at the heart of EFA. All stakeholders — teachers and students, parents and community members, health workers and local government officials — should work together to develop environments conducive to learning. To offer education of good quality, educational institutions and programmes should be adequately and equitably resourced, with the core requirements of safe, environmentally friendly and easily accessible facilities; well motivated and professionally competent teachers; and books, other learning materials and technologies that are context specific, cost effective and available to all learners.

66. Learning environments should also be healthy, safe and protective. This should include: (1) adequate water and sanitation facilities, (2) access to or linkages with health and nutrition services, (3) policies and codes of conducts that enhance the physical, psycho-social and emotional health of teachers and learners, and (4) education content and practices leading to knowledge, attitudes, values, and life skills needed for self-esteem, good health, and personal safety.

67. There is an urgent need to adopt effective strategies to identify and include the socially, culturally and economically excluded. This requires participatory analysis of exclusion at household, community and school levels, and the development of diverse, flexible, and innovative approaches to learning and an environment that fosters mutual respect and trust.

68. Assessment of learning should include an evaluation of environments, processes and outcomes. Learning outcomes must be well-defined in both cognitive and non-cognitive domains, and be continually assessed as an integral part of the teaching and learning process.

9 Enhance the status, morale and professionalism of teachers

69. Teachers are essential players in promoting quality education, whether in schools or in more flexible community-based programmes; they are advocates for, and catalysts of, change. No education reform is likely to succeed without the active participation and ownership of teachers. Teachers at all levels of the education system should be respected and adequately remunerated; have access to training and ongoing professional development and support, including through open and distance learning; and be able to participate, locally and nationally, in decisions affecting their professional lives and teaching environments. Teachers must also accept their professional responsibilities and be accountable to both learners and communities.

70. Clearly defined and more imaginative strategies to identify, attract, train and retain good teachers must be put into place. These strategies should address the new role of teachers in preparing students for an emerging knowledge-based and technology-driven economy. Teachers must be able to understand diversity in learning styles and in the physical and intellectual development of students, and to create stimulating, participatory learning environments.

10 Harness new information and communication technologies to help achieve EFA goals

71. Information and communication technologies (ICTs) must be harnessed to support EFA goals at an affordable cost. These technologies have great potential for knowledge dissemination, effective learning and the development of more efficient education services. This potential will not be realized unless the new technologies serve rather than drive the implementation of education strategies. To be effective, especially in developing countries, ICTs should be combined with more traditional technologies such as books and radios, and be more extensively applied to the training of teachers.

72. The swiftness of ICT developments, their increasing spread and availability, the nature of their content and their declining prices are

having major implications for learning. They may tend to increase disparities, weaken social bonds and threaten cultural cohesion. Governments will therefore need to establish clearer policies in regard to science and technology, and undertake critical assessments of ICT experiences and options. These should include their resource implications in relation to the provision of basic education, emphasizing choices that bridge the 'digital divide', increase access and quality, and reduce inequity.

73. There is a need to tap the potential of ICTs to enhance data collection and analysis, and to strengthen management systems, from central ministries through sub-national levels to the school; to improve access to education by remote and disadvantaged communities; to support initial and continuing professional development of teachers; and to provide opportunities to communicate across classrooms and cultures.

74. News media should also be engaged to create and strengthen partnerships with education systems, through the promotion of local newspapers, informed coverage of education issues and continuing education programmes via public service broadcasting.

11 Systematically monitor progress towards EFA goals and strategies at the national, regional and international levels

75. Achieving EFA goals requires setting priorities, defining policies, establishing targets and progress indicators, allocating resources, monitoring performance, and assessing qualitative and quantitative outcomes. Robust and reliable education statistics, disaggregated and based on accurate census data, are essential if progress is to be properly measured, experience shared and lessons learned. Information on the success of particular strategies, on national and international budget allocations for basic education and on civil society participation in Education for All must also be sought. These are all key elements in assessing the accountability of EFA partners. Ongoing monitoring and evaluation of EFA, with the full participation of civil society, should be encouraged.

76. When governments are truly committed to educational outcomes, they recognize the fundamental importance of statistics and the need for credible and independent institutions to produce them. The EFA 2000 Assessment identified the existence of important data gaps. Capacity

should be increased to fill these gaps, and to produce accurate and timely data, qualitative and quantitative, for analysis and feed-back to policy-makers and practitioners. Attention to collecting disaggregated data at lower levels of the system, both to identify areas of greatest inequity and to provide data for local-level planning, management and evaluation, is essential.

77. Progress towards meeting EFA goals and targets needs to be assessed regularly and systematically to allow for meaningful comparative analyses. The availability of better data at national and international levels will allow governments, civil society and other agencies to gain a clearer understanding of progress toward the goals, to identify regions, countries, and sub-national levels where there is particular success or difficulty, and then to take appropriate action.

12 Build on existing mechanisms to accelerate progress towards Education for All

78. In order to realize the six goals presented in this Framework for Action, broad-based and participatory mechanisms at international, regional and national levels are essential. The functions of these mechanisms will include, to varying degrees, advocacy, resource mobilization, monitoring, and knowledge generation and sharing.

79. The heart of EFA activity lies at the country level. National EFA forums will be strengthened or established and countries will prepare national EFA plans by 2002 at the latest. For those countries with significant challenges such as crises or natural disasters, special technical support will be provided by the international community. Members of the international community commit themselves to working in a consistent, co-ordinated and coherent manner in supporting national EFA plans.

80. Regional and sub-regional activities to support national efforts will be based on existing organizations, networks and initiatives, augmented where necessary. These will work in tandem with national EFA forums.

81. UNESCO will continue its mandated role in co-ordinating EFA partners and maintaining their collaborative momentum. In line with this, UNESCO will convene annually a high-level, small and flexible group to serve as a lever for political commitment and technical and financial resource mobilization. It will be composed of leaders from governments and civil society and development agencies. UNESCO

will refocus its education programme in order to place the outcomes and priorities of Dakar at the heart of its work.

82. Achieving Education for All will require that new, concrete financial commitments be made by national governments and by bilateral and multilateral donors including the World Bank and the regional development banks, civil society and foundations.

Bibliography

Alan K. Bowman and Greg Woolf, eds., *Literacy and Power in the Ancient World*, (Cambridge) 1994.

Aspin, David N. & Chapman, Judith D. (2007) "Lifelong Learning Concepts and Conceptions" in: David N. Aspin, ed.: *Philosophical Perspectives on Lifelong Learning*, Springer. ISBN 1-4020-6192-7

Beiter, Klaus Dieter. *The Protection of the Right to Education by International Law*. The Hague: Martinus Nijhoff. 2005.

Bernstein Tarrow, Norma, ed. *Human Rights and Education*. Oxford: Pergamon Press, vol. 3, Pergamon Comparative and International Education Series, 1987.

Best, Francine. *Education, Culture, Human Rights, and International Understanding: The Promotion of Humanistic, Ethical, and Cultural Values in Education*. Paris: UNESCO, 1990.

Blaschke, Lisa Marie. "Heutagogy and Lifelong Learning: A Review of Heutagogical Practice and Self-Determined Learning". *The International Review of Research in Open and Distance Learning*. Athabasca University. Retrieved 24 November 2012.

Commission of the European Communities: "Adult learning: It is never too late to learn". COM(2006) 614 final. Brussels, 23.10.2006.

Crisp, Jeff, Christopher Talbot and Daiana B. Cipollone, eds., *Learning for a Future: Refugee education in developing countries*, United Nations Refugee Agency, Geneva, 2001.

Dahlberg, Gunilla, Peter Moss and Alan Pence, *Beyond Quality in Early Childhood Education and Care*, Routledge/Falmer, London and New York, 1999.

Delors, Jacques, *Learning: The treasure within*, Report to UNESCO of the International Commission on Education for the Twenty-first Century, UNESCO Publishing, Paris, 1996.

Department of Education and Science (2000). Learning for Life: White Paper on Adult Education. Dublin: Stationery Office.http://eric.ed.gov/PDFS/ED471201.pdf]

Douglas A. Sylva. *The United Nations Children's Fund: Women or Children First?* Diss. Catholic Family and Human Rights Institute, 2003. New York, New York, 2003.

Dowd, Amy Jo; Greer, Heather. *Girls' Education: Community Approaches to Access and Quality. Strong Beginnings.* Westport: Save the Children Federation, Inc., 2001.

Education for All 2000 Assessment, submitted by countries to the World Education Forum, Dakar, April 2000.

Fischer, Gerhard (2000). "Lifelong Learning - More than Training" in *Journal of Interactive Learning Research*, Volume 11 issue 3/4 pp 265-294.

Fountain, Susan, *It's Only Right! A practical guide to learning about the Convention on the Rights of the Child*, United Nations Children's Fund, New York, 1993.

Geissinger, Helen. "Girls' Access to Education in a Developing Country." *International Review of Education.* V43 n5-6 (1999): 423-38. EBSCOhost. 15 Nov. 2006.

Graham-Brown, Sarah, 'The Role of the Curriculum', Chapter 6, *Education Rights and Minorities*, Minority Rights Group, London, 1994.

Jean Debiesse, "The Right to Free and Compulsory Education" in the *UNESCO Courier*, July-August 1951, p. 14.

Jean Piaget, "The right to education in the modern world" in *Freedom and Culture*, compiled by UNESCO, Wingate, London, pp. 69-116.

Jochnick, Chris, and Pauline Garzon, *Rights-based Approaches to Development,* CARE and Oxfam America, Atlanta, 2002.

Kattan, Raja Bentaouet, and Nicholas Burnett, *User Fees in Primary Education*, World Bank, Washington, D.C., 2004.

Kerr, David, *Citizenship Education in Primary Schools*, Institute for Citizenship Studies, London, 1999.

Knobel, M. (1999). *Everyday literacies: Students, discourse, and social practice.* New York: Lang; Gee, J. P. (1996). *Social linguistics and literacies: Ideologies in Discourses.*Philadelphia: Falmer.

Lawrence, John, *The Right to Education for Persons with Disabilities: Towards inclusion – An EFA flagship paper*, Inclusion International, London, 2004.

Mehrotra, S. (1998): Education for All: Policy Lessons From High-Achieving Countries:UNICEF Staff Working Papers, New York, UNICEF.

Right to Education project. "Right to education – What is it? Acceptability". Retrieved 2010-09-11

Stuart Selber (2004). *Multiliteracies for a digital age.* Carbondale: Southern Illinois University Press.

Torres, R.M. *One decade of 'Education for All': The challenge ahead.* Buenos Aires: IIPE-UNESCO, 2000.

UNESCO and UNICEF. *A Human Rights-Based Approach to Education for All.* 2007.

Whyte, Cassandra B/ (2002). "Great Expectations for Higher Education". Speech at Higher Education Round Table Event. Oxford, England.

World Education Report 2000 – The Right to Education: Towards Education for All Throughout Life, UNESCO Publishing, Paris, 2000.